Praise for *Visual Basic Developer's Guide to ADO*

Mike Gunderloy has researched the topics you need to understand in order to use ADO and Visual Basic together, and explained them in a clear, concise, and to-the-point manner.

You'll learn about ADO and find the answers to your questions in this book.

[The author has] provided a skillful, clear, patient explanation of topics that aren't patently obvious. We're happy that Mike's dug into this particular topic—now we don't have to do the research ourselves!

[W]atch carefully for the tidbits that Mike tosses out throughout the book. There's certain to be something you hadn't thought about already in here.

> —From the foreword by Ken Getz, Mike Gilbert, and Paul Litwin, nationally known database consultants and authors of the best-selling *Access Developer's Handbook*.

Visual Basic Developer's Guide to ADO

Visual Basic® Developer's Guide to ADO

Mike Gunderloy

SYBEX®

San Francisco • Paris • Düsseldorf • Soest • London

Associate Publisher: Richard Mills
Contracts and Licensing Manager: Kristine O'Callaghan
Acquisitions & Developmental Editor: Denise Santoro
Editor: Suzanne Goraj
Project Editors: Susan Berge, Raquel Baker
Technical Editor: Dianne Siebold
Book Designer: Kris Warrenburg
Graphic Illustrators: Tony Jonick, Jerry Williams
Electronic Publishing Specialist: Nila Nichols
Project Team Leader: Shannon Murphy
Proofreaders: Richard Ganis, Catherine Morris
Indexer: Lynnzee Elze
Cover Designer: Design Site
Cover Illustrator: Jack D. Myers

Library of Congress Card Number: 99-65206
ISBN: 0-7821-2556-5

Manufactured in the United States of America

10 9 8 7 6 5 4 3 2 1

To Dana, who keeps me going.

FOREWORD

ADO is easy. Therefore, you don't need this book.

At least, that's what Microsoft would like you to think, and you might agree if you simply picked up an object model diagram for ADO and compared it to other more complex data access technologies. Actually, mastering ADO is quite difficult—the number of tricks and details is daunting, and the amount of trivia involved in really getting to know this new data access technology can be overwhelming.

Should you use a single Connection object and keep it open? Or should you create implicit connections when you open recordsets? What about the new ADO Data controls? Are they worth using? How do you use ADO with multidimensional data? These are the sorts of things you might come to a reference like this to find out, and you won't be disappointed. Mike Gunderloy has researched the topics you need to understand in order to use ADO and Visual Basic together and has explained them in a clear, concise, and to-the-point manner.

You'll learn about ADO and find the answers to your questions in this book. That's a given. What you won't find out about is who Mike Gunderloy really is. Covering that topic is our job.

We've all worked with Mike on various projects over the past six years, starting with a two-week incarceration in a Civil War–era farmhouse in eastern Virginia, writing an application-development tool. Mike was the project lead. His memory of the experience was summed up once as being as easy as "herding cats" (his words). Since then, we've jointly worked on various projects, including revising some ugly add-in code for Microsoft Access, creating wizards for Visual InterDev and Office 2000, and writing courseware and certification exams. Each of these projects was piloted by Mike, a testament to both his superior talent and our disdain for managing anything other than our own time.

For three years, Mike traveled full-time, seeing the country from his recreational vehicle. Of course, Mike made several modifications that stretched the definition of "recreational." Our guess is that the high-tech equipment *in* the RV was worth far more than the RV itself. Along the way, he spent several weeks camped on our individual doorsteps. (And some of those doorsteps managed to get him wired up for ISDN, or 30-amp electricity for air-conditioning. Phone connectivity at these stops was assumed.) He's become a friend, a mentor, and a source of information about a wide range of topics.

Through all these projects (and while keeping our driveways warm), it's always been clear that Mike is one of the most astute developers we've run across. No one we know is able to push and pop the internal temporary stack with as much ease as Mike can—he can be working on three or four things at once, on a minute-by-minute basis, and keep track of them all. He's incredibly articulate, passionate, and caring. And we've always had a great time working with him.

We believe he's done the same for this book as he's done for us when we've worked on projects together. That is, he's provided a skillful, clear, patient explanation of topics that aren't patently obvious. We're happy that Mike's dug into this particular topic—now we don't have to do the research ourselves!

You may know some of the material in this book already, or perhaps not. In any case, watch carefully for the tidbits that Mike tosses out throughout the book. There's certain to be something you haven't already thought about in here. And we don't expect to see Mike's RV pulling up to our driveways anymore—he recently settled on a farm, with livestock to feed and crops to care for. Watch out, though: we're sure there are more books, waiting to be written, in between the milking and the feeding.

Ken Getz, Mike Gilbert, and Paul Litwin

ACKNOWLEDGMENTS

Thanks of course to the editorial team that whipped this book into shape: Denise Santoro, Susan Berge, Raquel Baker, Suzanne Goraj, and Dianne Siebold. Denise was particularly understanding when I took a month off in the middle of the manuscript in order to get married. Thanks also to Melanie Spiller at Sybex, who encouraged me to work on this book even though it delayed some of her own projects. Thanks also to the able production team of Nila Nichols, Shannon Murphy, Richard Ganis, Lynnzee Elze, and Catherine Morris.

Ken Getz was always happy to answer stupid questions and discuss puzzling code issues. Daniel Doris from Microsoft was a great help during the ADO 2.5 beta cycle.

I'd like to thank the staffs of Silver Tray Catering, Alpha Photography, the Dallas Botanical Gardens, and Celebrations Entertainment, as well as the wedding party (Steve White, Donna Covington, David Gunderloy, Julie Ackley, Danielle Bachelder, and Nancy Lopez) for making our wedding trouble-free enough that I was actually able to get some writing done even in the last few hectic weeks. Thanks a bunch, folks, and be relieved that we don't have to organize another one!

Last but certainly not least, thanks to Dana Jones for helping drive trucks, run fences, weed gardens, pack, unpack, and water livestock—and above all, for keeping me smiling while I was writing this book. I couldn't have done it without you, hon.

CONTENTS AT A GLANCE

TABLE OF CONTENTS

INTRODUCTION

Visual Basic and ADO are two of my favorite development tools.

I've been working with Visual Basic since VB3, and I remain delighted with it as a development environment. Sure, there are quirks and holes and even outright bugs; but really, VB provides a fast way to get attractive Windows applications up and running. When you're trying to work to deadline, that's important. Even more important, as far as I'm concerned, is that hooking together components and controls to build an application fills me with the same delight that Lego™ and Erector™ sets did when I was a (smaller) kid. Don't tell my clients how much fun this stuff is, though, and I won't tell yours.

As for ADO: Like many of you, I've been writing database applications with Microsoft tools since the first release of ADO quite a few years ago. Over the years, Microsoft has faced technical and political (both internal and external) challenges as it's honed its data-access strategy. At last, with the release of ADO, data access feels "right." ADO provides a combination of power and simplicity, and the extensible design of the library allows you to defer learning things like DDL and multidimensional data access until you really need to. I don't think we're ever going to be able to use absolutely identical code to retrieve data from every conceivable data source, but ADO is close enough to that ideal to be very useful.

You might not have been in this business as long as I've been, but I assume that you were experienced with Visual Basic before you picked up this book. I also assume that you're at least a bit tired of huge books that try to explain everything about a product in excruciating detail. This is a book for the experienced Visual Basic developer who wants to quickly understand what ADO has to offer and how to use it from Visual Basic. I've tried to keep the book focused on the synergies between VB and ADO, and to give you plenty of useful bits of code without overwhelming you with too much tedious detail. You should be able to work through this book in a week or so, and then start using ADO in your own applications.

How This Book Is Organized

This book is designed to offer something to developers at all levels of experience with Visual Basic and ADO. The first three chapters cover some basic background material. Then come four chapters on using the built-in user interface tools in VB in conjunction with ADO. The rest of the book is devoted to code, code, and more code.

Chapter 1 discusses the new features in Visual Basic 6 and ADO 2.5 and the ways in which they work together. Even if you've worked with previous versions of these programs, you should at least skim this chapter because Microsoft has added a lot of new features. It also covers where you can get the latest and greatest ADO releases.

Chapter 2 presents a roundup of the entire Microsoft data access universe. No matter how happy you are with ADO or how much Microsoft says it's the ultimate data access method, you need to recognize that sometimes it's not the perfect solution. In this chapter, you'll learn how to choose the appropriate data access library for your application.

Chapter 3 is devoted to the ADO object model. Although this object model is simpler than that of either DAO or RDO (previous data access libraries), there is still a lot of complexity hidden in a few objects. You should find this chapter a useful reference as you learn ADO. I also introduce the ADOX and ADO MD extension libraries in this chapter.

Chapter 4 focuses on the Visual Basic Data View and its associated tools. If you haven't used the Data View, you're probably working too hard when you need to investigate or update database schemas. Building the ability to perform simple database administration functions directly into Visual Basic was a major improvement in the product.

Chapter 5 covers the use of bound controls with ADO to quickly move information from a database to the user interface. If you've dismissed bound controls in the past, you may want to pay particular attention to this chapter. The ADO version of these controls is actually very fast and functional.

Chapter 6 introduces the Data Environment. The Data Environment is a new designer added to Visual Basic 6 that makes building hierarchical recordsets simple. This in turn leads to very nice user interfaces with minimal development time. You'll learn both how to construct a Data Environment and how to program it.

Chapter 7 covers the Data Report, a companion to the Data Environment. If you've had to choose between the inadequate and confusing Crystal Reports package and moving your data to Microsoft Access just to use the Access report engine, you'll find this new tool a real boon.

Chapter 8 gets down to serious coding with an examination of the various operations you need to perform to use ADO without the user interface widgets. This includes opening recordsets, working with records, searching and sorting, and many other techniques. Understanding the material in this chapter is essential if you're going to integrate ADO into your applications.

Chapter 9 shows you how to build your own data consumers in Visual Basic. VB 6 added the ability to do data binding in code, which opens up vast possibilities for integrating your own components into the Visual Basic data universe.

Chapter 10 covers the basics of data shaping. Data shaping is a Microsoft-invented technology for creating hierarchical recordsets. These recordsets can make operations involving multiple tables much more efficient. You'll learn how to create shaped recordsets and see what you can do with them.

Chapter 11 demonstrates how you can integrate ADO and Visual Basic with the Internet. You'll learn about DHTML applications and about using RDS for true three-tier data access. These technologies may be just what you're looking for to upgrade your corporate intranet.

Chapter 12 examines the ADO MD library and show you how this powerful extension to the base ADO library can help you pull information from large volumes of data.

Chapter 13 shows how you can use ADO and Visual Basic to create your own data providers. This technique opens up the possibility of using your own Visual Basic components to supply data to other data consumers. No longer do you need to turn to C++ to open your data up to the rest of the development universe.

Finally, there's also an appendix that teaches you the basics of the SQL SELECT statement, just in case your SQL background is a bit shaky. Though this appendix covers most of the SQL you'll need to use this book, you'll want to refer to your own database's documentation for the fine points implemented by your particular server.

Release Dependency

This book was written in spring and summer of 1999 using the then-current versions of the software it discusses:

- Windows NT 4 with Service Pack 5

- Visual Basic 6 with Service Pack 3

- SQL Server 7 with Service Pack 1

- Windows 2000 RC1

- ADO 2.5 beta 2

Inevitably, there will be updates and service packs and release versions that change this software. With luck, all of the samples will keep working, but if anything doesn't work, I'd appreciate it if you'd let me know. My e-mail address is MikeG1@mcwtech.com, and I'm always happy to hear from my readers.

About the Web Site

You'll notice that there's quite a bit of code in this book, which is as it should be for a developer-oriented book. But there's no CD-ROM. That's because all of the code is available on the Sybex Web site. Just go to http://www.sybex.com, look up this book (you can search by title, author, or ISBN from the Catalog page), and click the Downloads button. Accept the license agreement, and you'll go straight to a Web page where you can download any of the sample projects discussed in this book. I'll also use the Web site to post any necessary additions and corrections to the book.

NOTE   The author created reusable code in this publication expressly for reuse by readers in applications that they develop or distribute. Readers cannot publish the code in any way that allows other developers access to the code itself. Sybex grants readers limited permission to reuse the code for applications developed or distributed by the reader so long as the author is attributed in any application containing the reusable code and the code itself is never distributed, posted online by electronic transmission, sold, or commercially exploited as a stand-alone product..

CHAPTER
ONE

1

Overview of ADO and Visual Basic

- A Brief History of ADO

- What's New in ADO 2.5

- What's New in VB 6 Data Access

- Getting ADO

Welcome! That you're reading this book is a good indication that you care about one of the most exciting changes in Windows-based application development in recent years: the rise of ActiveX Data Objects (ADO) as a truly universal way to retrieve and change data from many diverse sources. These sources are not limited to traditional databases, but can include file systems, e-mail stores, and even data on the Internet. In this book, we'll concentrate on using this new data access technology from Microsoft's premiere rapid application development tool, Visual Basic. In this chapter, I'll introduce ADO and make sure you're up to speed on what's new and exciting in the most current versions of both ADO and Visual Basic.

A Brief History of ADO

Despite its low version number (especially compared to programs such as Office 2000!), ADO has in fact been through a number of major versions. On the one hand, this is a good thing, since it shows how actively Microsoft has been working on this library. But on the other, it leads to the disease of "versionitis," where it's hard to be entirely sure just what software is installed on a particular machine. Hence, it's worth taking a quick look at the history of ADO, to give some hint of which version has shipped where.

ADO 1.0 was released as an object library wrapping for OLE DB (a function that the current release still fulfills) in 1996, as a part of Microsoft Internet Information Server (IIS) 3. You'll learn a bit more about OLE DB, the collection of COM (Component Object Model) interfaces for retrieving data, in Chapter 2. This version included the first version of the Advanced Data Connector (ADC), which was superseded by the Remote Data Service (RDS) in later releases. I'll look at RDS in Chapter 11.

ADO 1 was also included in Visual Studio 97, both as a part of Visual Interdev and as a part of the OLE DB SDK (Software Development Kit). At this time, there was no single unified installation for ADO and OLE DB, resulting in version conflicts even among individual products within Visual Studio 97.

ADO 1.5 was released in 1997 as part of MDAC 1.5. MDAC stands for Microsoft Data Access Components, a single setup that was designed to bring more coordination to all the various bits of data-access technology that Microsoft's been shipping. MDAC 1.5 includes ADO 1.5, OLE DB 1.5, RDS 1.5, and ODBC (Open Database Connectivity) 3.5. Although OLE DB is replacing ODBC, it's doing so slowly, and the older ODBC drivers are still necessary to retrieve data from sources for which no OLE DB providers exist.

MDAC 1.5 was available for free download from the Internet, as have been all subsequent versions. Microsoft has been investing heavily in making data access a part of the operating system by offering it for free (well, for free if you have a free download connection, anyhow). MDAC 1.5 went through a series of bug-fix releases culminating in version 1.5d, which was included with Internet Explorer 4.01 Service Pack 1.

ADO 2 was shipped in MDAC 2, again as a free Web download, in 1997. In addition to ADO 2, MDAC 2 includes OLE DB 2 and RDS 2. ODBC has remained at version 3.5, since development on that component has practically ceased. ADO 2 added asynchronous operations and hierarchical recordsets to the basic ADO model. This version also introduced ADO MD, a set of multidimensional extensions for ADO that I'll cover in Chapter 12.

In early 1999, Microsoft released ADO 2.1 as a part of MDAC 2.1. A version of ADO 2.1 shipped with Microsoft SQL Server 7, but the final version wasn't available until just after the shipment of Office 2000. Referred to as MDAC 2.1.2.4202.3 (GA), this was the last stand-alone version of ADO before the release of ADO 2.5. This version introduced the Seek method and the Index property, as well as the ability to save a recordset as XML.

> **NOTE**
>
> ADO 2.5, the current version, was in late beta as this book was being written. However, it's already clear that this version will be released as a system component in Windows 2000. I expect that a stand-alone version of MDAC 2.5 will also be released to the Microsoft Universal Data Access Web site. (I'll discuss what being a system component means later in this chapter.) In the following section, I'll cover what's new in ADO 2.5. The sample code throughout this book is based on ADO 2.5.

So, what does all this mean for the developer of ADO-using applications? In practice, it's pretty simple:

- For legacy applications that don't use any of the new features in ADO 2.5, you'll want to download MDAC 2.1.2.4202.3 (GA) from the Internet, and use that to make sure that client computers are running the most recent available version of ADO 2.1.

- For new applications on Windows 95, Windows 98, or Windows NT 4, you'll need to obtain and install MDAC 2.5.

- For new applications on Windows 2000, you're all set: the software is in the operating system.

NOTE   You may find that there's a newer release of ADO 2.1 than 2.1.2.4202.3 (GA) available on Microsoft's Web site by the time this book is published, but that's the current version as I write this. Use the latest version for any legacy ADO 2.1 applications.

What's New in ADO 2.5

As the version number indicates, ADO 2.5 is an incremental update from ADO 2.1. But in the nine months or so between these two versions, Microsoft managed to sneak in several new capabilities, as well as the inevitable bug fixes. In this section, I'll briefly introduce you to the new features in ADO 2.5:

- ADO as a system component

- Record and Stream objects

- URLs as connection strings

- Provider-Supplied Fields

- New OLE DB Providers

If you're not already familiar with ADO, you might want to skip over this section. Don't worry; all these features are covered in their proper context later in this book.

ADO as a System Component

Starting with Windows 2000, ADO is a standard part of the Windows operating system. What this means is that ADO 2.5 is automatically installed as a part of the Windows 2000 installation. If you're writing applications that use ADO and intend to deploy them only on computers using Windows 2000 as an operating system, you don't have to worry about installing a data access library, because it's already there.

As a Windows 2000 system component, ADO 2.5 on Windows 2000 is subject to more stringent controls than past versions have been. Specifically, it can only be installed or updated by the Microsoft Installer, and only as a part of an operating system service pack. This is all part of Microsoft's broad strategy to make Windows a more robust operating system, and to eliminate the library version conflicts (commonly known as "DLL Hell") that have made debugging client-side installations a time-consuming and difficult activity. It's too soon to tell how well this strategy is going to work, but if all goes according to plan, you should be able to treat data access with the same casual disregard that you already have for finding and opening disk files.

Record and Stream Objects

ADO 2.5 introduces two new objects to the ADO hierarchy: the Record object and the Stream object. These objects are designed to help extend ADO to a wider understanding of what a "data source" can be.

A Record object can represent a single record within a Recordset object, but more typically it provides an object-oriented view of more heterogeneous data. For example, you might use a Record object to represent a file or folder in a file system, a message in an e-mail store, or a storage or stream within a COM compound file.

Record objects are also designed to represent hierarchically organized data. A Record object can represent either a node or a leaf within a tree of data. Properties of the Record object tell you whether any particular Record object represents a leaf or a non-leaf node. (A leaf node, of course, is one that doesn't have any child nodes of its own).

A Stream object represents binary data associated with a particular Record object. If you have a Record object representing a file, for example, its associated Stream object would contain the binary data for that file.

Record and Stream objects are discussed in more detail in Chapter 3.

URLs as Connection Strings

ADO 2.5 allows the use of Uniform Resource Locators (URLs) to specify the data source for a particular ADO Connection object. These URLs are then passed to an underlying OLE DB provider that can interpret them. For example, you can now use these as valid locations to open a connection:

```
file://MyServer/CDrive/SomeFile.txt
http://www.myserver.com/data.html
```

Using URLs as connection strings allows better integration with Web-based applications and simplifies the process of retrieving data from arbitrary files using ADO.

Provider-Supplied Fields

ADO 2.5 introduces the concept of a heterogeneous recordset. In previous versions of ADO, every record in a recordset contained exactly the same fields. Now, depending on the underlying OLE DB provider, this need not be the case.

For example, a provider that retrieves data from an electronic mail store might insert To, From, and Subject fields in every record. However, only records representing e-mail messages with attachments would have an Attachment field.

This new capability lets a custom provider represent almost anything as an ADO recordset. You could build a provider that represented a file system, for example, and set a ParentApplication field only on records representing documents. In general, this capability lets records in a recordset be as different from one another as is necessary for the current programming task.

In addition, a special class of providers known as Document Source Providers is devoted to managing documents—for example, in a file system. In this case, the properties of each record are not the documents themselves, but a description of the document. There are constants in ADO 2.5 that allow you to easily retrieve two special fields: one representing the Stream object with the actual contents of the document and one holding the URL that describes the document's contents.

New OLE DB Providers

In addition to the changes to ADO itself, MDAC 2.5 also includes several new OLE DB providers. These providers help extend the reach of ADO to new types of data:

- The Microsoft OLE DB Provider for Microsoft Active Directory Service allows ADO to connect to heterogeneous directory services. In addition to full access to the Active Directory Service in Windows 2000, this provider supplies read-only access to Windows NT 4 directory services, Novell Directory Services, and any other LDAP-compliant directory services provider.

- The Microsoft OLE DB Provider for Internet Publishing gives you access to Web resources under the control of Microsoft FrontPage and Microsoft Internet Information Server.

What's New in VB 6 Data Access

Although not as new as ADO 2.5, Visual Basic 6 has so many new features over the previous version that you may not be familiar with them all yet. In this book, I'm only going to cover data-related features that are of use with ADO. Here I'll briefly introduce these features; of course, they're covered in more detail later on in the book:

- ADO

- Data Environment and Data Report

- Enhanced data binding

- User-created data sources

- New controls

- Enhanced data wizards

ADO

Of course, the big news in Visual Basic 6 data access is the promotion of ADO as the preferred data-access technology. This wholehearted endorsement of ADO comes after a period of indecision, in which it first appeared that VB would promote Data Access Objects (DAO) and the Jet engine, and later the Remote Data Object (RDO) technology developed by the Visual Basic team. I'll review some of this history and consider when you might want to use an alternative data access library in Chapter 2.

Not only is ADO included in Visual Basic 6, but substantial parts of the product have been reengineered to make use of ADO. For example, there's a new ADO Data control that uses ADO (instead of DAO, which the older data control used as its underlying data access technology). As far as data access libraries go, it definitely seems that all of Microsoft is on a single wavelength now, since Office 2000 has also embraced ADO. So the good news is that the skills you pick up from working with ADO in Visual Basic 6 should serve you well in other Microsoft products in the future.

Data Environment and Data Report

Visual Basic 6 introduces two new designers. A *designer* is a tool that's hosted within the Visual Basic Integrated Development Environment (IDE) to allow you to work with objects. For example, Visual Basic has had a designer for forms since the earliest versions. You might also have experimented with the UserConnection Designer in Visual Basic 5, which was an RDO-centric data access tool.

The new designers in Visual Basic 6 are the Data Environment Designer and the Data Report Designer. Like forms, Data Environments and Data Reports have both user interface and code windows (though the Data Environment user interface window is only visible at design time). The Data Environment is designed to let you quickly create a hierarchy of ADO objects connected to a particular record source, while the Data Report Designer is a drag-and-drop reporting tool, conceptually similar to the Microsoft Access Report Designer.

Figure 1.1 shows a Visual Basic Data Report at runtime. You'll learn about the Data Environment in Chapter 6 and about Data Reports in Chapter 7.

FIGURE 1.1:

A Data Report in Visual Basic 6

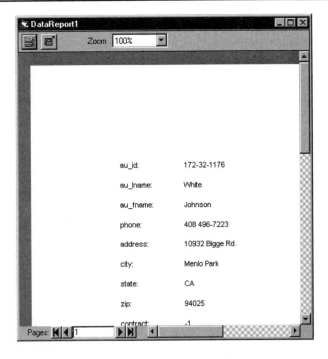

Enhanced Data Binding

Another exciting advance in Visual Basic 6 is enhanced data binding. Most developers saw data binding in previous versions as a joke, or perhaps a tool for prototyping, later to be replaced by "real code" in a production version. It's true that Visual Basic 5's data binding was inflexible, being based solely on the use of data controls. But no more.

Now, data binding is a programmatic technique. You can use code to bind any ADO data source to any ADO data consumer. The data source can be a data control or a command from a data environment or even an OLE DB provider written in Visual Basic itself. The data consumer can be a control or a structure in memory.

You can work with enhanced data binding simply by setting DataSource properties at run time. Or you can control enhanced data binding in detail by creating your own BindingCollection object and specifying exactly which ADO fields map to which properties of which controls. The possibilities are nearly endless, and the flexibility created by programmatic data binding is immense.

You'll see enhanced data binding used in several examples scattered throughout the book.

User-Created Data Sources

In older versions of Visual Basic, you could only use data sources that had been supplied by Microsoft. That is, if you wanted a control that was a data source, you used the Microsoft Data Control. (Or, if you were a truly advanced developer, you might build a data source using C++, but that's well beyond the scope of this book.)

Again, things have changed in this area. Now you can actually build a User-Control that's a data source—that is, one that you can bind other controls to at run time. You can create both simple data sources, which expose a single field, and complex data sources, which expose an entire row of data at one time. I'll cover this new technology in Chapter 13.

New Controls

Visual Basic 6 contains a number of new controls that can help you rapidly develop data-aware applications:

- The ADO Data control provides a way to access any data source using ADO and OLE DB. It's similar to the old DAO-based Data control, but with more advanced options.

- The Hierarchical FlexGrid control inherits all the functionality of the old Grid control. In addition, it can be bound to an entire hierarchy of records through the use of a shaped recordset.

- The Data Repeater control lets you create a form that shows multiple instances of other controls, one for each row in a recordset. If you've worked with continuous forms in an Access database, you'll recognize this concept.

- The DataGrid, DataList, and DataCombo controls provide new ways to bind ADO-supplied data to your user interface. These controls are OLE DB–aware and so can be bound to the new ADO Data control.

We'll take a look at all these controls in Chapter 5.

Enhanced Data Wizards

The Data Form Wizard underwent a major overhaul in Visual Basic 6. Now, like the rest of the product, it uses ADO by default. It can also create code-only forms, without any bound controls. It also understands the new FlexGrid control as a way to show data. You'll see this wizard in action in Chapter 5.

Getting ADO

Even though ADO 2.5 is a system component in Windows 2000, there are still multiple options for getting copies of the most recent ADO code. You should know about these, from the simple MDAC redistributable to the complex MDAC SDK.

MDAC

MDAC stands for Microsoft Data Access Components. In past versions of ADO, MDAC had been the only way to get ADO onto any system. Now, it's still the sole way to install ADO on a pre-Windows 2000 system. Even products that include ADO (such as Visual Studio) handle the installation by running the MDAC install program.

Usually, the install program is called `mdac_typ.exe`. This self-extracting setup program contains all the components needed to support ADO code on a client computer and does not require the user to make choices.

You should distribute the latest `mdac_type.exe` program along with any program that makes use of ADO. Although products such as Visual Basic include a version of this program, your best bet is to download the most current version from the Microsoft Universal Data Access Web site at `http://www.microsoft.com/data`. That way you're guaranteed the latest bug fixes and most recent versions of all ADO components.

WARNING   You may find references in some books to a minimum version, `mdac_min.exe`. Starting with ADO 2.1, there's no longer such a version. The only ADO to install is the full version.

Windows 2000

As I mentioned above, if you've installed Windows 2000, you've already installed ADO 2.5. In that case, you're all set. At least, you're all set until the first Service Pack for Windows 2000 comes out. Based on past experience, that won't be all that long after Windows 2000 itself is released. So you should monitor the Microsoft Web site for service packs, and install any that contain ADO-related fixes, if you want to stay up to date.

If you want to simplify your setup program, it's safe to try to run the MDAC install on a Windows 2000 computer. It just won't do anything.

MDAC SDK

Finally, if you're serious about database work, you should get a copy of the MDAC SDK (Microsoft Data Access Components Software Development Kit). This contains not only ADO but all the other data-related technologies that Microsoft is supporting as a part of Windows, along with sample code, tools, and more. Some of the components in the 2.5 version of the MDAC SDK include:

- Conformance tests for OLE DB drivers
- OLE DB
- OLE DB for OLAP
- Current ODBC drivers
- The OLE DB Simple Provider Toolkit
- ADO
- RDS
- ADO MD
- ADOX
- Jet Replication Objects
- Various OLE DB Providers
- Complete OLE DB documentation

Many parts of this SDK are written for C++ programmers rather than for Visual Basic programmers. Nevertheless, you'll find its documentation of ADO (and the ADO extensions such as ADOX and ADO MD) useful for Visual Basic programs.

You can download the MDAC SDK from the Microsoft Universal Data Access Web site at `http://www.microsoft.com/data`. Be warned, though, that it's quite large. But it's worth it, even if you're only working with ADO, to get the enhanced ADO documentation and help files. If you're a serious Windows developer, you should take a look at the Microsoft Developer Network program. This annual subscription program will deliver the entire Windows SDK, including the MDAC SDK, straight to your door four times a year.

2

Understanding Data Access Architecture

- ADO and OLE DB

- Other Data Access Libraries

- Choosing a Data Access Library

As I've already mentioned, ADO is one of the core pieces of the grandiosely named Universal Data Access (UDA) strategy. While the basic idea is simple—to use one method of programming to retrieve any data, anywhere—the implementation is complex. In this chapter, you'll learn about the basic architecture of ADO and OLE DB, and see how they work together to bring heterogeneous data to your applications. I'll also briefly review the older data-access strategies of Data Access Objects (DAO), Remote Data Objects (RDO), and Open Database Connectivity (ODBC), since you'll still run across these libraries in many applications. Finally, I'll give some pointers on choosing the appropriate data access library for particular circumstances.

ADO and OLE DB

ADO and OLE DB are really two faces of the same technology. OLE DB provides low-level connections to data via COM interfaces, while ADO provides an object model that simplifies the process of using OLE DB in your applications to retrieve data. If you've worked with traditional programming languages, you might think of OLE DB as being a sort of assembly language for databases, with ADO providing a higher-level language built atop that assembler.

In this section, I'll take a brief look at the overall architecture of OLE DB, and then look at what ADO adds to the picture. For the remainder of the book, I'll be concerned exclusively with the high-level ADO syntax, but it's important to realize that there's an entire layer beneath ADO that gets invoked implicitly every time an application uses ADO to retrieve data.

OLE DB Architecture

OLE DB is a set of interfaces that deal directly with data. OLE DB is built on top of COM, the Component Object Model, Microsoft's overall method of enabling communication between different data-processing components. OLE DB, in fact, is nothing more than a set of COM interfaces designed for data access.

The low-level details of using OLE DB are beyond the scope of this book, but it's worth understanding the high-level architecture that OLE DB uses. By understanding OLE DB on this overview level, you can more easily conceptualize how your data is being retrieved, as well as troubleshoot any problems that may occur.

NOTE   The gory details of OLE DB are covered in the Microsoft Data Access SDK (Software Development Kit). This SDK is included in the Microsoft Developer Network (MSDN) Platform SDK, or is available for downloading separately from `http://www.microsoft.com/data`.

OLE DB defines three types of data access components:

- *Data providers* contain data and expose it to other components.
- *Data consumers* use the data contained in data providers.
- *Service components* process and transport data.

For example, if you use OLE DB to retrieve SQL Server data and display it on a dedicated interface built in C++, SQL Server would be the data provider, your interface application would be the data consumer, and the cursor engine that maintained a set of records would be a service component.

When using Visual Basic and ADO to retrieve data, ADO itself is the OLE DB Data Consumer. All of the samples in this book use ADO as the OLE DB Data Consumer. Using ADO as the data consumer hides all the messy details of the COM interfaces that underlie OLE DB.

Most of the functionality of OLE DB is contained in the data providers and service components that retrieve and manipulate the data your application uses. However, there are a number of core components that are contained in the OLE DB libraries:

Data Conversion Library   Supports converting from one datatype to another across a wide variety of standard datatypes.

Row Position object   Keeps track of the current row in a recordset. This allows a variety of other components to agree on what data they're currently working with.

Root Enumerator   Can search the registry for known OLE DB Data Providers.

IDataInitialize interface   Contains functionality to allow working with data sources.

IDBPromptInitialize interface   Contains functionality to let applications work with the Data Link Properties dialog.

When working with ADO and Visual Basic, you won't be using any of these components directly. However, they're all being invoked as needed by OLE DB when you work with data through ADO.

What ADO Brings to OLE DB

In a word, ADO brings simplicity into the OLE DB picture. OLE DB is a call-oriented API (application programming interface). To perform operations using OLE DB, you may need to make many different API calls in a specific sequence. While there's nothing to prevent your learning and using this API directly, you won't often need the full power and flexibility of OLE DB.

ADO places another layer on top of OLE DB. The ADO layer is an object-oriented API. Rather than call functions in the OLE DB API directly, you manipulate the methods and properties of a few simple objects. Figure 2.1 shows the overall ADO object model. Chapter 3 covers this object model in depth. For now, the most important thing to understand is that you can manipulate nine objects instead of learning hundreds of API calls.

FIGURE 2.1:

ADO object model

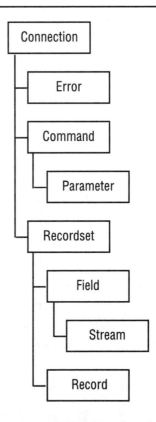

The ADO object model includes these objects, which can be used to abstract almost any data access operation:

Connection object   Represents a persistent connection to a data source.

Error object   Represents a single error during the data access process.

Command object   Represents a stored procedure or other data access object that can return data. The Command object can also be used to execute stored procedures that do not return data.

Parameter object   Represents a run-time parameter used to specify the data desired from a command object.

Recordset object   Represents a set of records retrieved from a data source.

Field object   Represents a single field of data within a recordset.

Record object   Represents a single record within a recordset. It's also possible to have stand-alone Record objects based on a data source that allows retrieving individual nodes from a hierarchy.

Stream object   Represents a binary stream of data contained within a Record object.

Property object   Defines a characteristic of an object. It is not shown on the figure, because each of the other objects has its own collection of Properties. The Properties collection is extensible with custom properties, which lets individual providers customize the core ADO objects.

In addition to the core ADO objects mentioned above, ADO also defines a special set of objects that are part of the Remote Data Service (RDS). RDS defines a separate object model and programming sequence that can be used to retrieve data in a three-tier system, typically with RDS running on a client that communicates with an intermediary such as Microsoft Internet Information Server (IIS), which in turn uses ADO to retrieve data from the ultimate data source. The goal of RDS is to hide all the complexity of this model and to make three-tier development as easy as two-tier development (in which your client program talks directly to the data source). RDS is most often used for retrieving data over the Internet or from a corporate intranet.

I'll cover RDS in more detail in Chapter 11. The basic steps for using RDS are as follows:

1.   Create an RDS.DataSpace object to connect to a specific server.

2.   Use the RDS.DataFactory object to create a recordset on the server.

3. Pass the recordset to the client.

4. Pass changes back to the RDS.DataFactory object to write back to the data source.

RDS also defines the RDS.DataControl object. This object provides a bindable source of data that can be used directly on client interfaces such as Web pages, and is designed to encapsulate as many of the details of data access as possible.

Available OLE DB Components

There are many OLE DB components already available, and the number is growing every day as new companies add OLE DB functionality to their products. In this section, I'll review the components that ship as part of the Microsoft Data Access Components (MDAC). You can generally expect this set of components to be available on any computer that's had ADO and OLE DB installed. ADO and OLE DB components can be installed from their own dedicated setup programs, or as part of another product. Currently, ADO and OLE DB are shipped in a variety of Microsoft products, including Microsoft Office 2000, Microsoft SQL Server 7.0, and Windows 2000.

Data Providers

Data providers connect to data sources and supply data, either directly to client applications or to service providers. Microsoft currently supplies these data providers as part of MDAC:

- Microsoft OLE DB Provider for ODBC
- Microsoft OLE DB Provider for Microsoft Indexing Service
- Microsoft OLE DB Provider for Microsoft Active Directory Service
- OLE DB Provider for Microsoft Jet
- Microsoft OLE DB Provider for SQL Server
- Microsoft OLE DB Provider for Oracle
- Microsoft OLE DB Provider for Internet Publishing

In addition, other OLE DB providers are shipped as part of other Microsoft products. For example, SQL Server installs the Microsoft OLE DB Provider for DTS Packages.

The Microsoft OLE DB Provider for ODBC allows ADO to use any ODBC dri-ver to retrieve data. (ODBC—Open Database Connectivity—is an older standard for connecting to heterogeneous data sources.) In other words, this is a way to use OLE DB to get data from data sources that do not have an OLE DB driver. If you omit the Provider keyword from an OLE DB connection string, this is the default provider that OLE DB will try to use to retrieve data. Currently, this is a very important driver, since there still exist many data sources for which there is no native OLE DB driver. However, you need to be aware of several problems when using this provider. First, because retrieved data goes through additional process-ing layers, using this provider is necessarily slower than using a native provider. Second, because OLE DB calls do not map perfectly to ODBC calls, some OLE DB functionality isn't available through this driver.

The Microsoft OLE DB Provider for Microsoft Index Server supplies read-only access to the information maintained by Microsoft Index Server. Microsoft Index Server, a component of IIS, maintains both full-text and property indexes of files and Web pages on a specific server. For example, you might have a set of Web pages describing all the components offered for sale by an electrical supply com-pany. If you deploy Index Server on the computer containing the Web pages, you can run Index Server queries via ADO and this provider in order to retrieve the names of, say, all Web pages containing information on circuit breakers.

The Microsoft OLE DB Provider for Microsoft Active Directory Service can retrieve read-only information from Windows NT 4 directories, as well as Novell Directory Services and any other LDAP-compliant directory service. (LDAP—Lightweight Directory Access Protocol—is an industry standard describing the format that directory information should be supplied in.) Using this provider lets you explore the various namespaces maintained by servers within your organization.

The OLE DB Provider for Microsoft Jet is used to retrieve information directly from Microsoft Jet databases. These can be Microsoft Access databases or other databases created directly with the Jet database engine, for example from a Visual Basic program. In addition, this driver can also use the Jet ISAM (Indexed Sequential Access Method) drivers to retrieve data from other client-side data-base formats, including Paradox, FoxPro, dBASE, text, and Excel files. We'll use this provider in many of the examples in this book. The Jet provider doesn't sup-port dynamic cursors; if you request a dynamic cursor, you'll get a keyset cursor instead.

The Microsoft OLE DB Provider for SQL Server is a native provider designed to retrieve information directly from Microsoft SQL Server databases. Many of the examples in this book use this provider.

The Microsoft OLE DB Provider for Oracle is a native provider for data in Oracle databases (although the provider was developed by Microsoft). Some of the examples in this book use this provider to retrieve data from Oracle databases.

The Microsoft OLE DB Provider for Internet Publishing uses OLE DB to communicate with Microsoft FrontPage Server Extensions or Microsoft Internet Information Server. It's designed to retrieve or create files on a Web site or another server that's accessible over the Internet or an intranet.

Service Providers

Service providers consume data from data providers and modify it. The modified data can be made available directly to client applications or to other service providers. Microsoft currently supplies these service providers:

- Microsoft Data Shaping Service for OLE DB

- Microsoft OLE DB Persistence Provider

- Microsoft OLE DB Remoting Provider

- Microsoft Cursor Service for OLE DB

The Microsoft Data Shaping Service for OLE DB supports the construction of "shaped" (hierarchical) recordsets. When using this service provider, you specify a data provider, which is an OLE DB Data Provider that will supply the actual data from the underlying data source. After the data is retrieved by the data provider, the Data Shaping Service turns it into a hierarchical recordset. You'll learn more about data shaping in Chapter 10.

The Microsoft OLE DB Persistence Provider allows you to use an ADO recordset that has been saved as a file. You can use the Save method of any Recordset object to create such a file, and then use the Persistence Provider at a later date to open the saved file:

```
Dim con As New ADODB.Connection
Dim rst As New ADODB.Recordset
con.Open "Provider=MSPersist"
Set rst = con.Execute("c:\SavedRecordset.adtg")
```

The saved file includes information on where the data originally came from, and ADO operations can transparently span the saving and restoring operations. For example, you can create a recordset, edit some records, save the recordset, and at a later date open the persisted recordset and commit the changes.

The Persistence Provider supports two data formats. One, the Advanced Data Tablegram (ADTG) format, is a proprietary Microsoft format designed to minimize storage and transmission requirements. Starting in ADO 2.5, this provider also supports Extensible Markup Language (XML). XML is a standard for storing heterogeneous data across a variety of products. In addition to persisting data to a file, the Persistence Provider can also store data in an ADO Stream object.

The Microsoft OLE DB Remoting Provider supports using data sources on remote computers (for example, servers connected to the Internet) as if you were logged on locally. For the most part, you won't need to deal directly with this provider. It's automatically invoked if you use RDS to retrieve data from a remote server. For more details on RDS, see Chapter 11.

The Microsoft Cursor Service for OLE DB enhances the cursor support built into many providers. A cursor is simply a pointer to a particular row in a recordset that might move backwards and forwards. When you use the MoveNext method of the Recordset object, for example, you're manipulating a cursor. Although many products support cursors, this support is somewhat uneven. The effect of the Microsoft Cursor Service is to hide this unevenness. Invoking the cursor service does not require modifying the OLE DB connection string. Rather, it's automatically used any time you specify a client-side cursor:

```
Dim con As New ADODB.Connection
Dim rst As New ADODB.Recordset
con.CursorLocation = adUseClient
rst.CursorLocation = adUseClient
```

ADO Extensibility

One of the key features of ADO is that it's extensible. That is, although the basic object model of ADO is quite sparse, it's designed so that other libraries may add additional objects that interact with the core ADO objects. There are two sets of these extensions shipped with ADO: the Microsoft ADO Extensions for DDL and Security and the Microsoft ADO (Multidimensional) Extensions.

ADO Extensions for DDL and Security

The ADO Extensions for DDL and Security (ADOX) include objects for manipulating the schema of your database and for controlling the security of objects within the database. (DDL stands for Data Definition Language, a standard set of SQL keywords for defining objects.) ADOX adds these objects to the standard ADO objects:

Catalog object   Represents the entire schema of a data source.

Table object   Represents design information on a single table.

Column object   Represents design information on a single column (field) within a table, index, or key.

Index object   Represents design information on a single index within a table.

Key object   Represents design information on a primary key or foreign key.

Group object   Represents a group of users with uniform security.

User object   Represents an individual database user.

Procedure object   Represents a stored procedure within a database.

View object   Represents a view within a database.

ADO Multidimensional Extensions

The Microsoft ActiveX Data Objects (Multidimensional) Extensions (ADO MD) provide additional objects to allow you to work with multidimensional data from an ADO client application. Multidimensional data is typically supplied by an Online Analytical Processing (OLAP) server such as Microsoft OLAP Server, which ships with SQL Server 7. OLAP servers are designed to summarize large amounts of data and make totals and other statistics available for querying. For example, if you had individual sales data on five million sales, you could use an OLAP server to quickly provide information on the number of sales in Massachusetts during April, without having to run a slow and expensive query directly on the original data.

The ADO MD library adds these objects to the standard ADO objects:

Catalog object   Represents schema information for a single OLAP database.

CubeDef object   Represents a cube from an OLAP Server. A cube contains data summarized in many different ways.

Dimension object   Represents a dimension within a cube. A dimension is a single way of summarizing data—for example, by geographic location.

Hierarchy object   Represents a way in which a dimension can be summarized or "rolled up."

Level object   Represents a single part of a hierarchy—for example, the city information in a geographic level.

Cellset object   Represents the results of a single multidimensional query. It's analogous to a Recordset object in regular ADO.

Cell object   Represents one piece of information from a single multidimensional query. It's analogous to a Field object in regular ADO.

Axis object   Represents filtering information for a Cellset object.

Position object   Provides additional information about the location of a Cell or Axis object.

Member object   Represents the basic unit of information that's summarized in a particular data cube.

You'll learn about the basics of using ADO MD to retrieve multidimensional data in Chapter 12.

The Big Picture

Figure 2.2 is an attempt to give you an overview of how these components all fit together. Depending on your application, there can be many layers of components between the user interface and the data.

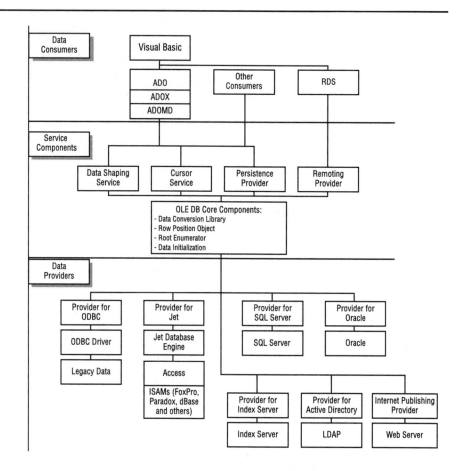

The good news is that you don't have to comprehend this picture as one seamless entity. The ADO programming model is designed so that you can concentrate on two simple tasks to do most of the work you want to do with data:

- Connecting to the desired data source

- Retrieving the desired data

The first task revolves around building OLE DB connection strings, while the second centers on creating and manipulating recordsets. In coming chapters you'll learn how to do both of these operations, first using the built-in tools that Visual Basic 6 provides for rapid data access, and then using straight Visual Basic code with the ADO object model.

Other Data Access Libraries

ADO is a tool for retrieving data, but (despite its position in the Universal Data Access scheme) it's not the only such tool. Although ADO should be your first choice for new applications, you're likely to find a variety of other data access libraries used in older applications. Three of these libraries in particular are common enough that you should be familiar with them:

- Open Database Connectivity (ODBC)
- Data Access Objects (DAO)
- Remote Data Objects (RDO)

ODBC

In many ways, ODBC is the father of OLE DB. ODBC is an earlier attempt at universal data access; like OLE DB, it was designed largely by Microsoft with some industry participation. Also like OLE DB, ODBC depends on data source–specific driver software being written to actually retrieve data.

However, ODBC is pretty well limited to retrieving data from relational databases, rather than from the more widely defined OLE DB data sources such as e-mail, HTML pages, or files, since the core software expects all data to be retrieved with SQL queries. Ultimately, this proved to be enough of a limiting factor to convince Microsoft to design a replacement, OLE DB, which is also better integrated with the core Windows operating systems than ODBC ever was.

To retrieve data via ODBC, an application first converts its request into a standard dialect of SQL defined by ODBC. This ODBC SQL is an attempt to create a universal SQL language that can cover all the variants implemented by different database providers. The ODBC Manager locates an appropriate ODBC driver and passes the request to the driver, which translates it from ODBC SQL into database-specific SQL. This SQL is then fed to the database, which returns results to the driver. These results are passed back to the ODBC Manager and ultimately to the client application.

While it's possible to write an application that uses the ODBC API directly, this is rather complicated. In order to tame this complexity, Microsoft introduced a pair of object models, Data Access Objects and Remote Data Objects, which allow object-oriented access through the procedural ODBC API.

DAO

Data Access Objects (DAO) is the native object model shipped with Microsoft Access. It can use the Jet engine directly to retrieve data from Access databases, but it's also capable of using ODBC to retrieve data from any database for which you have an ODBC driver.

Figure 2.3 shows a portion of the DAO object model. As you can see, it's similar to the ADO object model.

FIGURE 2.3:

DAO object model

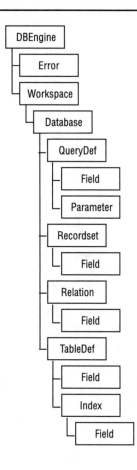

Because it's been distributed with every copy of Microsoft Access or Visual Basic, there may be more applications using DAO for data access than any other data access library. However, DAO has certain weaknesses. First, it was designed for local data access, and client-server data access via ODBC was added on later. This resulted in some performance compromises for using server-based data. Second, DAO isn't extensible. Rather, it tries to encompass all possible data operations, including DDL and security operations, within one large object model. This has resulted in a very complex object model that takes a long time to learn and uses up a lot of computer resources.

DAO also suffers from a strictly hierarchical approach to objects. To use DAO, you always need to start with the top-level DBEngine object and work your way down the hierarchy to the objects you're interested in. ADO, by contrast, allows you to create a Recordset object directly and immediately use it to retrieve data.

RDO

Remote Data Objects provides yet another data access library layered on top of ODBC. First shipped with Visual Basic 4, RDO has been a feature of Visual Basic ever since. Figure 2.4 shows the RDO object model.

RDO was a conscious attempt to correct some of the problems of DAO, especially with regard to client-server data. The RDO object model is simpler than the DAO model (though not as simple as the ADO model) and correspondingly faster. However, RDO keeps the SQL orientation and the hierarchical approach of DAO. The idiosyncratic naming of objects and exclusivity to Visual Basic also put off many developers. Although RDO represents a distinct advance over DAO, especially with regard to raw speed, it's not as optimized for general-purpose data access as ADO.

FIGURE 2.4:

RDO object model

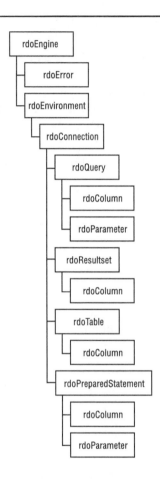

Choosing a Data Access Library

Given the variety of choices for moving data from a database to a client application, how do you decide which data access library to use? The easy answer is to just go for the latest model, ADO. But this might not be the correct answer in all circumstances. Here are a few things to think about when you're deciding how to retrieve data:

- If you need a feature that's only available in ADO, such as the ability to use the Stream object to retrieve binary data from a file considered as a record in a set of records supplied by a directory service provider, you've got no choice but to use ADO.

- If you require the absolutely fastest data access and development costs are no object, you should think about using OLE DB directly by writing a custom data consumer. You should be aware, though, that this will take *much* longer than using ADO, and result in, at best, a modest performance gain.

- If you need data from nontraditional data sources such as e-mail storage or file systems, and there's an OLE DB provider for the data you're interested in, you should seriously consider using ADO.

- If you need portability to older 16-bit (Windows 3.1 or Windows for Workgroups) platforms and don't want to maintain multiple code bases, you need to use one of the older data access interfaces. DAO and ODBC are both available in 16-bit versions, making it easier to maintain one code base for both old and new platforms.

- If you're updating an existing application that uses one of the older methods (such as DAO), you've got a hard problem. Staying with the current data access library will likely result in the fastest development cycle, but at the cost of not being able to use the latest features. If there are substantial problems with your existing application, you might find it worth your while to upgrade to ADO while you're fixing the other problems and take all the development hits in a single cycle.

Ultimately, in the foreseeable future (say, two to four years) most new applications will benefit from using ADO as the data access library. Now that Microsoft has committed its substantial resources to ADO and OLE DB, you can expect other vendors to join the parade and devote more effort to OLE DB providers than to ODBC drivers. Microsoft has announced that they are standardizing on ADO in their own applications, but you should take this with a grain of salt. There are still many shipping Microsoft applications that use older data access methods. And, as always, it will be easier to get technical support on new interfaces than on old ones. So, let's move forward on the assumption that you'll be using ADO in your application. In the next chapter, I'll explore the ADO object model in more depth and show you what you can do with each of the nine basic ADO objects.

CHAPTER

THREE

3

The ADO Object Model

As an experienced developer, you know that COM components expose their functionality through objects with methods, properties, and events. ADO is no exception to this. The ADO library contains surprisingly few objects, considering the amount of functionality it exposes. In this chapter, I'll discuss all the ADO objects, together with their characteristics. I'll show some examples of using these objects as well, though of course you'll be using them throughout the rest of the book.

The ADO Object Hierarchy

If you've worked with older Microsoft data access libraries such as Data Access Objects (DAO) or Remote Data Objects (RDO), ADO's object model will seem somewhat familiar. However, as Figure 3.1 shows, the object hierarchy is not nearly as complex in ADO as it was in previous libraries. You should also realize that ADO is not as strictly hierarchical as previous libraries were. For example, using DAO, in order to create a Recordset object you first needed to create the DBEngine, Workspace, and Database objects that were its ancestors in the object model. With ADO, you can simply create the Recordset object directly.

FIGURE 3.1:

ADO object hierarchy

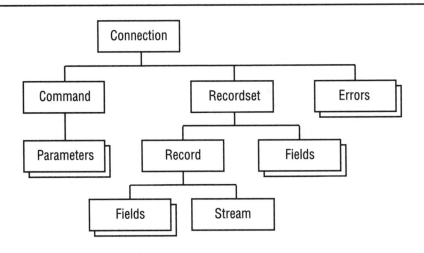

In addition to the objects shown in Figure 3.1, the Connection, Command, Parameter, Recordset, Record, and Field objects each have a Properties collection of Property objects. This enables your code to easily enumerate the properties of these objects. Objects shown in Figure 3.1 with multiple boxes are collections. For example, the Command object contains a Parameters collection containing individual Parameter objects.

The Connection Object

The Connection object represents an open connection to an OLE DB data source. You can create a Connection object and use it to create other objects further down the ADO object hierarchy. However, if you only need a single Recordset object from a particular Connection, it's probably more efficient to just create the Recordset directly and it will create a Connection object implicitly. You should reserve explicitly creating actual Connection objects for situations where you'll need to perform multiple, diverse operations on the connection.

You choose which data source a particular Connection will point to by using its ConnectionString property. This can be either an ODBC Data Source Name (DSN) that you've previously defined or a string of arguments and values using this syntax:

```
Provider=value;File Name=value;Remote Provider=value; ➡
  Remote Server=value; URL=value;
```

- The Provider argument specifies the name of the OLE DB provider to use.

- The File Name value specifies a file containing connection information—for example, an ODBC file data source. If you use the File Name argument, you must omit the Provider argument.

- The Remote Provider value specifies the name of a provider to use on the server when opening a client-side connection. This option applies to Remote Data Service (RDS) connections only. See Chapter 11 for more information on RDS.

- The Remote Server value specifies the name of a server to retrieve data from when using RDS.

- The URL value specifies the connection string as a URL rather than as an ODBC-style string.

All these arguments are optional. You can include additional arguments in the ConnectionString property in which case they are passed to the OLE DB provider without any alteration by ADO.

Methods, Properties, and Events

Table 3.1 details the functionality of the Connection object. You may find in practice that not all of these properties and methods apply to a particular Connection, since the properties are dependent on the data provider you're using. That's a reflection of the wide diversity of OLE DB providers. While there is a common core of functionality that every provider is required to support, the ADO library includes wrappers for some optional functionality as well.

NOTE In Table 3.1 and the tables following, the Type column indicates whether a particular listing is a property (P), method (M), event (E), or collection (C) of the parent object.

TABLE 3.1: Connection Object Details

Name	Type	Explanation
Attributes	P	Bitmapped property that indicates whether the data source supports retaining commits and retaining aborts.
BeginTrans	M	Begin a transaction.
BeginTransComplete	E	Occurs after a BeginTrans method is completed.
Cancel	M	Cancel a pending asynchronous Open or Execute method.
Close	M	Terminate the connection with the data source.
CommandTimeout	P	Number of seconds to wait for a response from the data provider when using the Execute method.
CommitTrans	M	Commit a transaction.
CommitTransComplete	E	Occurs after a CommitTrans method is completed.
ConnectComplete	E	Occurs when a connection is successfully connected to a data source, or when an asynchronous connection attempt is cancelled.

Continued on next page

TABLE 3.1 CONTINUED: Connection Object Details

Name	Type	Explanation
ConnectionString	P	Data source name or arguments to use for this connection.
ConnectionTimeout	P	Number of seconds to wait for a connection after executing the Open method.
CursorLocation	P	Controls whether cursors are created on the client (adUse-Client) or the server (adUseServer).
DefaultDatabase	P	Database that other objects using this Connection will use by default.
Disconnect	E	Occurs after the connection to a data source is closed.
Errors	C	Collection of Error objects.
Execute	M	Execute a command on the connection without creating a Command object.
ExecuteComplete	E	Occurs after a command is executed on this connection.
InfoMessage	E	Occurs when this connection receives an informational message from the underlying provider.
IsolationLevel	P	Constant indicating the isolation level of transactions in this connection from those in other connections.
Mode	P	Set to one of adModeUnknown, adModeRead, adModeWrite, adModeReadWrite, adModeShareDenyRead, adModeShare-DenyWrite, adModeShareExclusive, or adModeShareDenyNone to indicate the permissions for this Connection.
Open	M	Initialize the connection with the data source.
OpenSchema	M	Obtain schema information from the provider.
Properties	C	The collection of Property objects describing this connection.
Provider	P	OLE DB provider used for this connection.
RollbackTrans	M	Roll back a transaction.
RollbackTransComplete	E	Occurs when a RollbackTrans operation is completed.
State	P	Constant indicating whether the Connection is open or closed.
Version	P	Version of ADO.

Continued on next page

TABLE 3.1 CONTINUED: Connection Object Details

Name	Type	Explanation
WillConnect	E	Occurs just before an attempt to connect to a data source. Can be cancelled.
WillExecute	E	Occurs just before an attempt to execute a command on this connection. Can be cancelled.

Using the Connection Object

I'm not going to try to teach you everything about using the ADO objects in this book. That would be an entire book all by itself. But the Objects.vbp sample project includes some samples of basic ADO operations, just to get you up to speed. In this section, we'll look briefly at the Connection object.

Figure 3.2 shows frmConnect from the Objects.vbp sample project. It demonstrates three ways that you can open a Connection object:

- Synchronously with a connection string
- Asynchronously with a connection string
- Using a URL instead of a connection string

FIGURE 3.2:

Opening Connections

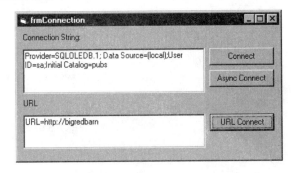

Synchronous Connections

The frmConnection sample uses this connection string to open a connection:

```
Provider=SQLOLEDB.1; Data Source=(local);User ID=sa; ➡
Initial Catalog=pubs
```

The form presents this connection string in a text box so you can easily edit it before attempting to connect to a server. This string will work as is if you've got SQL Server installed on the same computer where you're running the example, and the default sa user has the default blank password. If that's not the case, you might need to change the Data Source or User ID arguments, or add a Password argument.

The only part of this string that's understood by the ADO Connection object is Provider=SQLOLEDB.1. This tells ADO to use the native Microsoft SQL Server OLE DB provider. The rest of the options in the connection string are passed to the provider to be interpreted. This interpretation is provider-specific. To find out which options are accepted by a provider, you'll need to refer to the documentation supplied by that provider. Or you can use this technique to create a valid connection string from a Data Link file:

1. Create a new text file on your hard drive.

2. Change the name of the text file to use the extension .UDL.

3. Double-click the UDL file. This will open the Data Link Properties dialog box.

4. Choose the provider you want to use and set the appropriate properties to connect to your data.

5. Close the Data Link Properties dialog box.

6. Open the UDL file in Notepad. You'll see that it contains a complete connection string for your chosen provider.

Once you've created a connection string, the basic ADO code to open a connection is quite simple:

```
Private Sub cmdConnect_Click()
    ' Connect via an OLE DB Connection string
    Dim cnn As ADODB.Connection
    Set cnn = New ADODB.Connection
    cnn.ConnectionString = txtConnectionString.Text
    cnn.Open
```

```
    MsgBox "Connection succeeded"
    cnn.Close
    Set cnn = Nothing
End Sub
```

Here txtConnectionString is the text box that contains the connection string. Once you call the Open method, this code uses the connection string to locate the appropriate OLE DB provider, passes it the remaining arguments in the connection string, and waits for the connection to be made.

Asynchronous Connections

It's not always convenient to wait for an OLE DB provider to make a connection. Particularly if you're connecting to a server over the Internet, this may take a substantial amount of time. Rather than lock the user out of your application entirely while the connection is made, you may want to connect asynchronously. To do this, you'll need a module-level variable for your ADO Connection object, declared with the WithEvents keyword:

```
Private WithEvents mcnn As ADODB.Connection

Private Sub cmdAsyncConnect_Click()
    ' Connect asynchronously via an
    ' OLE DB Connection string
    Set mcnn = New ADODB.Connection
    mcnn.ConnectionString = txtConnectionString.Text
    mcnn.Open , , , adAsyncConnect
End Sub

Private Sub mcnn_ConnectComplete( _
 ByVal pError As ADODB.Error, _
 adStatus As ADODB.EventStatusEnum, _
 ByVal pConnection As ADODB.Connection)
    MsgBox "Asynchronous connection succeeded"
    mcnn.Close
    Set mcnn = Nothing
End Sub
```

Supplying the asAsyncConnect argument to the Open method of the Connection object tells ADO not to block on the operation. Instead, your other code is free to continue executing while ADO locates the data via OLE DB. When the connection is made, the Connection object's ConnectComplete event is fired. In production code, you'll want to check the pError argument to this event procedure, because the ConnectComplete event is also fired if a connection cannot be made.

URL Connections

New in ADO 2.5 is the ability to connect to data simply by supplying a URL that can be interpreted by an OLE DB provider. For example, on the frmConnection user interface you can see the following URL used:

```
URL=http://bigredbarn
```

In this case, `bigredbarn` is a computer that's running Internet Information Server on my network. You'll need to modify this URL to point to your own IIS server. Once you've got a valid URL, though, it's simple to connect via ADO:

```
Private Sub cmdURLConnect_Click()
    ' Connect via a URL
    Dim cnn As ADODB.Connection
    Set cnn = New ADODB.Connection
    cnn.ConnectionString = txtURL.Text
    cnn.Open
    MsgBox "Connection succeeded"
    cnn.Close
    Set cnn = Nothing
End Sub
```

As you can see, there's no code difference between using a full connection string and using a URL. When you use a URL, ADO checks to see which provider interprets that particular type of resource URL, and calls that provider. For HTTP URLs, ADO uses the Microsoft OLE DB Provider for Internet Publishing.

WARNING   The Microsoft OLE DB Provider for Internet Publishing is not installed as a part of ADO 2.5. It's already part of the operating system if you're using Windows 2000. If you're using another platform, you need to install either the Web Folders component of Internet Explorer 5 or the Web Folders component of Office 2000 to obtain this provider.

The Command Object

Think of a Command object as a single instruction to your data source to produce data. Depending on the back end, this might be a SQL query, a stored procedure, or something else entirely.

The easiest way to use a Command object is to create an independent command object, set its other properties, and then set its ActiveConnection property to a valid connection string. This will cause ADO to create an implicit Connection object for use by this Command only. However, if you're going to execute multiple Commands on a single Connection, you should avoid this technique, since it will create a separate Connection object for each Command. Instead, you can set the ActiveConnection property to an existing Connection object.

TIP Depending on whether you're using a connection string or a Connection object, the ActiveConnection property might be a string or an object. Be sure to use the Set keyword in the latter case.

Methods, Properties, and Events

Table 3.2 shows the functionality of the Command object.

TABLE 3.2: Command Object Details

Name	Type	Explanation
ActiveConnection	P	Connection object or string to execute this command on.
Cancel	M	Cancels a pending asynchronous command.
CommandText	P	Text (SQL statement, stored procedure name or table name) of the Command.
CommandTimeout	P	Number of seconds to wait for a response from the data source.
CommandType	P	One of adCmdText, adCmdTable, adCmdStoredProc, or adCmd-Unknown.
CreateParameter	M	Creates a new Parameter object associated with this Command.

Continued on next page

TABLE 3.2 CONTINUED: Command Object Details

Name	Type	Explanation
Execute	M	Executes the Command and returns any recordset(s) it generates.
Name	P	String identifying this Command object.
Parameters	C	Collection of Parameter objects associated with this Command.
Prepared	P	If set to True, causes the data provider to save a compiled version of the command on the first execution.
Properties	C	The collection of Property objects describing this Command.
State	P	Constant indicating whether the object is open, closed, executing a command, or fetching records.

Using the Command Object

There are two major uses for Command objects:

- Executing statements against an OLE DB connection

- Retrieving a recordset based on a SQL statement or stored procedure

You'll see the latter technique below, in the sections on the Recordset and Parameter objects. In the Objects.vbp sample project, frmCommand demonstrates the use of Command objects to execute SQL statements. Figure 3.3 shows frmCommand, which displays two fields from the authors table in the SQL Server pubs database. It then lets you change all the instances of "CA" to "CO," or vice versa.

FIGURE 3.3:

The frmCommand sample form

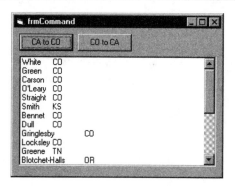

The code to change from CA to CO uses the Execute method of the Command object:

```
Private Sub cmdCO_Click()
    ' Change all instances of "CA" to "CO"
    Dim cmd As ADODB.Command
    Set cmd = New ADODB.Command
    ' Set the SQL statement to execute
    cmd.CommandText = "UPDATE authors SET state='CO' " & _
     "WHERE state='CA'"
    ' Set the connection
    Set cmd.ActiveConnection = mcnn
    ' And execute the command
    cmd.Execute
    ' Refresh the list
    RefreshList
End Sub
```

The CommandText property of a Command object holds the statement that should be sent through the OLE DB provider to the data source. Naturally, this needs to be in a syntax understood by the data source (here, Microsoft SQL Server). This code also sets the ActiveConnection property of the Command object to refer to an existing connection (set up in the Form_Load procedure) that points to the appropriate database.

Alternatively, the code to change from CO to CA uses a different ability of Command objects. Once you've associated a Command object with a Connection object, you can use the name of the Command object as if it were a method of the command object:

```
Private Sub cmdCA_Click()
    ' Change all instances of "CO" to "CA"
    Dim cmd As ADODB.Command
    Set cmd = New ADODB.Command
    ' Assign a name to the command
    cmd.Name = "ChangeToCA"
    ' Set the SQL statement to execute
    cmd.CommandText = "UPDATE authors SET state='CA' " & _
     "WHERE state='CO'"
    ' Set the connection
    Set cmd.ActiveConnection = mcnn
    ' And execute the command by name
    mcnn.ChangeToCA
```

```
      ' Refresh the list
      RefreshList
End Sub
```

This code differs from the previous example by explicitly assigning a name to the Command object. You must do this before assigning the CommandText or setting the ActiveConnection property; otherwise, you'll get a run-time error. Note that the code no longer uses the Execute method to actually run the Command. Instead, once you've named a Command, ADO treats that name as a method of the parent Connection object.

While using Command names as methods is a good technique for making your code look simpler, it has one major drawback in Visual Basic: Because this "method" of the Connection object doesn't exist in the ADO type library, you don't get the benefits of IntelliSense when you're writing your code.

The Recordset Object

A Recordset object represents a set of records retrieved from a data provider (similar to the DAO Recordset and RDO Resultset objects). Because this is the object that allows you to directly retrieve data, it's indispensable to ADO processing. ADO allows you to open a Recordset object directly, or to create one from a Connection or Command object.

ADO Recordset objects support four types of cursor (although, of course, not all cursor types will be available from all data providers):

Dynamic   Lets you see changes to the data made by other users, and supports all types of movement that don't rely on bookmarks. It may allow bookmarks if the data provider supports them.

Keyset   Is dynamic but does not let you see records added or deleted by other users. (It does allow you to see changes to the data made by other users.) Keyset cursors support bookmarks and all other kinds of movement through the recordset.

Static   Provides a frozen copy of the data at the time the recordset was opened. Additions, changes, and deletions by other users have no impact on the recordset, since it is never refreshed after it is created. Static cursors support bookmarks and all other kinds of movement through the recordset.

Forward-only   Is a static cursor that only allows you to move forward through the recordset. This is ADO's default cursor.

ADO Recordset objects support both immediate and batch updating. You can also use disconnected recordsets to obtain the optimistic batch updating functionality first introduced in RDO.

Methods and Properties

Table 3.3 lists the methods and properties supplied by the ADO Recordset object. Remember, not all of these will apply to every recordset. Which methods and properties are relevant depends on both the recordset type and the underlying data provider.

TABLE 3.3:   Recordset Object Details

Name	Type	Explanation
AbsolutePage	P	Number of data pages the current record is into the recordset.
AbsolutePosition	P	Ordinal position of the current record in the recordset.
ActiveCommand	P	Command this recordset was created from.
ActiveConnection	P	Connection this recordset was created from.
AddNew	M	Prepares a new record to be added to the recordset.
BOF	P	True if you have moved before the beginning of the recordset.
Bookmark	P	Unique identifier for the current row of the recordset.
CacheSize	P	Number of records that are cached in local memory.
Cancel	M	Cancels an asynchronous Open method.
CancelBatch	M	Cancel all pending changes in the recordset.
CancelUpdate	M	Throws away an AddNew or Edit without saving changes.
Clone	M	Produces a second recordset identical to the current recordset.
Close	M	Closes the recordset.
CompareBookmarks	M	Determine which of two bookmarks points to an earlier row in the recordset.

Continued on next page

TABLE 3.3 CONTINUED: Recordset Object Details

Name	Type	Explanation
CursorLocation	P	Constant indicating the location of the cursor used for this recordset. Can be adUseClient or adUseServer.
CursorType	P	Constant indicating the type of cursor used for this recordset. Can be adOpenDynamic, adOpenForwardOnly, adOpenKeyset, or adOpenStatic.
DataMember	P	Specifies which member of a particular data source to bind this recordset to when using bound recordsets.
DataSource	P	Specifies the data source to use for a bound recordset.
Delete	M	Deletes the current record.
EditMode	P	Enumerated value indicating whether the current record is being edited and can be adEditNone, adEditInProgress, adEditAdd, or adEditDelete.
EndOfRecordset	E	Occurs when a MoveNext method fails because there are no more records in the recordset.
EOF	P	True if you have moved past the end of the recordset.
FetchComplete	E	Occurs when all the records in an asynchronous operation have been fetched.
FetchProgress	E	Occurs periodically during an asynchronous record retrieval operation.
FieldChangeComplete	E	Occurs after the value in a field is changed.
Fields	C	Fields collection of the recordset.
Filter	P	Allows you to select a subset of the recordset to work with.
Find	M	Find a record matching some criterion.
GetRows	M	Fills an array with records from a recordset.
GetString	M	Returns the recordset as a delimited string.
Index	P	Sets the index to use when performing a Seek operation.
LockType	P	Controls the type of locks placed during editing. Can be adLockReadOnly, adLockPessimistic, adLockOptimistic, or adLockBatchOptimistic.

Continued on next page

TABLE 3.3 CONTINUED: Recordset Object Details

Name	Type	Explanation
MarshalOptions	P	Controls the marshalling of records to the server for a client-side recordset. Can be adMarshalAll or adMarshal-ModifiedOnly.
MaxRecords	P	Maximum number of records to be returned in the recordset.
Move	M	Moves to an offset from the current record (you can specify the number of records to move).
MoveComplete	E	Occurs after the record pointer is repositioned.
MoveFirst	M	Moves to the first record.
MoveLast	M	Moves to the last record.
MoveNext	M	Moves to the next record.
MovePrevious	M	Moves to the previous record.
NextRecordset	M	Returns the next recordset from the current Command object.
Open	M	Opens a recordset.
PageCount	P	Number of data pages in the recordset.
PageSize	P	Size of a single data page.
Properties	C	Collection of Property objects describing this recordset.
RecordChangeComplete	E	Occurs when a change to an entire record has been saved.
RecordCount	P	Number of records in the recordset. May return adUnknown (-1) if ADO cannot determine how many records are in the recordset.
RecordsetChangeComplete	E	Occurs when all changes to the recordset have been committed.
Requery	M	Reruns the original query that created the recordset.
Resync	M	Synchronizes the recordset with the underlying data.
Save	M	Persists the recordset to a file.
Seek	M	Search for a record using an index. Can only be used on client-side recordsets, and only if the provider supports this functionality.

Continued on next page

TABLE 3.3 CONTINUED: Recordset Object Details

Name	Type	Explanation
Sort	P	Specifies the field(s) to sort the recordset on.
Source	P	Command or SQL query that's the source of the recordset.
Status	P	Array of values containing the results of batch update operations.
StayInSync	P	Applies to hierarchical recordsets only. If True, the child recordset pointers are automatically updated whenever a parent pointer is changed.
Supports	M	Operator to determine which operations a recordset supports.
Update	M	Commit the work since an Edit or AddNew method.
UpdateBatch	M	Commit all pending changes on a batch cursor.
WillChangeField	E	Occurs before a Field object's value is changed.
WillChangeRecord	E	Occurs before a row is changed.
WillChangeRecordset	E	Occurs before changes to a recordset are committed.
WillMove	E	Occurs before the record pointer is repositioned.

Using Recordset Objects

I'll cover some advanced Recordset operations in Chapter 8. For now, I'll just concentrate on the basics. In order to make the best use of ADO, you need to understand the distinct types of recordset that are available. After I've covered that, I'll show you several ways to open Recordset objects.

Types of Recordsets

In addition to the connection and the record source, there are three parameters that characterize recordsets:

- Cursor Location
- Cursor Type
- Lock Type

Each of these parameters corresponds to a property of the Recordset object, and each can be set when the recordset is opened. ADO supplies constants for the allowable values for these parameters.

The CursorLocation property can be either adUseServer, for server-side cursors, or adUseClient, for client-side cursors. A cursor is a set of records in memory, and of course some software has to be responsible for keeping track of this set of records. Server-side cursors are maintained by the actual data source the records are retrieved from. Client-side cursors are maintained by the Microsoft Cursor Service for OLE DB, which attempts to level the playing field by supplying capabilities that are lacking in some servers. If no CursorLocation is specified, a server-side cursor is the default.

Some functionality is available only in client-side cursors—for example, re-sorting recordsets, or using an index to find records. If you need these capabilities, you should use client-side cursors. Otherwise, you may find that server-side cursors provide better performance.

The CursorType parameter further specifies the desired behavior of the Recordset object. You can specify one of four constants here:

- To open a dynamic recordset, use adOpenDynamic. A dynamic recordset allows all types of movement through the recordset, and keeps you up to date with changes made by other users.

- To open a keyset recordset, use adOpenKeyset. A keyset recordset functions like a dynamic recordset, except that you won't see new records added or records deleted by other users.

- To open a static cursor, use adOpenStatic. A static recordset does not show you any changes made by other users while the recordset is open, and is therefore most useful for reporting or other applications that don't need to be kept completely up to date. Disconnected recordsets must have a static CursorType.

- Finally, to open a forward-only cursor, use adOpenForwardOnly. A forward-only cursor is identical to a static cursor, except that you can only move forward in the recordset to go to a different record. This offers the fastest performance of any of the cursor types, at the expense of flexibility.

Note that the forward-only recordset is more flexible than you might think at first. In addition to using the MoveNext method, you can also use the Move method to skip intervening records, as long as you're moving forward. A forward-only recordset also supports the MoveFirst method, although this seems contradictory. Be aware, though, that this may be an expensive operation, as it might force the provider to close and reopen the recordset.

In general, if you stick to a cursor type that has no more functionality than you need in your application, you'll get the best possible performance. If you don't specify a cursor type, ADO defaults to the fastest type, which is a forward-only recordset.

Finally, you can use the LockType parameter to specify the record-locking behavior that will be used for editing operations. Here again you have four choices:

- adLockReadOnly, for recordsets that cannot be edited

- adLockPessimistic, for pessimistic locking (record locks are taken for the duration of all editing operations)

- adLockOptimistic, for optimistic locking (record locks are taken only while data is being updated)

- adLockBatchOptimistic, for recordsets that will use the UpdateBatch method to update multiple records in a single operation

If you don't specify a lock type, ADO defaults to the fastest type, which is a read-only recordset.

WARNING   The default recordset in ADO is server-side, forward-only, and read-only. If you want to move through records at random, or edit records, you must specify the cursor type and lock type to use!

Just to make things more interesting, what you ask for isn't always what you get. Not every provider supports every possible combination of these parameters. In almost every case, though, you'll get something close to what you asked for. But, for example, if you try to open a client-side, static, pessimistic recordset on a SQL Server data source, what you actually get will be a client-side, static, batch optimistic recordset. If you aren't sure what you're getting, you need to check the values of the CursorType, CursorLocation, and LockType properties of the Recordset object after calling its Open method to see what ADO delivered. You should also realize that different recordsets can have very different performance implications. In general, the recordsets with fewer capabilities are faster, but you'll want to test this in your own application to determine the best type of recordset to open.

Opening Recordsets

To open a recordset, you call the Open method of the Recordset object:

```
Recordset.Open Source, ActiveConnection, CursorType, ➡
LockType, Options
```

All these arguments are optional, because they can all be supplied by setting properties of the Recordset object before calling the Open method. For example, you can omit the LockType argument here if you have already set the LockType property of the Recordset object, or if you're happy with the default read-only locking. The Source argument specifies where the records should be retrieved from. Because providers are so flexible, there are a lot of possibilities for the Source argument. It can be:

- A Command object that returns records

- A SQL statement

- A table name

- A stored procedure name

- The name of a file containing a persisted recordset

- The name of a Stream object containing a persisted recordset

- A URL that specifies a file or other location with data

Not all of these options, of course, are valid for all providers.

The ActiveConnection argument specifies the ADO connection to use. This can be either a Connection object that you've already opened or a connection string. In the latter case, ADO creates a connection "behind the scenes" specifically for this Recordset object to use.

The CursorType and LockType arguments correspond to the cursor type and lock type parameters discussed in the previous section.

The Options argument supplies additional information to the provider. Generally, you can omit this argument, but some Open methods may be faster if you can include it. Valid Options include:

- adCmdUnknown, which is the default and supplies no additional information to the provider.

- adCmdText, which tells the provider that the CommandText property is a textual command like a SQL string.

- adCmdTable, which tells the provider that the CommandText property is the name of a table.

- adCmdStoredProc, which tells the provider that the CommandText property is the name of a stored procedure.

- adCmdFile, which tells the provider that the CommandText property is the name of a file.

- adCmdTableDirect, which tells the provider that the CommandText property is the name of a table that should be opened using low-level calls. Most providers don't support this.

- adCmdURLBind, which tells the provider that the CommandText is a URL.

- adAsyncExecute, which tells the provider that the command should be executed asynchronously.

- adAsyncFetch, which tells the provider that the cache should be filled synchronously, and then additional rows fetched asynchronously.

- adAsyncFetchNonBlocking, which tells the provider to fetch records asynchronously if it can be done without blocking the main thread of execution.

You'll find additional information on opening and manipulating recordsets in Chapter 8, and throughout the book.

The Parameter Object

A Parameter object represents a single parameter for a Command object. This might be a runtime parameter in a SQL query or an input or output parameter in a stored procedure. More generally, parameters are used with any type of parameterized commands, where an action is defined once but can have its results changed depending on the values set for variables. If you know the properties of a particular Parameter, you can use the CreateParameter method to make appropriate Parameter objects for a Command object, which allows you to initialize parameters without any server-side processing. Otherwise, you must call the Refresh method on the Command object's Parameters collection to retrieve parameter information from the server, a resource-intensive operation.

Methods and Properties

Table 3.4 lists the methods and properties for Parameter objects.

TABLE 3.4: Parameter Object Details

Name	Type	Explanation
AppendChunk	M	Stores data in a long binary parameter.
Attributes	P	Bitmapped set of attributes for the parameter.
Direction	P	Indicates whether a parameter is input, output, both input and output, or a return value from a stored procedure.
Name	P	Name of the parameter.
NumericScale	P	Scale (number of digits to the right of the decimal point) for a numeric parameter.
Precision	P	Precision (total number of digits) for a numeric parameter.
Properties	C	Collection of Property objects describing this parameter.
Size	P	Maximum data a parameter can hold.
Type	P	Constant indicating the datatype of the parameter.
Value	P	Current value of the parameter.

Using Parameter Objects

As I mentioned above, you can interrogate a Command object for its parameters using the Refresh method on the Parameters collection, or you can explicitly declare parameters in your Visual Basic application. As an example of the first technique, consider this code from frmParameters in the Objects.vbp sample project:

```
Private Sub cmdGetParameters_Click()
    ' Get the parameters for a
    ' specified stored procedure
    Dim cmd As ADODB.Command
    Dim prm As ADODB.Parameter
    Dim rst As ADODB.Recordset
```

```
lboResults.Clear

' Create a command and retrieve its
' parameters collection
Set cmd = New ADODB.Command
Set cmd.ActiveConnection = mcnn
cmd.CommandText = "byroyalty"
cmd.CommandType = adCmdStoredProc
cmd.Parameters.Refresh

' Step through the parameters, filling
' in the input parameters
For Each prm In cmd.Parameters
    If prm.Direction = adParamInput Then
        prm.Value = InputBox(prm.Name, _
          "Enter parameter value")
    End If
Next prm

' Get a recordset from the stored proc
Set rst = cmd.Execute

' And display the results
If Not rst.EOF Then
    Do Until rst.EOF
        lboResults.AddItem rst.Fields(0).Value
        rst.MoveNext
    Loop
End If

End Sub
```

In this code, the call to the Parameters.Refresh method instructs ADO to actually connect to the data source and retrieve the parameters (if any) for the stored procedure represented by the Command object in the CommandText property. If you check the Parameters.Count property before the call to the Refresh method, it will tell you that there are zero parameters. Make sure to test the count before setting the ActiveConnection and stored procedure name; if you do it afterwards, it will automatically go to the stored procedure and retrieve the ParameterCount even before the Refresh. Afterwards, though, the collection has been initialized, and you can walk through it with a typical For Each loop. Note the use of the Parameter's Direction property to identify parameters that you need to supply a value for in order to execute the stored procedure.

Alternatively, if you know in advance the details of the parameterized command you'll be working with, you can create parameters in your code. This method has the advantage of speed, because you don't have to connect to the data source to retrieve parameter information. Again, there's an example in frm-Parameters in the Objects.vbp sample project:

```
Private Sub cmdGetResults_Click()
    ' Execute a stored procedure
    ' by supplying a parameter
    Dim cmd As ADODB.Command
    Dim prm As ADODB.Parameter
    Dim rst As ADODB.Recordset

    lboResults.Clear

    ' Create a command
    Set cmd = New ADODB.Command
    Set cmd.ActiveConnection = mcnn
    cmd.CommandText = "byroyalty"
    cmd.CommandType = adCmdStoredProc

    ' Create and initialize a parameter
    Set prm = cmd.CreateParameter("@percentage", _
     adInteger, adParamInput)
    prm.Value = txtPercentage.Text

    ' Append the parameter to the command
    cmd.Parameters.Append prm

    ' Get a recordset from the stored proc
    Set rst = cmd.Execute

    ' And display the results
    If Not rst.EOF Then
        Do Until rst.EOF
            lboResults.AddItem rst.Fields(0).Value
            rst.MoveNext
        Loop
    End If
```

The drawback to this method is that you must have correct information about parameters in advance. For example, in this case, if the parameter had been named something other than @percentage or was of a type other than integer, the procedure would not have worked properly. However, creating your own parameters is much faster than using the Refresh method to retrieve them from the data source.

The Field Object

A Field object represents a single column of data in a recordset. Once you've retrieved a recordset, you'll usually work with the Fields collection to read the data in the recordset. However, since the Fields collection is the default property of the Recordset object, you won't often see its name in your code. The following two lines of code produce an identical result:

```
Recordset.Fields(0).Value
Recordset(0)
```

Methods and Properties

Table 3.5 shows the methods and properties available from the Field object.

TABLE 3.5: Field Object Details

Name	Type	Explanation
ActualSize	P	Size of the data actually stored in the field.
AppendChunk	P	Stores a chunk of data in a long binary field.
Attributes	P	Bitmapped value indicating some of the characteristics of the field, including whether it may be updated and whether it is valid for long binary operations.
DataFormat	P	For a bound field, represents the DataFormat object that controls formatting for the field.
DefinedSize	P	Maximum data the field can store.
GetChunk	M	Retrieves a chunk of data from a long binary field.

Continued on next page

TABLE 3.5 CONTINUED: Field Object Details

Name	Type	Explanation
Name	P	Name of the field.
NumericScale	P	Scale (number of digits to the right of the decimal point) for a numeric field.
OriginalValue	P	Value in the field before another user changed it.
Precision	P	Precision (total number of digits) for a numeric field.
Type	P	Constant indicating the datatype of the field.
UnderlyingValue	P	Value currently stored in the database for this field (might have changed since the field's Value property was set).
Value	P	Data stored in the field.

Using Field Objects

The basic use of a Field object is to retrieve and update information stored in the original data source. Of course, in order to update a field's value you must be sure that you've opened the recordset in some mode that allows writing. But other than that, there's not much to know about fields.

In the Objects.vbp sample project, the frmField form demonstrates the different syntaxes that you can use to refer to a field's value:

```
Private Sub cmdGo_Click()
    ' Demonstrate different ways to
    ' refer to a Field's value
    Dim cnn As ADODB.Connection
    Dim rst As ADODB.Recordset
    Dim fld As ADODB.Field

    ' Open a recordset
    Set cnn = New ADODB.Connection
    cnn.Open _
     "Provider=SQLOLEDB.1;Data Source=(local);" & _
     "User ID=sa;Initial Catalog=Northwind"
    Set rst = New ADODB.Recordset
    rst.Open "Customers", cnn
```

```
' Using the field's index
lboResults.AddItem rst.Fields(0).Value
lboResults.AddItem rst.Fields(0)
' Using the field's name
lboResults.AddItem _
 rst.Fields("CustomerID").Value
lboResults.AddItem _
 rst.Fields("CustomerID")
' Fields is the default collection
lboResults.AddItem rst(0).Value
lboResults.AddItem rst(0)
lboResults.AddItem rst("CustomerID").Value
lboResults.AddItem rst("CustomerID")
' And finally, using a variable
Set fld = rst.Fields(0)
lboResults.AddItem fld.Value
lboResults.AddItem fld

End Sub
```

If you run this sample, you'll see that all 10 of these ways of referring to the field's value return exactly the same result.

The Record Object

The Record object is a dual-purpose object. It can represent a row in a recordset. It can also represent a file or folder in a file system. However, it's important to realize that these are not actually distinct features of the Record object. Rather, the Record object is designed to represent a row in a recordset when the underlying OLE DB provider naturally supports a hierarchical data store. For example, Record objects can be used with providers that supply information from file systems or e-mail storage. They can't be used with providers that supply information from standard relational databases (even if there's a hierarchy within the database).

The Record, Stream, and Recordset objects work together to help you navigate through hierarchical storage:

- You can open a Record object at the root level of a storage.

- Using the Record's GetChildren method, you can open a Recordset object containing all the children of a node. You can in turn set a Record object equal to one of these children.

- Using the Record's associated Stream object, you can retrieve the actual binary data from within the record. You can think of Records as directory entries and Streams as the data contained within the files that those entries refer to.

WARNING   There's no easy way to tell whether an arbitrary OLE DB provider supports the Record object. Perhaps the best way is to attempt to open a Record object using the provider. If it can't supply one, it will generally return error 3251, Operation Not Supported.

Methods and Properties

Table 3.6 describes the Record object.

TABLE 3.6: Record Object Details

Name	Type	Explanation
ActiveConnection	P	The OLE DB connection that this record was retrieved from.
Cancel	M	Halts execution of an asynchronous operation.
Close	M	Removes the connection between this object and the original data source.
CopyRecord	M	Copies the contents of the record object to another location.
DeleteRecord	M	Deletes the contents of the record.
Fields	C	Field objects contained within this record.
GetChildren	M	Opens a recordset containing the subdirectories and files contained below this record.
Mode	P	Controls the permissions to this record. Takes the same values as the Mode property of the Connection object.
MoveRecord	M	Moves the contents of this record to another location.

Continued on next page

TABLE 3.6 CONTINUED: Record Object Details

Name	Type	Explanation
Open	M	Associates the record with a data source.
ParentURL	P	Returns the URL of the folder containing this record.
Properties	C	Collection of Property objects describing this record.
RecordType	P	Indicates the type of data represented by this object. Can be adCollectionRecord, adSimpleRecord, or adStructDoc.
Source	P	Contains the URL or recordset that this record was derived from.
State	P	Contains information on the state of an asynchronous operation. Can be adStateClosed, adStateConnecting, adStateExecuting, adStateFetching, or adStateOpen.

Using Record Objects

You can use the frmRecord form in the Objects.vbp sample project to investigate the behavior of Record objects. This form, shown in Figure 3.4, allows you to enter a URL for a server that you have rights to, and then opens a Record object pointing to that URL. It then fills the list box with the names of all the records that are children of the Record object you just opened. If you double-click one of those records, either its children will be displayed (if it's a collection) or the contents of the record's associated Stream will be displayed (if it's a simple record).

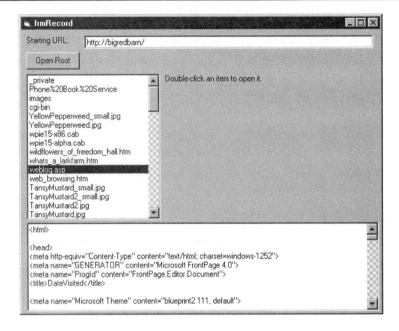

The code to open the root Record object is fairly simple:

```
Private Sub cmdOpenRoot_Click()
    ' Open a record pointing to the specified URL
    Set mrec = New Record
    mrec.Open "", "URL=" & txtURL.Text, , _
    adOpenIfExists Or adCreateCollection
    ' Open a recordset containing this record's
    ' children. This recordset is forward-only,
    ' read-only, server-side: that's all set
    ' by the choice of OLE DB provider.
    Set mrstChildren = mrec.GetChildren
    lstChildren.Clear
    Do Until mrstChildren.EOF
        lstChildren.AddItem mrstChildren(0)
        mrstChildren.MoveNext
    Loop
    lblDoubleClick.Enabled = True
End Sub
```

In the sample project, the txtURL control is pre-filled with `http://bigredbarn/`, which happens to be the internal network URL of my Web server. Of course, you'll need to replace that with the name of your own Web server to successfully run this code.

This bit of code demonstrates the first way to use the Record object's Open method: use an empty string for the first argument, and a URL for the second argument. This tells ADO to find the OLE DB provider that can interpret the supplied URL, and open a Record object pointing to the selected root item. Using the adOpenIfExists and adCreateCollection flags simultaneously make the code do the right thing whether this URL refers to an individual file or to a folder (as it does in this case).

Once the code has a Record object referring to the root, it uses the record's GetChildren method to populate a recordset of all the children of that record. Using the Internet Publishing Provider, as I'm doing here, means that this recordset will contain all the files and folders that are children of the root. The rest of the code in this procedure simply displays the names of those files (which are stored in the first field of the recordset) in a list box.

The code that handles double-clicking the list box demonstrates the other way you can use the Open method of a Record object:

```
Private Sub lstChildren_DblClick()
    ' Deal with double-click on an item. If it's
    ' a collection, open it. If it's a simple
    ' item, show the associated stream

    ' First, get to the selected record. Since
    ' both the recordset and the listbox are
    ' zero-indexed, we can use the move method
    ' to get there easily. Also note that the
    ' MoveFirst method is valid on a forward-
    ' only recordset.
    mrstChildren.MoveFirst
    mrstChildren.Move lstChildren.ListIndex
    ' Now get this child into a record
    mrec.Close
    mrec.Open mrstChildren
    ' Check the type and act accordingly
    Select Case mrec.RecordType
        Case adSimpleRecord
```

```
            ShowRecord
        Case adCollectionRecord
            ' Reset the recordset to the
            ' new children and repopulate
            ' the listbox
            Set mrstChildren = mrec.GetChildren
            lstChildren.Clear
            Do Until mrstChildren.EOF
                lstChildren.AddItem mrstChildren(0)
                mrstChildren.MoveNext
            Loop
    End Select
End Sub
```

First, this procedure uses a combination of the MoveFirst and Move methods to position the recordset so that the selected item is the current row (remember, you can use the MoveFirst method even on a forward-only recordset). Then, it uses the Open method of the Record object, passing the recordset as the source. This causes the Record object to contain the current recordset in the source.

What the code does next depends on the RecordType property of the record. If the RecordType is adCollectionRecord, this is another directory (or, more generally, a record containing a collection of other records). In this case, the code flushes out the list box and lists the children of the new record. Otherwise, the code calls the ShowRecord procedure to display the contents of the Record object's associated Stream in a text box. You'll learn about Stream objects in the next section.

The Stream Object

The Stream object represents binary data. Most often, you'll want to open a Stream object to retrieve the data associated with a Record object. You can also create your own stand-alone Stream objects and use them as handy spots to store binary data.

Methods and Properties

Table 3.7 describes the functionality of the Stream object.

TABLE 3.7: Stream Object Details

Name	Type	Explanation
Cancel	M	Cancels an asynchronous operation.
Charset	P	Character set to be used when storing this stream.
Close	M	Disassociates this object from its data source.
CopyTo	M	Copies the contents of this stream to another stream.
EOS	P	True if the end of the stream has been input.
Flush	M	Writes data from the ADO buffer to the hard drive.
LineSeparator	P	Specifies the character used to separate logical lines within the stream.
LoadFromFile	M	Loads the contents of a local disk file into an open Stream.
Mode	P	Specifies the permissions of the Stream.
Open	M	Retrieves data into the Stream.
Position	P	Location of the current position in the stream.
Read	M	Reads data from a binary stream.
ReadText	M	Reads data from a text stream.
SaveToFile	M	Writes the contents of the Stream to a local disk file.
SetEOS	M	Sets the end of the Stream.
Size	P	Number of bytes in the stream.
SkipLine	M	Skips a logical line when reading a text stream.
State	P	State of a Stream during an asynchronous operation.
Type	P	Specifies whether the stream is binary (adTypeBinary) or textual (adTypeText) information.
Write	M	Writes data to a binary stream.
WriteText	M	Writes data to a text stream.

Using Stream Objects

One use of Stream objects is to retrieve the binary data (if any) associated with a Record. There's an example of this in the frmRecord form in the Objects.vbp sample project. When you double-click the name of a record that corresponds to an actual disk file, it calls the ShowRecord procedure:

```
Private Sub ShowRecord()
    ' Show the contents of the current
    ' record. Assumes the record is already
    ' known to be of type adSimpleRecord
    Dim stm As Stream
    ' Open the stream from the record associated
    ' with the current recordset pointer
    Set stm = New Stream
    mrec.Close
    mrec.Open mrstChildren
    stm.Open mrec, adModeRead, _
     adOpenStreamFromRecord
    ' Check the type of the stream and
    ' read its contents into the textbox
    If stm.Type = adTypeBinary Then
        txtContents.Text = stm.Read(adReadAll)
    Else ' stm.type=adTypeText
        stm.Charset = "ascii"
        txtContents.Text = stm.ReadText(adReadAll)
    End If
End Sub
```

For purposes of this code, there's already a recordset in the module-level mrstChildren variable, and we already know it's a simple record rather than a collection. The mrec variable, a Record, is also declared at the module level.

The code first retrieves the actual record from the recordset, and then calls the Open method of the Stream object to grab the binary data of the record. Given the Stream object, you call either the Read or the ReadText method to obtain the actual data, depending on whether the Stream is binary or text (which you can determine from the Stream object's Type property).

Note the use of the Charset property of the Stream object. The data in the Stream is always stored in Unicode. However, it's a fact of life that you probably want a non-Unicode character set for display. The ASCII character set, as shown in this example, is usually a safe bet. If you'd like to know what other options are available on your computer, check the Registry under HKEY_CLASSES_ROOT\ Mime\Database\Charset.

You can also create your own Stream objects and use them as handy buckets to hold any sort of data that you care to store. One use for this technique is integrated directly into ADO. You can persist the contents of a recordset to a Stream, or take a Stream that has such contents and reload it into a recordset. There's a sample of this technique in the frmStream form in the Objects.vbp sample project. This sample first loads a recordset from a local Jet database and displays its contents in a list box on the form:

```
Private Sub Form_Load()
    ' Open a Recordset and show its contents
    Set mrst = New ADODB.Recordset
    mrst.CursorLocation = adUseClient
    mrst.Open "Customers", _
     "Provider=Microsoft.Jet.OLEDB.4.0;" & _
     "Data Source=C:\Program Files\Microsoft " & _
     "Visual Studio\VB98\Nwind.mdb;", _
     adOpenKeyset, adLockBatchOptimistic
    Do Until mrst.EOF
        lboCustomers.AddItem mrst("CompanyName")
        mrst.MoveNext
    Loop
End Sub
```

Then, when the user clicks the Persist To Stream command button, the form calls the Recordset's Save method to transfer the entire contents of the recordset to a Stream variable:

```
Private Sub cmdPersist_Click()
    ' Persist the recordset to a stream
    Set mstm = New ADODB.Stream
    mrst.Save mstm, adPersistADTG
End Sub
```

The Clear And Close button removes the data from the form and the recordset:

```
Private Sub cmdClear_Click()
    ' Disconnect from the data source
    mrst.Close
    Set mrst = Nothing
    ' And clear the listbox
```

```
        lboCustomers.Clear
    End Sub
```

And, if you want to see the data again, the "Reload from Stream" button dumps the Stream back into a recordset and displays it on screen again:

```
Private Sub cmdReload_Click()
    ' Reload the records from the stream
    Set mrst = New ADODB.Recordset
    mrst.Open mstm
    Do Until mrst.EOF
        lboCustomers.AddItem mrst("CompanyName")
        mrst.MoveNext
    Loop
End Sub
```

Of course, this technique is only useful for as long as your program maintains the Stream variable in memory. However, there's a level of additional flexibility available by saving the Stream to a disk file. You can use the Stream's SaveToFile method to write an entire stream out, or the LoadFromFile method to read a disk file and make its contents into a Stream. So, for example, your application might use Stream variables to hold data that the user is currently working with, and then write any pending data out to disk files when the application is shut down.

The Error Object

An Error object represents a single error. Since one data access operation can generate multiple errors, Error objects are contained in an Errors collection. If the last operation succeeded, this collection will be empty. Otherwise, you can use the For Each operator to examine each Error in turn.

Note that if there is no valid Connection object, you will have to use the Visual Basic Err object instead. This is the case if you've directly opened a recordset using a connection string, for example.

Methods and Properties

Table 3.8 lists the properties of the Error object.

TABLE 3.8: Error Object Details

Name	Type	Explanation
Description	P	Text of the error.
HelpContext	P	Help topic for the error.
HelpFile	P	Help file for the error.
NativeError	P	Original provider-specific error number.
Number	P	Error number.
Source	P	Object that raised the error.
SQLState	P	Original ODBC SQLState constant.

Using Error Objects

The Error object is refreshingly straightforward when compared to the rest of the ADO object model. If errors occur in the OLE DB layer, each one is translated to an Error object, and these Error objects are used to populate the Connection object's Errors collection.

For example, the frmError sample form in the Objects.vbp sample project attempts to use the SQLOLEDB Provider to connect to a nonexistent server:

```
Private Sub cmdConnect_Click()
    ' Attempt to connect, trapping errors
    Dim cnn As Connection
    Dim er As Error

    On Error GoTo HandleErr

    Set cnn = New Connection
    cnn.Open txtConnectionString

ExitHere:
    Exit Sub

HandleErr:
    For Each er In cnn.Errors
```

```
        MsgBox "Error " & er.Number & " " & _
            er.Description
        Next er
        Resume ExitHere
    End Sub
```

If you execute this procedure, you'll see a message box with the message shown in Figure 3.5.

FIGURE 3.5:

Sample information from an Error object

WARNING   The Errors collection is populated only when errors are bubbled up from an OLE DB provider. So, for example, if you change the connection string to refer to a nonexistent provider, you won't get anything in the Errors collection. In that case, the error will be passed to the Visual Basic Errors collection by ADO, which can't find the specified driver.

The Property Object

The Property object is the building block of the other ADO objects. That is, properties describe the other objects. Table 3.9 lists the properties of a Property object.

TABLE 3.9: Property Object Details

Name	Type	Explanation
Attributes	P	Information about the property. Can be a combination of adPropNotSupported (not supported by this Provider), adProp-Required (must be specified before initializing the data source), adPropOptional, adPropRead (the user can read the property), and adPropWrite (the user can change the value of the property).

Continued on next page

TABLE 3.9 CONTINUED: Property Object Details

Name	Type	Explanation
Name	P	Name of the property.
Type	P	Datatype of the property.
Value	P	Current value of the property.

If you've worked with other data access libraries in the past, you might expect the Properties collection of an object to contain all the properties of the object. In ADO, this is *not* the case. The Properties collection contains only the properties added to the object by the provider. It does not contain the intrinsic properties of the object.

Figure 3.6 shows the frmProperty form from the Objects.vbp sample project. This form shows both the hard-wired and the dynamic properties of a Connection object—in this case, one connected to a SQL Server provider.

FIGURE 3.6:

Built-in and Dynamic properties

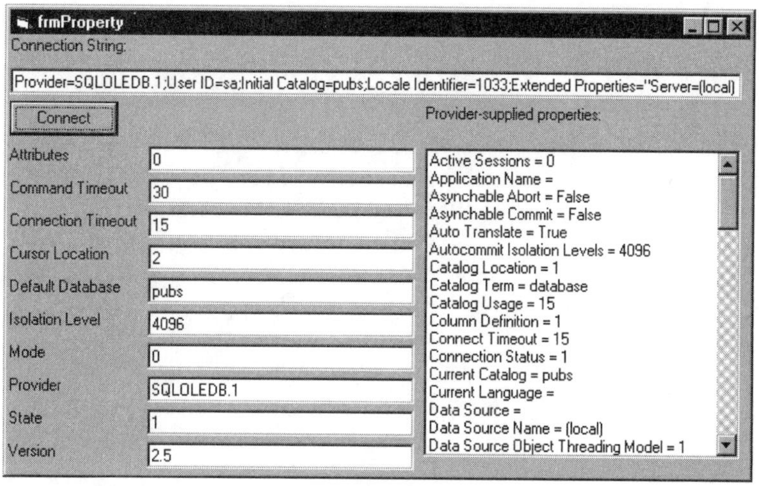

As you can see, the built-in properties don't appear in the Properties collection, and vice versa. What this means is that if you want to fully iterate the properties of an ADO object, you need to know in advance what the built-in properties are named. The code for frmProperties demonstrates this principle:

```
Private Sub cmdConnect_Click()
    ' Connect to a provider, and
    ' then show the properties of
    ' the connection
    Dim cnn As New Connection
    Dim prp As Property

    cnn.Open txtConnectionString.Text

    With cnn
        ' Retrieve the built-in properties
        txtAttributes.Text = .Attributes
        txtCommandTimeout.Text = .CommandTimeout
        txtConnectionString.Text = _
         .ConnectionString
        txtConnectionTimeout.Text = _
         .ConnectionTimeout
        txtCursorLocation.Text = .CursorLocation
        txtDefaultDatabase.Text = _
         .DefaultDatabase
        txtIsolationLevel = .IsolationLevel
        txtMode.Text = .Mode
        txtProvider.Text = .Provider
        txtState.Text = .State
        txtVersion.Text = .Version
        ' Retrieve the dynamic properties
        lboProperties.Clear
        For Each prp In .Properties
            lboProperties.AddItem prp.Name & _
            " = " & prp.Value
        Next prp
    End With

End Sub
```

You can't create or destroy ADO object properties—unless, of course, you're writing an OLE DB Provider!

ADO Extensions

ADO supports the notion of extension libraries. An extension library is a collection of additional objects that work together with the existing ADO objects to accomplish some special task. Though you won't see much about extension objects in this book, you should at least be aware of the two major extension libraries:

- The ADO Extensions for Data Definition Language and Security, usually called ADOX, contains objects for working with schema and security information.

- The Microsoft ActiveX Data Objects (Multidimensional), usually called ADO MD, contains objects for working with consolidated data warehouse information.

To use the objects in these libraries, you must set a reference to an additional type library in your Visual Basic project. By splitting out functionality in this way, Microsoft accomplishes several goals. First, it makes the core ADO functionality easier to learn and understand. Second, it keeps the memory footprint of ADO lower and its speed higher by not loading objects that are rarely needed unless the developer explicitly asks for them.

ADOX

Figure 3.7 shows the ADOX object model. As you can see, it has objects to represent most underlying objects in a typical relational database. ADOX properties and methods allow you to create and manipulate these objects.

FIGURE 3.7:

The ADOX object model

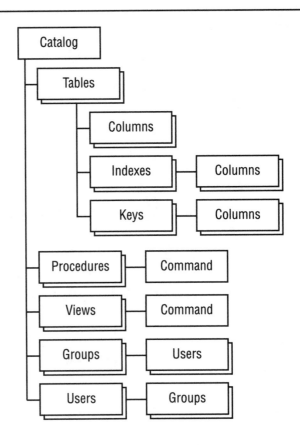

For more information on using ADOX, see the *Access 2000 Developer's Handbook, Volume 1: Desktop Edition* (by Ken Getz, Paul Litwin, and Mike Gilbert, ISBN 0-7821-2370-8, Sybex, 1999). That book covers the use of ADOX with Microsoft Jet databases. Of the available Microsoft drivers, the Jet OLE DB driver does the best job of supporting ADOX.

ADO MD

Figure 3.8 shows the ADO MD object model. Multidimensional data is data that's been stored and aggregated in such a way as to make summary queries quick and easy to run. Usually this is called Online Analytical Processing, or OLAP. Microsoft OLAP Server is one source of such data.

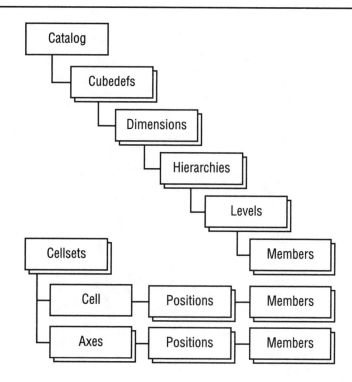

You'll learn more about using ADO MD to retrieve data in Chapter 12.

CHAPTER
FOUR

4

Exploring Data from Visual Basic

- Using the Data View Window

- Using the Query Designer

- Creating and Debugging Stored Procedures

Now that you've seen the ADO object model and have some sense of what you can do with ADO, it's time to start working with data. A few years ago, this would have meant writing a lot of code to connect to data sources, retrieve information about the data, examine the data, and update it. You can still do all these operations in code (and we'll look at some of that code in Chapter 8). But that's not the best way to go if you want to get up and running with data quickly.

Starting with Visual Basic 5, the developers at Microsoft began working hard to make basic database operations easier to perform. You can now do a wide variety of database operations using visual tools without ever having to write a line of code. This makes it possible for you to be vastly more productive as a database developer. If you need to be a database administrator as well, you'll still need to use your database's native tools for some operations. For example, these tools don't offer any support for creating users or performing other security operations.

In this chapter, you'll learn about the Data View window and the tools that you can call from this window. These tools are collectively known as the Visual Database Tools, and they're shared by many Microsoft products, including Visual Basic, Visual C++, Visual J++, Visual Interdev, and even Microsoft Office 2000. In addition, these tools can work with data from any OLE DB or ODBC provider. The net effect is that they let you concentrate on what you want to do instead of on the tedious syntax of how to do it. Let's start by looking at the Data View window itself.

Using the Data View Window

To open the Data View, choose View ➢ Data View Window from the Visual Basic menus, or click the Data View Window button on the Visual Basic Standard Toolbar. Figure 4.1 shows the default state of the Data View window. As you can see, it's a TreeView-based interface, similar to the left pane of Windows Explorer.

FIGURE 4.1:

The Data View window

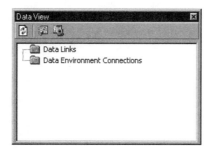

The Data View includes two top-level nodes:

Data Links   Represent connections to individual databases. These connections are stored independently of any particular Visual Basic project. You'll see the same set of connections reappear if you close your Visual Basic project and open another project, or close and reopen Visual Basic itself. Data links are useful for data that you need to have available all or most of the time.

NOTE   Don't confuse data links in the Data View with Microsoft Data Link files that you'll find in Windows Explorer. A Microsoft Data Link file contains the information needed to open an OLE DB connection to a data source. Microsoft Data Link files are covered in Chapter 5.

Data Environment Connections   Represent connections made through the Visual Basic Data Environment Designer. These connections are specific to a particular Visual Basic project. You'll learn about the Data Environment in Chapter 6.

An empty Data View isn't particularly useful. Figure 4.2 shows what the Data View might look like after adding a couple of data links and expanding parts of the TreeView. In the next section, you'll learn how to add new data links to the Data View.

FIGURE 4.2:

Data View window with
some data links

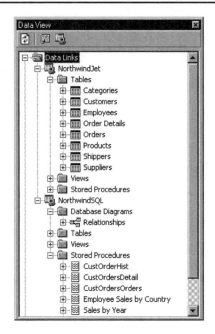

Connecting to Data

The simplest way to connect the Data View to actual data is to create a new data link. You can do this by right-clicking in the Data View window and choosing Add A Data Link, or by clicking the Add A New Data Link button on the Data View toolbar.

When you add a new data link, the Data View will display the Data Link Properties dialog box shown in Figure 4.3. You'll get very familiar with this dialog box as you work with ADO data sources; it's used any time you need to connect something to an OLE DB provider. As you can see, the first tab allows you to choose a particular OLE DB provider to use for the current data link. Once you select a provider, you can navigate through the other tabs of this dialog box to set provider-specific information.

FIGURE 4.3:

The Provider tab of the
Data Link Properties
dialog box

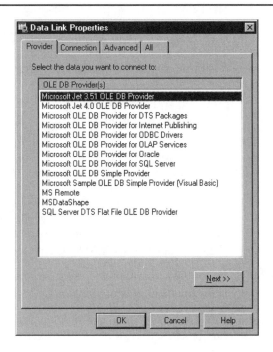

You'll probably see a different list of providers than that shown in Figure 4.3. As you install software on your computer, you'll end up with more and more OLE DB providers. The computer from which this screenshot was taken has had Visual Basic 6, SQL Server 7, ADO 2.5, the OLE DB Simple Provider Toolkit, Internet Explorer 5, and Microsoft Internet Information Server 4 installed. Here's a brief rundown of the OLE DB providers shown in this example:

- The Microsoft Jet 3.51 and Microsoft Jet 4 providers are used to read data from Microsoft Access databases and other databases that rely on the Jet database engine. The 4 driver doesn't remove the 3.51 driver, because they have slightly different default behaviors and the provider developers are wary of breaking existing applications.

- The Provider for DTS Packages and the SQL Server DTS Flat File OLE DB Provider are used to connect to SQL Server 7 Data Transformation Services packages. These packages are used in data warehousing applications to convert data from one format to another. We won't cover DTS in this book, but there's a summary in *SQL Server 7 In Record Time* (by Mike Gunderloy and Mary Chipman, ISBN 0-7821-2155-1, Sybex, 1998).

- The Provider for Internet Publishing is used to retrieve information from Web and FTP servers on the Internet or (more likely) your corporate intranet. It's installed by Office 2000 or Internet Explorer 5.

- The Provider for ODBC Drivers gives you a handy way to use ADO to connect to older data sources for which you do not yet have an OLE DB provider. You'll recall that Open Database Connectivity, or ODBC, was the old standard for connecting to heterogeneous databases. This provider allows you to use existing ODBC drivers to retrieve data, at the cost of some performance. If you have a native OLE DB provider specifically for your target data, you should use it instead of this provider.

- The Provider for OLAP Services retrieves data from the Microsoft Online Analytical Processing (OLAP) Server. This server ships with SQL Server 7, and is used to generate summary data from large databases. Using OLAP from Visual Basic with ADO is covered in Chapter 12.

- The Provider for Oracle is used to retrieve data from Oracle databases. There are examples of using this provider in this and later chapters.

- The Provider for SQL Server can retrieve data from Microsoft SQL Server versions 6.5 and 7. Many of the examples in this book use this provider.

- The Simple Provider implements a reduced set of OLE DB interfaces designed to present tabular data on Web pages. We'll use this provider for some of the examples in Chapter 13.

- The Sample OLE DB Simple Provider (Visual Basic) is an example from Microsoft that demonstrates the use of the Simple Provider interfaces from Visual Basic. The samples in Chapter 13 build on this example.

- The MS Remote provider is used to send data requests across the Internet to a remote database. This provider is an essential part of the Remote Data Service, covered in Chapter 11.

- The MSDataShape provider is designed to retrieve hierarchical recordsets. Data shaping is covered in Chapter 10.

Connecting to SQL Server Data

After choosing the SQL Server provider, you need to fill in the information on the Connection tab of this dialog box. This information tells OLE DB where to find the data you'd like to connect to. Each provider can control which prompts appear on this tab—you'll notice that they change depending on which provider you choose. Figure 4.4 shows the information that the SQL Server provider prompts for. In this case, the information is already filled in to connect to the Northwind database on a server named Beaver. The Test Connection button on this tab allows you to make sure that you've filled in all the required information correctly. With the SQL Server provider, no database names appear in the combo box until you've been authenticated by the server. If your network uses SQL Server 7 with integrated security, this authentication will happen based on your Windows NT login identity. Otherwise, you'll need to fill in a SQL Server username and password to see the list of available databases.

FIGURE 4.4:

The Connection tab of the Data Link Properties dialog box for a SQL Server database

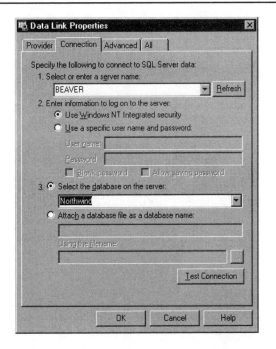

The other two tabs of this dialog box (Advanced and All) contain settings that you probably won't need to touch. The All tab in particular allows you to tweak any of the initialization properties for the OLE DB connection. Figure 4.5 shows what this tab might look like in the case of the SQL Server OLE DB provider.

FIGURE 4.5:

The All tab of the Data Link
Properties dialog box for a
SQL Server database

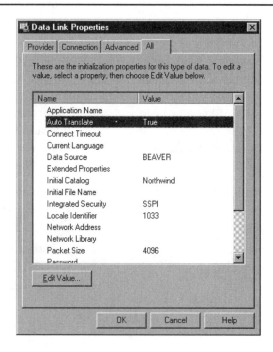

When you click the OK button on the Data Link Properties dialog box, the Data View will create the new link and assign it a default name such as DataLink1. You can change this name immediately, or change it at any time by right-clicking the name and choosing Rename from the context menu.

Connecting to Jet or Oracle Data

Adding a Jet or Oracle database (or a database from any other OLE DB provider, for that matter) follows the same steps. The only difference is that the tabs of the dialog box after the first one will contain information specific to the chosen provider. Figure 4.6, for example, shows the Connection tab for a Jet database.

FIGURE 4.6:

The Connection tab of the
Data Link Properties dialog
box for a Jet database

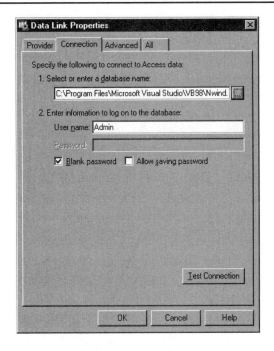

To connect to a Jet database using either the 3.51 provider or the 4 provider, you
have to supply three pieces of information:

- The database path and name

- The username

- The password (which may be blank)

If the database requires a password, you have the option of whether or not to
save the password with the connection information.

WARNING   Passwords are saved in plain text in the Windows Registry, so saving passwords
can represent a significant security risk.

Figure 4.7 shows the Connection tab for an Oracle database.

FIGURE 4.7:

The Connection tab of the Data Link Properties dialog box for an Oracle database

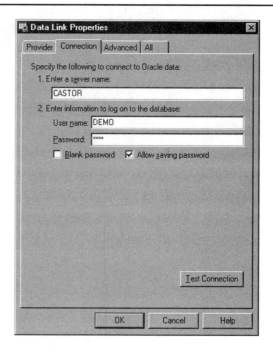

Again, you have to supply three pieces of information to connect to an Oracle database:

- The server name
- The username
- The password (which may be blank)

Once again, the password is stored in plain text if you allow it to be saved.

NOTE   The Oracle samples for this book use the default Oracle username and password of DEMO and DEMO. You may need to modify the connection properties to use them with your own test server if your DBA has disabled the DEMO account.

Information in the Data View

The information shown in the Data View varies depending on the type of OLE DB provider you're using. For a Jet database, the Data View will show you:

- Tables and their fields

- Views and their fields

- Stored procedures, their fields, and their parameters

 For a SQL Server database, the list is somewhat more extensive:

- Database diagrams, their tables, and their fields

- Tables, their fields, and their triggers

- Views and their fields

- Stored procedures, their fields, and their parameters

 An Oracle database has an even more extensive list:

- Database diagrams, their tables, and their fields

- Tables, their fields, and their triggers

- Synonyms and their fields

- Views and their fields

- Stored procedures, their fields, and their parameters

- Functions and their parameters

 When you use the Data View, you're actually using ADO and OLE DB for everything. Behind the scenes, the Visual Database Tools are generating SQL statements and sending them off to the database. You don't have to worry about the details, though; you can just point and click in the Data View interface. In the rest of this chapter, you'll learn about some of the operations that you can perform with the Data View.

Data Link Storage

Since connection information in the Data View persists between Visual Basic sessions, it obviously must be stored somewhere. Although the method of storage is undocumented, an understanding of it is helpful for a couple of reasons. First, you may need to manually inspect the OLE DB connection string for a particular data link if something has changed, or for troubleshooting purposes. Second, you may wish to transfer or propagate the persistent link information from one computer to another, perhaps to share it with other developers in your organization.

Not surprisingly, this information is stored in the Windows Registry. You can use the Registry Editor to inspect or edit the information contained in the key

```
HKEY_CURRENT_USER\Software\VB and VBA Program Settings\ ➥
Microsoft Visual Basic AddIns\VBDataViewWindow
```

This key contains a list of pairs of values. Each pair contains the name and OLE DB connection string for a single node in the Data Links section of the Data View window. For example, if you have the two links shown in Figure 4.2 in your Data View, you'd have this data in the Registry (this is the format that the Registry will export it to as text):

```
"DisplayOnConnect"="0"
"DataLinkName1"="NorthwindSQL"
"DataLinkString1"="Provider=SQLOLEDB.1; ➥
 Integrated Security=SSPI;Persist Security Info=False; ➥
 Initial Catalog=Northwind;Data Source=BEAVER"
"DataLinkName2"="NorthwindJet"
"DataLinkString2"="Provider=Microsoft.Jet.OLEDB.4; ➥
 Persist Security Info=False;Data Source= ➥
 C:\\Program Files\\Microsoft Visual Studio\\ ➥
 VB98\\Nwind.mdb"
```

The DataLinkName and DataLinkString values contain the information for each persistent data link in the Data View. The DisplayOnConnect value controls whether the Data View window is shown (the data in the value will be 1 in this case) or hidden (the data in the value will be 0) when Visual Basic is first launched.

Creating and Using Database Diagrams

One good use for the Visual Database Tools is to explore the structure of a database. Microsoft Access developers are used to the Relationships window in Access, which graphically displays tables and their relationships. Starting with the Data View, you can build such a view for other databases, such as SQL Server databases.

To create a database diagram in a SQL Server database, for example, right-click the Database Diagrams folder and choose New Diagram. This will give you a blank window within the Visual Basic design space. Now you can populate this window with tables. The easiest way to start this process is by simply dragging a table from a Data Link or Data Environment connection in the Data View into your new database diagram. By default, it will be displayed as a list of column names. This is the view used for the Customers table in Figure 4.8. But there are four other views available, which you can select by right-clicking the table in the database diagram.

FIGURE 4.8:

A database diagram for part of the SQL Server Northwind database

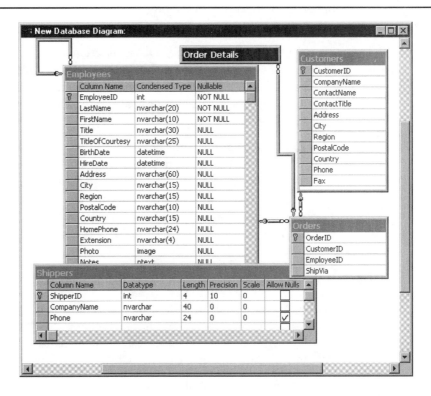

The four other views are as follows:

Column Properties   Displays all the properties of the columns in the table. The Shippers table in Figure 4.8 uses this view.

Keys   Shows only column names for primary and foreign keys in the table. The Orders table in Figure 4.8 uses this view.

Name Only   Shrinks the table display to a title bar only. The Order Details table in Figure 4.8 uses this view.

Custom   Shows a selection of the properties for the column in the table (you can change the properties shown by choosing Modify Custom View from the shortcut menu for the table). The Employees table in Figure 4.8 is displayed using this view.

No matter which view you choose, the database diagram will show the relationships between the tables in the view. These are the "pipes" between the tables. The key symbols identify primary keys, while the infinity symbols identify foreign keys. In a self-join the pipe will make a loop, as shown for the Employees table in Figure 4.8.

Shortcut menus within the database diagram let you control its appearance. You can add text annotations to the diagram, show or hide the names of the relationships, set up the page for printing, automatically arrange the tables, and control the zoom of the display. You can also right-click any table or relationship to view its properties.

The database diagram is not simply a display; it's also a workspace for designing databases. You can create new relationships by dragging and dropping a foreign key field to a primary key field. You can delete relationships using the shortcut menu for the relationship. You can even create new tables by right-clicking in the diagram and selecting New Table. This will open a blank table designer. The next section covers the use of the table designer.

Working with Tables

Working with the data in tables from the Data View is simple. Choose the appropriate database, expand the tree until you can see the table in question, and double-click it (or right-click and choose Open). This will open the table in a datasheet. You can add, edit, and delete data just by typing within this datasheet.

Depending on the provider, you can also do design work on the tables in your database. Right-click the table in the Data View window and choose Design. (If there's no Design choice, then the OLE DB provider for this data link doesn't support designing tables.) Figure 4.9 shows a table from a SQL Server database open in the table designer.

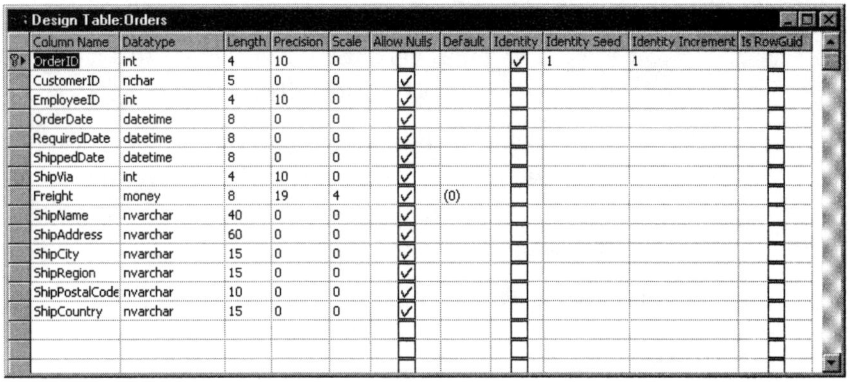

FIGURE 4.9:

The Visual Database Tools table designer

Column Name	Datatype	Length	Precision	Scale	Allow Nulls	Default	Identity	Identity Seed	Identity Increment	Is RowGuid
OrderID	int	4	10	0			✓	1	1	
CustomerID	nchar	5	0	0	✓					
EmployeeID	int	4	10	0	✓					
OrderDate	datetime	8	0	0	✓					
RequiredDate	datetime	8	0	0	✓					
ShippedDate	datetime	8	0	0	✓					
ShipVia	int	4	10	0	✓					
Freight	money	8	19	4	✓	(0)				
ShipName	nvarchar	40	0	0	✓					
ShipAddress	nvarchar	60	0	0	✓					
ShipCity	nvarchar	15	0	0	✓					
ShipRegion	nvarchar	15	0	0	✓					
ShipPostalCode	nvarchar	10	0	0	✓					
ShipCountry	nvarchar	15	0	0	✓					

You can design entirely new tables with this interface or alter existing tables. If you've worked with server databases in the past, you'll be pleasantly surprised at the ease with which you can alter existing tables. For example, to change the length of an nvarchar field in a SQL Server database, just highlight the existing length and type the new value. When you close the designer, the Visual Database Tools will commit the changes.

WARNING   Whether the designer displays them on screen or not, changes are not saved until you close the designer and confirm that you want to make changes. If your computing environment is unstable, you'll want to take this step often.

By right-clicking in the table designer and choosing Properties, you can also alter table-level properties. Again, the available selection will vary with the OLE DB provider you're using to get to the table. For a SQL Server table, for example, you can perform these operations in the property sheet:

- Add and remove CHECK constraints.
- Edit the table's relationships.
- Set or remove a primary key.
- Create and delete indexes.

Using Triggers

Client-server databases (such as SQL Server and Oracle, but not Jet) typically support triggers: bits of SQL code that run when a row is inserted, deleted, or updated in a table. (If you're not familiar with SQL, the standard Structured Query Language, there's a brief introduction in Appendix A.) The Data View lets you edit existing triggers or add new triggers to a table, provided the underlying database supports this functionality.

Figure 4.10 shows the insert trigger from the employee table in the SQL Server pubs database open for editing. (The SQL Server Northwind database doesn't contain any triggers.) The editor automatically color-codes the SQL according to this scheme:

- Red for SQL keywords
- Blue for arguments
- Green for comments
- Light blue for punctuation
- Black for other text
- Orange for functions

FIGURE 4.10:

Editing a SQL Server trigger

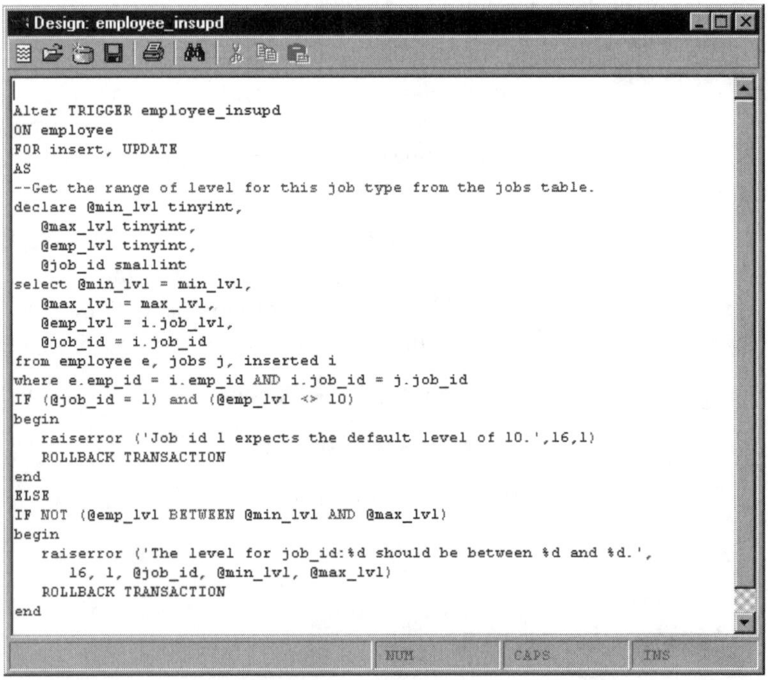
Design: employee_insupd
Alter TRIGGER employee_insupd
ON employee
FOR insert, UPDATE
AS
--Get the range of level for this job type from the jobs table.
declare @min_lvl tinyint,
@max_lvl tinyint,
@emp_lvl tinyint,
@job_id smallint
select @min_lvl = min_lvl,
@max_lvl = max_lvl,
@emp_lvl = i.job_lvl,
@job_id = i.job_id
from employee e, jobs j, inserted i
where e.emp_id = i.emp_id AND i.job_id = j.job_id
IF (@job_id = 1) and (@emp_lvl <> 10)
begin
raiserror ('Job id 1 expects the default level of 10.',16,1)
ROLLBACK TRANSACTION
end
ELSE
IF NOT (@emp_lvl BETWEEN @min_lvl AND @max_lvl)
begin
raiserror ('The level for job_id:%d should be between %d and %d.',
16, 1, @job_id, @min_lvl, @max_lvl)
ROLLBACK TRANSACTION
end
NUM
CAPS
INS

You may not be familiar with triggers, but this one is fairly straightforward. The ALTER TRIGGER statement at the top is inserted by the editor. This is the SQL statement that changes an existing trigger when you run it, so that the effect of running this statement (using the Save To Database toolbar button) is to modify the existing trigger. ALTER TRIGGER isn't part of the saved trigger, but rather an editing convenience.

The declare section specifies four variables used in the trigger and sets their datatypes. The SELECT statement (which includes FROM and WHERE clauses) then fills in these variables with values based on the current row. Note the use of the special table named "inserted" (here aliased to the name "i"), which contains the row that caused this trigger to be invoked.

The trigger then uses logic in a pair of IF statements to determine whether the job_lvl field for the newly inserted employee is within an acceptable range, determined from the jobs table. If it is outside this range, the trigger executes a ROLLBACK TRANSACTION statement, which has the effect of discarding the attempted insertion.

NOTE   Many older databases use triggers to enforce referential integrity between tables. This is essentially what's happening in this case, though the design of the pubs database would need to be slightly changed in order to use FOREIGN KEY constraints to enforce this exact condition.

You can also use the Visual Database Tools to create a new trigger for a table. To do this, right-click the table in the Data View and choose New Trigger. The same editing window will open, but this time it will have a skeletal trigger, as shown in Figure 4.11.

FIGURE 4.11:

Creating a new trigger for the Customers table

Here the only thing provided by the editor is the CREATE TRIGGER statement, which is used to save a new trigger to the database. The text in green between the /* and */ symbol pairs is comments, ignored by SQL Server when it interprets the trigger.

Using the Query Designer

Probably the most important job of ADO is to retrieve data from a database. In most cases, you'll do this by running a query, a collection of SQL commands that tell the database which data you want. (Some products call these *views* instead of queries.) The Visual Database Tools include a powerful Query Designer that lets you design new queries and modify or run existing queries through a graphical interface, instead of by writing SQL statements directly. Whatever job you're doing with ADO, you'll find the Query Designer, launched from the Data View, to be a quick and easy way to build the queries you need. Even if you're planning to execute queries in code, instead of persisting them to the database, you'll find that the Query Designer's ability to generate the SQL statements you need is very helpful. The Query Designer is limited to generating SELECT queries.

Designing a Query

To open a query, locate the appropriate object in the Data View TreeView (usually it will be under Views), right-click it, and choose Design. You'll see the Query Designer open, displaying the design of this query. If you then right-click in the query and choose Run, the Query Designer will retrieve the records specified by the query. Figure 4.12 shows a query open in the Query Designer.

NOTE   If you don't see Design on the right-click menu for a particular view, it means one of two things: either the OLE DB provider for that data link doesn't support the interfaces required by the Query Designer or the particular query cannot be represented within the Designer. In this case, there's no alternative to using the native tools supplied with the database to inspect this particular view.

FIGURE 4.12:

Query open in the Query Designer

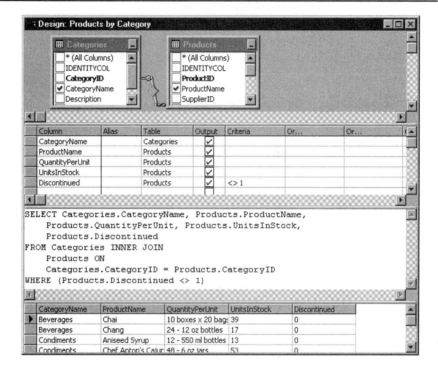

The Query Designer shows you four different views of your query. From top to bottom, these are:

The Diagram pane   Provides a graphical representation of the tables and fields used as the sources of data for your query. Lines show how the tables are joined, and check marks show the fields included in the resultset of the query.

The Grid pane   Provides a way to further control the fields that are included in the query. Here you can specify sorting, grouping, and searching conditions, the results of action queries, or the names of aliases.

The SQL pane   Shows you the SQL statement that represents this query in the database. You can verify the syntax of this statement or edit it by hand.

The Results pane   Shows you the data retrieved by running the query. You can both view and edit data in the Results pane.

The Query Designer keeps the information in all four panes synchronized. For example, if you check a new field in the Diagram pane, it will appear in the Grid and SQL panes and show up in the Results pane the next time that the query is executed.

The Diagram Pane

Usually, you'll start designing queries in the Diagram pane. To create a new, blank query, just right-click the Views node in a data link and choose New View.

To add a new table to the query, drag the table from the Data View. With certain types of data sources, you'll need to limit yourself to tables from a single data link. However, if you're using SQL Server 7, which supports distributed queries, you can drag in a table from just about any data source and add it to your query. To remove a table, right-click within the table and choose Remove.

To add or remove a column from the query's output, check or uncheck the check box to the right of the field. In addition to individual columns, you can check the box for "* (All Columns)" to include all the columns from this table in the resultset. Some databases, such as SQL Server, include an additional choice named IDENTITYCOL. This column will include the column with its Identity property set to True (if there is one) from this table in the query's output.

To see the datatype of a column, just hover the cursor over that column name in the Diagram pane, and the information will appear in a ToolTip.

If your query includes multiple tables, you'll almost certainly want to specify a join between the tables. If the database includes referential integrity information (PRIMARY KEY and FOREIGN KEY constraints), the Query Designer will automatically include these joins when you drop related tables. Otherwise, you can create joins by dragging a column from the many-side table and dropping it on the corresponding one-side column. The Query Designer also makes it easy to create non-equijoins (joins that include something other than the matching data from both tables) and outer joins. To create a join other than an equijoin, first create the equijoin and then right-click the join line and choose Properties. This will open the Join Properties dialog box shown in Figure 4.13.

FIGURE 4.13:

Editing join properties

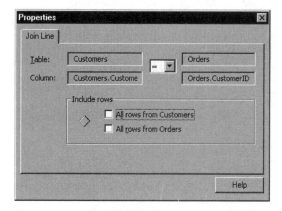

To create a non-equijoin, select a different join criterion from the combo box. To create an outer join, select one of the two check boxes in the Include Rows section of the dialog box. In either case, the Query Designer will alter the appearance of the graphic on the join line, so you can determine the type of join without looking at the join properties.

If there's a criterion set on a field, you can remove it by right-clicking the field and choosing "Remove Filter." This isn't all that useful, since there's no way to put the criterion back in this pane. Usually, you'll want to make filtering changes in the Grid pane instead.

Finally, by right-clicking and selecting Properties within the Diagram pane, you can select options for the query as a whole. The most common of these is the TOP option, which allows you to limit the size of the resultset returned by the query.

The Grid Pane

The Grid pane allows you to fine-tune the resultset of the query. This includes creating aliases for columns, setting criteria used to filter the query, and selecting grouping options.

To add a new column to the resultset, select the column and table names from the combo boxes in a blank row of the Grid pane. The drop-down arrows for these boxes are hidden until you click in the grid, but they're always there.

To create an alias for a column, just type the new name into the Alias column of the grid on that column's row. An Alias specifies the name used to refer to that column within the query's resultset.

To create a calculated column, type an arbitrary name into the Alias column and type the expression itself into the Column column. Remember that you need to use the syntax that the underlying OLE DB provider uses for this data source. For example, with a Jet database you might use [Company] & [Contact] to define a concatenated field, while with a SQL Server database you'd use Company + Contact.

To set a criterion used to filter the resultset (part of a SQL WHERE clause), type the appropriate restriction in the Criteria column of the Grid on the row with the column you want to restrict. You can set multiple criteria by using more of the grid. To connect two criteria on the same field with an OR, type the criteria into successive columns on the same row. To connect them with an AND, create a second row for the same field and enter the criteria on successive rows.

To transform your query into a grouping query, right-click in the Grid pane and select Group By. This will add a Group By column to the grid. You can then select an appropriate aggregate expression for each row in the grid by clicking in this column and choosing from the drop-down list that is displayed.

The SQL Pane

The SQL pane is primarily there as a reference for new users and a tool for advanced SQL authors. You can use it as a tool to learn SQL by constructing a query with the Diagram and Grid panes and watching to see what the Query Designer does with it. Alternatively, if you already know SQL well, you can make changes in this pane and they'll be propagated back to the other panes. You can also use the Query Designer to create queries graphically, and then cut and paste the generated SQL to other places where you need it, such as in code.

If you make a change in the SQL pane, it's not reflected in the other panes until you move out of the SQL pane. This allows you to edit and revise without worrying about extraneous error messages.

Although not all SQL statements are supported by the Query Designer, there are some statements that are supported in the SQL pane but not in the Diagram and Grid panes—for example, the basic union query:

```
SELECT CompanyName
FROM Customers
UNION
SELECT CompanyName
FROM Suppliers
```

This query can be successfully designed and executed by the Query Designer, but only by starting in the SQL pane. When you move out of that pane, the Query Designer warns you that the query cannot be displayed graphically. If you choose to continue, the Diagram and Grid panes will be grayed out, but you can still work with the query's data.

The Results Pane

At first glance, the Results pane might seem straightforward: just a place where the results of executing your query are displayed. But this pane is more than just a static display. Within certain broad limits (discussed below) you can edit the data shown in this pane as well.

To edit data in the Results pane, just navigate to the cell containing the value you wish to change, using the arrow keys, scroll bars, or mouse. Highlight the value and type in the new data. To enter a null, type **Ctrl+0**. When you leave the row that you're editing, the Query Designer will attempt to save the data back to the database.

Of course, the Designer might not succeed for a variety of reasons. Here are some of the limits on what you can edit using the Results pane:

- You can only edit memo and other long text columns that contain fewer than 900 characters of data.

- You cannot edit binary large object (BLOB) data.

- You must have the appropriate permissions to change data in the database.

- The resultset must contain the primary key of the output, or enough other information to uniquely identify the source rows for the data being edited.

- You cannot edit data if the query contains a table that isn't joined to the other tables in the query.

- You cannot edit data if the query displays multiple tables in a many-to-many relationship.

- You cannot edit aggregate queries.

- You cannot edit queries that use the DISTINCT keyword.

- You cannot edit columns based on expressions.

- You cannot edit timestamp columns.

In addition, there are differences between the support that the various OLE DB providers offer for updating. So changes that can be made when you're connected to one provider might not work with a different provider.

Creating and Debugging Stored Procedures

The last major class of objects in the Data View is *stored procedures*. Stored procedures are pieces of compiled SQL code that run exclusively on the server, and that may or may not deliver a resultset to the client. This powerful tool is often overlooked by Visual Basic developers who are accustomed to file-server databases instead of client-server databases.

The Data View offers the ability to view the design of stored procedures, execute them, and (if you've installed Microsoft SQL Server) debug them. Each of these features is covered in this section.

NOTE   Debugging stored procedures is supported only for Microsoft SQL Server 6.5 Service Pack 3 or higher, or Microsoft SQL Server 7.

WARNING   By default, SQL Server installation does not include the necessary support for the Visual Database Tools stored procedure debugger. If you're using SQL Server 6.5, there's a setup program named `sdi_nt4.exe` on the SQL Server CD-ROM. If you're using SQL Server 7, be sure to check "Development Tools" when you're selecting the components to include.

Viewing Stored Procedure Definitions and Resultsets

To view the definition of a stored procedure, navigate to the stored procedure node in the appropriate data link, expand it, right-click the stored procedure, and select Design. (As always, if this choice doesn't appear on the shortcut menu, either the OLE DB provider or the underlying database doesn't support designing stored procedures.) This will open the stored procedure in an editing window that uses the same color-coding as the trigger editor, covered earlier in the chapter. Figure 4.14 shows a sample stored procedure open in this editor.

FIGURE 4.14:

Editing a stored procedure

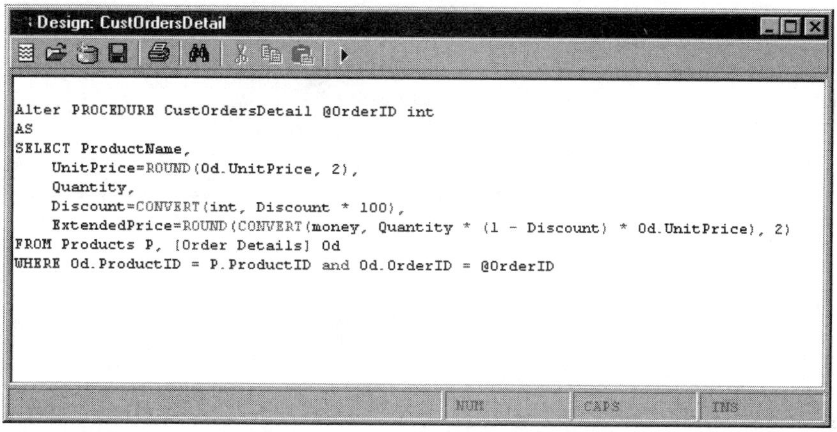

```
Alter PROCEDURE CustOrdersDetail @OrderID int
AS
SELECT ProductName,
    UnitPrice=ROUND(Od.UnitPrice, 2),
    Quantity,
    Discount=CONVERT(int, Discount * 100),
    ExtendedPrice=ROUND(CONVERT(money, Quantity * (1 - Discount) * Od.UnitPrice), 2)
FROM Products P, [Order Details] Od
WHERE Od.ProductID = P.ProductID and Od.OrderID = @OrderID
```

Seeing the data (if any) returned by the stored procedure is a bit harder. You might think you could just right-click and choose Run, but that's not a choice when the Visual Database Tools are hosted inside of Visual Basic (though, oddly, that choice is available when the same tools are hosted inside of Visual C++). Instead, you have to load the stored procedure into the T-SQL Debugger and run it from there. I'll cover the T-SQL Debugger in the next section.

The T-SQL Debugger

T-SQL stands for Transact SQL, Microsoft's flavor of Structured Query Language. Although you can use the T-SQL Debugger directly from the Data View, for maximum flexibility you'll also want to install it as a Visual Basic Add-In. To do this, choose Add-Ins ➤ Add-In Manager from the Visual Basic menus, scroll down the list until you find "VB T-SQL Debugger," and change the Load Behavior to

Loaded. (If you're going to use it frequently, you should also check the Load On Startup check box.) This will add two items to the Visual Basic menus. Add-Ins ➤ T-SQL Debugger will let you launch the debugger at any time. Tools ➤ T-SQL Debugging Options will open the dialog box shown in Figure 4.15.

FIGURE 4.15:

T-SQL Debugging Options

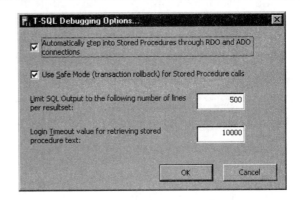

This dialog box offers four options:

- Checking Automatically Step Into Stored Procedures Through RDO And ADO Connections will bring up the debugger whenever you invoke a stored procedure. This option is useful if you're testing an application that makes some use of stored procedures and you suspect an error in their use.

- Checking Use Safe Mode (Transaction Rollback) For Stored Procedure Calls automatically rolls back any testing you do at design time.

- The Limit SQL Output To The Following Number Of Lines Per Resultset controls the maximum number of rows that will be shown in the debugger itself. It does not limit the data actually returned from the stored procedure.

- The Login Timeout Value For Retrieving Stored Procedure Text value keeps the debugger from hanging forever in case you don't have design permissions for the stored procedure in question.

To invoke the debugger, you can right-click a stored procedure in the Data View and choose Debug. The debugger will prompt you to fill in values for any input parameters that the stored procedure requires to do its work. Once any input parameters are supplied, the debugger window opens. This window is shown in Figure 4.16.

FIGURE 4.16:

The T-SQL Debugger

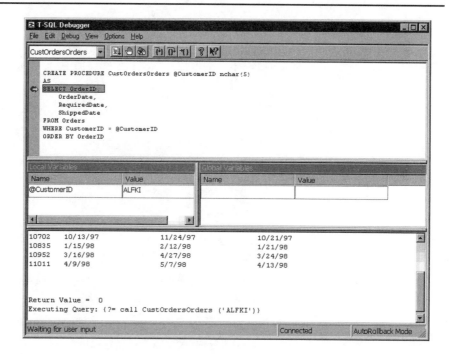

The T-SQL Debugger includes many of the standard features of other debuggers. The topmost pane shows you the text of the stored procedure that you're working with. The middle two panes give the values of local and global variables in the stored procedure, if any. The lower pane shows the results as you execute the stored procedure.

CHAPTER

FIVE

Using Bound Controls to Present ADO Data

- Using the ADO Data Control

- Binding Simple Controls

- The Data Form Wizard

- Programming the ADO Data Control

- The Hierarchical FlexGrid Control

Broadly speaking, there are two ways of getting data from a database to the user interface with Visual Basic. The first is to use *bound controls*, which are user interface gadgets that are connected to a data control at design time. The second is to use code for everything, placing the data in *unbound controls* that have no connection of their own to a database.

Historically, bound controls have been frowned on by serious Visual Basic developers. This dates back to Visual Basic 3, where using bound controls with DAO involved serious performance and functionality trade-offs. For several years, professional developers have been advising that bound controls are useful only in prototyping, and that serious applications use unbound controls.

With the release of Visual Basic 6 and the new ADO Data control, the situation has changed. This second-generation data control is flexible and fast enough to make serious applications using bound controls a distinct possibility. In this chapter, I'll look at the ADO Data control and show you how it can be used to quickly produce some sophisticated data-aware applications.

Using the ADO Data Control

The ADO Data control provides a way to connect other controls on Visual Basic forms to data via any OLE DB provider. At design time, you set the properties of the control to indicate where it should retrieve its data from. At run time, the control makes a connection to the selected provider and retrieves data for other controls on the form.

At run time, the ADO Data control displays buttons for first, last, next, and previous records on the form, so it can also be used to navigate through the resultset it has retrieved.

Connecting to Data

As with any other control, the first step when using the ADO Data control is to place it on a Visual Basic form and set the properties of the control. The simplest way to start is to click the builder button for the control's Custom property, which opens the property pages for the control shown in Figure 5.1.

WARNING   Don't confuse the ADO Data control with the standard Data control that appears by default in the Visual Basic Toolbox. You'll have to add this control to the Toolbox yourself. The easiest way to do this is to press Ctrl+T and choose Microsoft ADO Data Control 6 (OLEDB) from the list of available controls in the Components dialog box.

FIGURE 5.1:

Property Pages for the ADO Data control

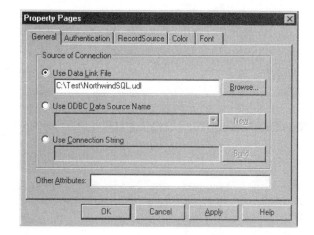

As you can see, there are five tabs in the Property Pages:

General   Lets you specify the data source to use. This can be a Data Link file (see sidebar), an ODBC data source, or an OLE DB connection string. Data Link files are convenient for applications that connect to a single OLE DB data provider. ODBC connections are useful if you need to connect to an older data source for which an OLE DB provider does not yet exist. OLE DB connection strings are most useful if you need to set or alter the properties of the connection in code. This tab also provides a text box where you can enter additional OLE DB attributes to be passed back to the provider.

Authentication   Allows you to specify the username and password that should be used to connect to the OLE DB provider. You can leave this blank if the provider doesn't require this information (for example, if you're using the SQL Server OLE DB provider with integrated security) or if you'd rather prompt the user to fill in this information at run time.

RecordSource   Lets you specify the actual resultset that this Data control will deliver to controls that are bound to the Data control. You can choose to supply a table or stored procedure or a SQL statement that returns records here.

Color   Lets you specify the foreground and background colors that are used to paint the inside of the control at run time.

Font   Lets you set the font used for the text displayed inside the ADO Data control.

As soon as you've filled in the first three tabs here, you can start binding controls to the data. I'll cover data binding a bit later in the chapter. But first let's look at some of the other properties of the ADO Data control.

Creating a Data Link File

One of the problems with the older ODBC standard for connecting to data is that connection information was stored in the Windows Registry where it was difficult to view and change. (This was fixed in later releases by the introduction of File DSNs.) Data Link files provide a way around this problem by saving the information necessary to connect to an OLE DB provider into a simple text file.

To create a new Data Link, open the Windows Explorer and navigate to the folder where you want to save the file. Right-click in the window and choose New ➤ Text Document. This will create the file and allow you to assign it a name. Choose a name with the extension .UDL and confirm the name change. After you've named the file, right-click it and choose Properties—or simply double-click it—to open the Data Link Properties dialog box. See Chapter 4 for a discussion of the options in this dialog box.

ADO Data Control Properties

Like any other control, the ADO Data control has a number of standard properties. These properties, such as ToolTipText, Top, Left, and Font, are shared with many other controls, and won't be covered in this book. More important, though, are the data properties that dictate the interaction of the control with its data source. A firm grasp of these properties will help you design applications that use bound controls to retrieve data via ADO.

The BOFAction and EOFAction properties control what happens when the user navigates beyond the beginning or the end of the resultset. You can set the BOF-Action property to adDoMoveFirst (the default) or adStayBOF. Similarly, you can set the EOFAction property to adDoMoveLast (the default), adStayEOF, or adDoAddNew. If you stick with the defaults, the user can never move outside of the retrieved records; they can navigate from one end to the other of the resultset, but that's it. Setting BOFAction to adStayBOF or EOFAction to adStayEOF allows the user to move "off the end" of the resultset, with the side effect of validating any changes to the first or last record, but it doesn't allow the user to do anything with the blank record that is displayed. Setting EOFAction to adDoAddNew automatically adds a new record when the user moves past the end of the result-set, and then positions the resultset to that record for editing.

The CacheSize property sets the size of the control's internal cache of records. By default, this is 50; you can set it to any positive long integer. When you first display a form containing an ADO Data control, it retrieves enough records to fill its internal cache. After this, it does not communicate with the server again until the user moves outside of the cached records, at which point it will flush the cache and retrieve enough records to fill it again. If there aren't enough records left in the data source to fill the cache, all remaining records are fetched; no error is raised in this case. Data in the cache is kept with the form, so it doesn't reflect any changes other users might make to the data. If you want to make sure the cache contains the latest data, you can call the Resync method of the underlying resultset. For example, if you have an ADO Data control named adodcCustomers, you could execute

```
adodcCustomers.Recordset.Resync
```

NOTE   The CacheSize property has no particular effect if you're using client-side cursors, since the client-side cursor engine does its own caching.

The CommandTimeout property sets the maximum number of seconds that the control will wait for data to be returned before giving up and generating an error. By default, this is 30 seconds. You may need to increase the timeout on slow networks, or if you're using the Internet to retrieve data via the Remote Data Service. You can also set this property to zero to force an indefinite wait.

The CommandType property indicates to ADO what the source of the resultset will be. This is one of the properties that you set on the RecordSource tab of the control's property pages. You can set this to adCmdText to supply a SQL statement as the connection's source, to adCmdTable to supply a table name (in this case, ADO generates its own internal query to return the contents of the table), to adCmdStoredProc to supply a stored procedure name, or to adCmdUnknown if you don't know where the records are coming from. This last choice is useful primarily if you're going to set both the CommandType and CommandText properties at run time.

The ConnectionString property holds the information that you supply on the General tab of the control's property pages. If you're using a Data Link file, this string will be of the form

```
FILE NAME=C:\Test\NorthwindSQL.udl
```

If you're using an ODBC data source, this property will be of the form

```
DSN=NorthwindSQL
```

If you're using an OLE DB connection string, this property will contain the full text of the connection string.

The ConnectionTimeout property sets the maximum number of seconds that the control will wait to connect to the data source before giving up and returning an error. By default, this is 15 seconds. You may need to increase the timeout on slow networks, or if you're using the Internet to retrieve data via the Remote Data Service. You can also set this property to zero to force an indefinite wait.

The CursorLocation property controls whether the cursor engine (the part of the data access architecture that returns data) is located on the client or on the server. The possible settings are adUseClient (the default) and adUseServer. Generally, adUseClient is more flexible, but if you need to conserve client-side resources, you may want to switch this to adUseServer. Also, using client-side cursors limits you to using static cursors (see the CursorType property), which may not be what you want.

The CursorType property controls the type of cursor that is used. The default is adOpenStatic, which returns a static set of records that doesn't show changes of any sort by other database users. You can also set this to adOpenKeyset, which will show you changes and deletions, but not additions, by other users, or adOpenDynamic, which shows you all changes that are made by other users.

NOTE   Don't be confused into thinking that an adOpenStatic cursor represents read-only data. You are quite free to make changes in your copy of the data, and these changes will be saved back to the server (assuming that the data isn't read-only for some other reason).

The LockType property controls the record locking used when you're editing records that are displayed via the ADO Data control. The default is adLockOptimistic, which (not surprisingly) provides optimistic locking, holding locks only when the record is actually being updated. You can also set this to adLockReadOnly to make your copy of the data read-only; generally, this will consume less resources, and of course it prevents users from accidentally altering the data. The adLockPessimistic setting enforces pessimistic locking, which will lock the record as soon as you start updating it. The fourth setting, adLockBatchOptimistic, is used for client-side disconnected resultsets that may need to be edited when they're not connected to the server. This is the only type of lock that can be used by disconnected recordsets.

The MaxRecords property specifies the maximum number of records that the provider should return from the data source. If you set this to zero, all records are returned without limit. Depending on the OLE DB provider you're using, the MaxRecords property might work by retrieving all records but only returning a certain number of them to the data control. In this case, you won't save any server processing by setting MaxRecords low. You'd be better off limiting the number of records with SET COUNT on the server, or some other server-side means.

The Mode property sets the access permissions on the data. By default, this is set to adModeUnknown, which indicates that no particular permissions are being requested. Table 5.1 shows the possible settings for the Mode property. You may be able to improve performance by setting the Mode to adModeRead. Setting the Mode property at run time has no effect if data has already been retrieved by the control.

TABLE 5.1: Settings for the Mode Property

Constant	Description
adModeUnknown	No permissions requested
adModeRead	Read-only permissions
adModeWrite	Write-only permissions
adModeReadWrite	Read/Write permissions
adModeShareDenyRead	Prevents others from opening a connection with read permissions

Continued on next page

TABLE 5.1 CONTINUED: Settings for the Mode Property

Constant	Description
adModeShareDenyWrite	Prevents others from opening a connection with write permissions
adModeShareExclusive	Prevents others from opening a connection at all
adModeShareDenyNone	Prevents others from opening a connection with any permissions

The UserName and Password properties supply security settings for the connection to the data source and display the information from the Authentication tab in the control's property pages. You can leave these blank if the provider doesn't require this information or if you want to fill in these properties at run time. Remember, if you do provide a password it will appear in plain text in the control's Password property, and so will be available to anyone who has access to the source code.

The RecordSource tells the ADO Data control precisely where to get the data it should display. What you put in this property depends on the setting of the CommandType property. If the CommandType is adCmdText, then the Record-Source should be a SQL statement. If the CommandType is adCmdTable, then the RecordSource should be a table name (or, with providers that treat views the same as tables, a view name). If the CommandType is adCmdStoredProc, then the RecordSource should be a stored procedure name.

For most purposes, you'll probably find that the default settings of these data properties are sufficient. If you need to change or optimize the characteristics of the database connection that's being made, take a look first at the CursorLocation, CursorType, LockType, and Mode properties. If you want to alter the actual data being retrieved, you should be working with the ConnectionString, Command-Type, and RecordSource properties instead.

Binding Simple Controls

Of course, retrieving data to a form isn't of all that much use if you don't display it. The ADO Data control has the ability to bind to any control that has the Data-Source property and display data in that control. This includes not just the controls shipped with Visual Basic, but ActiveX controls from third parties and data-aware UserControls (data-aware UserControls are covered in Chapter 9). You can bind any of these controls shipped with the Enterprise Edition of Visual Basic 6 to the ADO Data control:

- CheckBox
- ComboBox
- DataCombo
- DataGrid
- DataList
- DateTimePicker
- Image
- ImageCombo
- Label
- ListBox
- Microsoft Chart
- Microsoft Hierarchical FlexGrid
- MonthView
- PictureBox
- Rich TextBox
- TextBox

To bind a control to the ADO Data control, you generally set two properties on the target control. First, set the control's DataSource property to the name of the ADO Data control. Second, set the control's DataField property to the name of a field in the resultset supplied by the ADO Data control. If you set the properties in this order, Visual Basic will helpfully populate the DataField property with a combo box that lets you choose from all available fields.

A Simple Data-Aware Form

For an example of simple data binding, take a look at frmSimpleData in the BoundControls sample project. You can get to this form by running the Bound-Controls project and selecting Simple Data-Bound Form from the main menu. Figure 5.2 shows this simple form.

About the Code Samples

Remember, the samples are just that—samples. This is not production-quality code, and I've taken some shortcuts in order to keep the code simple. In particular, note that there's no trapping for unexpected errors in many of the samples.

FIGURE 5.2:

A simple data-bound form

This form contains an ADO Data control and two bound controls: a text box and a date picker. (The date picker, one of the Microsoft Windows Common Controls in this version of Visual Basic, provides a calendar-based way to select the value for a date field.) As you navigate through the records by clicking the buttons on the ADO Data control, you'll find that the data shown in these controls changes as new records are retrieved from the data source. You can also change these values manually, and the new values will be automatically saved to the data source when you move to another record.

WARNING   The samples for this chapter were compiled with the .UDL file in the C:\Sybex\Samples folder. If you install the samples to another folder, you'll have to modify the properties of the ADO Data control to include the folder you've used.

This sample also introduces a pair of other features: the ability to swap data sources and a rough indication of where you are in the recordset as you navigate using the arrow buttons.

The option buttons on the form allow you to select either a Jet or a SQL Server data source. Since both Visual Basic 6 and SQL Server 7 ship with versions of the

Northwind sample database, the required data for this form is available in either one. The code that runs when you select these buttons is fairly simple:

```
Private Sub optJet_Click()
    ' Switch to the Jet data provider
    If optJet.Value Then
        adodcNwind.ConnectionString = _
          "FILE NAME=" & App.Path & "\NorthwindJet.udl"
        adodcNwind.Refresh
    End If
End Sub
Private Sub optSQLServer_Click()
    ' Switch to the SQL Server data provider
    If optSQLServer.Value Then
        adodcNwind.ConnectionString = _
          "FILE NAME=" & App.Path & "\NorthwindSQL.udl"
        adodcNwind.Refresh
    End If
End Sub
```

Switching data sources is done by changing the ConnectionString property of the ADO Data control. In each case, the sample uses the FILE= syntax to pull connection information out of a saved Data Link file. This change has no immediate effect on the data control—in order to actually load the new data, you need to call the Refresh method of the control. (There's more on ADO Data control methods and events later in this chapter.)

NOTE   The sample Data Link files assume that you've got everything, including SQL Server, installed to default locations on a single machine and that SQL Server has Windows NT integrated security enabled. If these assumptions aren't correct, simply right-click each Data Link file individually in Windows Explorer, choose Properties, and direct them at your copies of the data. One of the big advantages of using Data Link files is that they can be edited without recompiling the application that uses them.

The caption of the ADO Data control shows recordset position information (for example, "8 of 830"). This is not the default behavior; by default, the control's caption is static. To get this dynamic caption, the sample uses the MoveComplete event of the ADO Data control:

```
Private Sub adodcNwind_MoveComplete( _
  ByVal adReason As ADODB.EventReasonEnum, _
  ByVal pError As ADODB.Error, _
  adStatus As ADODB.EventStatusEnum, _
  ByVal pRecordset As ADODB.Recordset20)
    adodcNwind.Caption = _
    adodcNwind.Recordset.AbsolutePosition & " of " & _
    adodcNwind.Recordset.RecordCount
End Sub
```

This event is triggered every time the control is positioned to a new row in the resultset. Here the code takes advantage of the Recordset property of the ADO Data control, which returns the underlying ADO recordset that the control is using to retrieve the data. Once you've retrieved this property, you have complete access to all the ADO Recordset properties and methods that we covered in Chapter 3. With OLE DB providers that support this functionality (including both the Jet and SQL Server providers), the AbsolutePosition property provides a pretty good indication of where the user is in the recordset.

WARNING   Note that the last parameter of the MoveComplete procedure is declared **As ADODB.Recordset20**. When Visual Basic creates the event procedure, this parameter will be declared **As ADODB.Recordset**. You need to make this change manually each and every time you use an event procedure from the ADO Data control, if that event procedure includes a Recordset object as a parameter. That's because Microsoft changed the recordset interface between ADO 2 (which is the version that the ADO Data control was compiled with) and ADO 2.5. It's unfortunate that Microsoft chose to break backwards compatibility in this fashion, since it can require you to change substantial portions of existing code. A better solution for developers would have been to release a new version of the ADO Data control along with the new version of ADO. Unfortunately, for whatever reason, Microsoft chose not to do this. We'll have to wait for Visual Basic 7 to ship before this issue is resolved.

Is Jet Dead?

From time to time you will hear people (even some Microsoft employees, who really ought to know better) claim that the Jet engine is "dead." Usually these people go on to assure you that some other database engine is the only one with a future, and urge you to convert all your old, "obsolete" Jet applications to use the new engine as quickly as possible.

Nonsense.

As this book was being written, Microsoft shipped Office 2000. This version of Office includes a brand-new version of the Jet engine, Jet 4. Far from being a dead or obsolete piece of software, the new Jet engine features significant new capabilities, including:

- Row-level record-locking
- Unicode support
- Increased ANSI SQL support
- Better repair capabilities
- Additional SQL data types
- Heterogeneous replication with SQL Server
- Maximum database size of 2GB

If that's not enough to convince you, consider the wide range of products that use the Jet engine. It's shipped not only with Microsoft Access and Visual Basic, but also with SQL Server, Microsoft Money, Microsoft Publisher, and dozens of other products. The Jet engine is a critical core piece of Microsoft's technology.

What *is* rapidly becoming obsolete is Data Access Objects (DAO), the original object library interface to the Jet engine. The DAO libraries are still being maintained, but the Office 2000 versions show no major improvements over previous versions. The new features are all in the new object library, ADO—which is probably why you're reading this book!

DataList and DataCombo

The DataList and DataCombo controls are designed to help you easily present relational data on a form. Each of these controls can connect to two data sources: one that supplies items for the list of available choices and one that stores the chosen item. In the sample for this chapter, choose Data List and Data Combo to see a sample form using the DataList and DataCombo controls, as shown in Figure 5.3.

FIGURE 5.3:

DataList and DataCombo controls

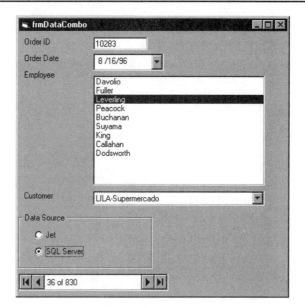

NOTE   If you browse the Components list (from the Project ➢ Components menu) on a computer that has a variety of recent Microsoft software installed, you'll find several data-bound list controls. The one that comes with Visual Basic and is used in this section is called Microsoft DataList Controls 6 (OLEDB).

Because they shuttle data from one table to another, the DataList and DataCombo controls require two ADO Data controls each. One control supplies the data for the list, and the other tells the list where to save the bound value. There are five essential properties you need to set for these controls:

The DataSource property   Specifies the name of the ADO Data control that contains the bound values. This is typically the one side of a one-to-many relationship.

The BoundColumn property   Specifies the name of the field in the data source that values are saved to.

The RowSource property   Specifies the name of the ADO Data control that supplies the list of possible values. This is typically the many side of a one-to-many relationship.

The DataField property   Specifies the name of the field that actually contains the data to be saved. This is the field that's the same in both tables.

The ListField property   Specifies the name of the field that should be displayed in the list portion of the DataList or DataCombo. By using different fields for ListField and DataField, you can save a numeric ID while still displaying user-friendly information. Of course, if the RowSource is a view rather than a table, you can also use a calculated field for the ListField.

Figure 5.4 shows these properties for the DataCombo on the sample form. You can think of the DataCombo as a control that takes values from the DataField of the RowSource and stores them in the BoundColumn of the DataSource.

FIGURE 5.4:

Properties for the Customer DataCombo

NOTE   Though Figure 5.3 displays only a single ADO Data control, there are actually three such controls on the form, as you can verify by opening it in Design View. The ADO Data controls that connect to the Employee and Customer tables have their Visible property set to False, since they are only used by the DataList and Data-Combo controls, not directly by the user.

DataGrid

Visual Basic 6 also includes the DataGrid control—more formally, the Microsoft DataGrid Control 6 (OLEDB). This control is useful when you want to display the contents of an entire resultset in a pseudo-spreadsheet form. No matter how much you explain that databases and spreadsheets are different animals, some users persist in wanting that old familiar grid display. This control fills that need nicely.

The basic DataGrid, shown in Figure 5.5, is ridiculously simple to set up. You can see this form by choosing Data Grid from the menu form in the sample project. All you need to do is drop the DataGrid and an ADO Data control on a form, set the ADO Data control's properties, and then set the DataGrid's DataSource property to the name of the ADO Data control. That's it! The form will display all the data from the table in rows and columns and allow you to edit values directly in the cells.

FIGURE 5.5:

DataGrid control in action

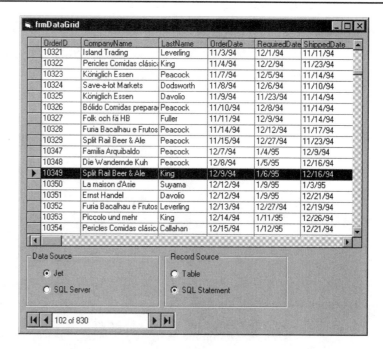

The DataGrid sample form demonstrates changing the RecordSource property of the ADO Data control at run time. This form allows a choice between the raw Orders table or a query constructed to return Customer and Employee names instead of their record IDs:

```
Private Sub optSQLStatement_Click()
    ' Display the results of a SQL query in the grid
    If optSQLStatement.Value Then
        adodcNwind.CommandType = adCmdText
        adodcNwind.RecordSource = "SELECT ➥
Orders.OrderID, Customers.CompanyName, " & _
        "Employees.LastName, Orders.OrderDate, ➥
Orders.RequiredDate, " & _
        "Orders.ShippedDate, Orders.ShipVia, ➥
Orders.ShipName, Orders.Freight," & _
        "Orders.ShipAddress, Orders.ShipCity, ➥
Orders.ShipRegion, " & _
        "Orders.ShipPostalCode, Orders.ShipCountry, ➥
Orders.CustomerID, " & _
        "Orders.EmployeeID FROM ((Orders INNER JOIN " & _
        "Customers ON Orders.CustomerID = ➥
Customers.CustomerID) INNER JOIN " & _
        "Employees ON Orders.EmployeeID = ➥
Employees.EmployeeID)"
        adodcNwind.Refresh
        ' Hide the redundant key columns
        dgOrders.Columns(14).Visible = False
        dgOrders.Columns(15).Visible = False
    End If
End Sub

Private Sub optTable_Click()
    ' Display the raw table in the grid
    If optTable.Value Then
        With adodcNwind
            .CommandType = adCmdTable
            .RecordSource = "Orders"
            .Refresh
        End With
    End If
End Sub
```

There are three steps to this process. First, choose the appropriate Command-Type. Next, set the RecordSource to something that makes sense for that CommandType. Finally, call the ADO Data control's Refresh method to tell it to reload the new data. When you do this, the DataGrid will automatically refresh itself.

The SQL statement in the first case here contains several columns of information that we don't want to display. You can see that the DataGrid control supports a Columns collection (zero-based), which can be used to modify the properties of the columns that it displays. Here it's used to make two columns in the grid completely invisible.

The DataGrid is a complex control with many other capabilities. Here are a few of them:

- At run time, the user can resize either rows or columns by dragging the separator lines with the mouse. If the rows are tall enough, text in a cell will automatically word-wrap, but only while the cell is being edited.

- The user can move from cell to cell with the arrow keys if the AllowArrows property of the control is set to True.

- You can control the user's ability to change data with three Boolean properties: AllowAddNew, AllowDelete, and AllowUpdate. If you set all three of these properties to False, the grid becomes a read-only view of the data and is safe to turn almost anyone else loose on.

- The DataGrid supports 35 different events that let you react to user editing and navigation actions. You can determine in its object model exactly which data is being changed and verify or modify it before the data is returned to the data source.

- You can set the font, border, and word wrap properties for each column independently.

- The user can split the DataGrid into multiple views (called splits) at run time by clicking and dragging the split tab, the small vertical bar to the left of the DataGrid's horizontal scrollbar. Figure 5.6 demonstrates how a split DataGrid lets you see widely separated columns in a single recordset. You can also control and create splits programmatically.

FIGURE 5.6:

Split DataGrid control

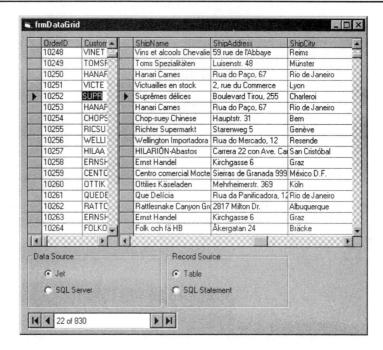

NOTE

If you'd like to learn how to create splits in the standard DataGrid programmatically, you should refer to the Visual Basic help files. However, before you go too far down that road, you should take a look at the Hierarchical FlexGrid. You may find that this newer control is capable of all the display flexibility you need without the bother of programming splits.

The Data Form Wizard

Building simple data forms can get tedious. Fortunately, Visual Basic 6 includes a tool to make it easier: the Data Form Wizard. To make this wizard available to your copy of Visual Basic, choose Add-Ins ➤ Add-In Manager and select the VB6 Data Form Wizard as an add-in to be loaded. You may also want to choose to load it on startup to make it available every time you launch Visual Basic.

Once it's loaded, you can launch the Data Form Wizard by choosing Add-Ins ➤ Data Form Wizard. This will bring up a standard wizard interface. The first screen asks what profile you want to use. A profile is a list of saved settings from a previous use of the wizard. If this is the first time you've used the wizard, you won't have a saved profile, so just click Next.

The next step is to choose a database format. Even though there are a bunch of choices available to you on any VB6 machine for OLE DB Providers, the only choices here are "Access" and "Remote(ODBC)." Choosing the former results in a connection string that uses the Jet 3.51 OLE DB provider. Choosing the latter results in a connection through the OLE DB provider for ODBC data sources. Neither one of these is really what you want in most cases. The best bet, though, is to pick the Remote(ODBC) format and reconfigure the ADO Data controls that the wizard creates to use the appropriate OLE DB provider after the form has been created.

Assuming you choose an ODBC connection, the next step is to provide connection information. You can either supply an existing ODBC DSN or supply the necessary information (User ID, Password, Database, Driver, and Server) to allow a DSN-less ODBC connection. This tab verifies the database connection settings you enter before continuing. Note that you cannot create a new DSN from this wizard panel, so if you don't know all your connection information by heart, and haven't created a DSN in the past, you'll need to abort here, create the DSN, and restart the wizard.

The next step is to name the form and pick a layout. You can choose from five form layouts:

Single Record   Creates a form with individual controls for each column in the record source. This form will display a single row of data at a time.

Grid (Datasheet)   Uses the DataGrid to display the records on the form.

Master/Detail   Joins several tables to present "drill-down" information on a single form.

MS HFlexGrid   Uses the Hierarchical FlexGrid control to display the data. This control is covered later in this chapter.

MS Chart   Uses the Microsoft Chart control to display graphical summaries of the data. This layout isn't especially useful for most database applications, and isn't covered here.

You can also choose the binding type to use on this page. Depending on the layout you choose, you'll have a choice of using the ADO Data control, straight ADO Code, or a Class module. All the examples in this chapter use the ADO Data control.

The next panel of the wizard lets you select a record source for your data form and then fields from that record source. You can also choose a single field (column) to sort the records by. The wizard will build a SQL statement based on your choices.

The next panel lets you choose which buttons the wizard should create on the form. You have seven choices here:

Add   Adds new records to the database.

Update   Immediately saves any data changes in the current record back to the database.

Edit   Allows editing of the current record. Although the wizard will always allow you to select this choice, you won't see this option unless you base your form on ADO Code. The ADO Data control automatically allows editing with no further user interaction.

Delete   Deletes the current record.

Refresh   Requeries the database to get any changes to the current record since it's been displayed. This button only makes sense if the data source is multiuser.

Close   Closes the form.

Show Data Control   Makes the ADO Data control visible (this choice only applies to forms that use the Grid (Datasheet) layout.

The final screen of the wizard lets you choose a profile name to save the settings you just used. This is useful if you're going to need to create the same form many times in different applications or want to try the form and then possibly make some slight adjustments. The form is then created and added to the current project.

Single Record Forms

Figure 5.7 shows a single record form created by the Data Form Wizard. (This form is in the sample project for this chapter and you can get to it from the Data Form Wizard Single button.) It's based on the Orders table in the Northwind database. The only changes that were made to this form after the wizard created it were the ones needed to hook it up to either the Jet or the SQL Server version of Northwind.

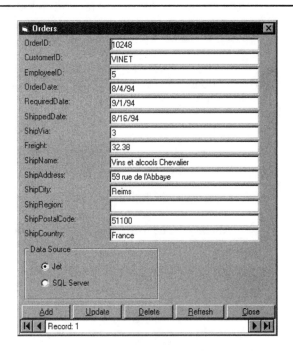

In addition to building the form and its controls, the Data Form Wizard also creates some code, most of it tied to events of the ADO Data control. This code is helpfully commented to allow you to customize it for your own application. The wizard writes procedures for these events:

- The Error event has a hook for trapping data errors in general.

- The MoveComplete event updates the record counter at the bottom of the form.

- The WillChangeRecord event lets you validate data before it's saved to the database. The code that the wizard creates shows you how you can use the adReason argument of this event to validate only in response to certain actions, while ignoring others:

```
Private Sub datPrimaryRS_WillChangeRecord( _
  ByVal adReason As ADODB.EventReasonEnum, _
  ByVal cRecords As Long, _
```

```
adStatus As ADODB.EventStatusEnum, _
ByVal pRecordset As ADODB.Recordset20)
 'This is where you put validation code
 'This event gets called when the following actions occur
Dim bCancel As Boolean

Select Case adReason
Case adRsnAddNew
Case adRsnClose
Case adRsnDelete
Case adRsnFirstChange
Case adRsnMove
Case adRsnRequery
Case adRsnResynch
Case adRsnUndoAddNew
Case adRsnUndoDelete
Case adRsnUndoUpdate
Case adRsnUpdate
End Select

If bCancel Then adStatus = adStatusCancel
End Sub
```

The wizard also writes code for all the buttons it creates:

- The Add button calls the recordset's AddNew method.

- The Delete button calls the recordset's Delete method and then makes sure that a valid record is displayed.

- The Refresh button calls the data control's Refresh method.

- The Update button calls the recordset's UpdateBatch method.

WARNING   As with the event procedures you write, you'll need to modify the Recordset objects in event procedures that the Wizard creates in order to use the Recordset20 datatype.

Grid Forms

Figure 5.8 shows a grid form created by the Data Form Wizard (again, it's been modified to use our code for switching data sources for the ADO Data control).

To see it, click the Data Form Wizard Grid button. You'll notice that it's very similar to the single record form, except that it uses a DataGrid control rather than a series of text boxes to display the data.

FIGURE 5.8:

Grid form created by the Data Form Wizard

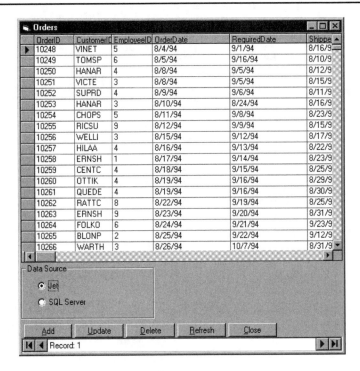

The grid form also includes a bit more code than the single record form:

- The Form_Resize event is used to automatically adjust the size of the grid itself to fill the bulk of the form. This is an easy way to let the user adjust the view for different video settings or working conditions.

- The code for the Add button uses a hack: it sends the focus to the last row in the grid and then uses SendKeys to send a Down arrow, thus forcing the focus onto the new record row. This is necessary because the grid doesn't have a method for adding a new record programmatically.

Master/Detail Forms

Master/Detail forms, such as the one shown in Figure 5.9, are ideal for displaying both halves of a one-to-many relationship. For example, the master section might display customers while the detail section displays the orders for the selected customer. Or the master section might display orders while the detail section displays the order detail for the selected order.

FIGURE 5.9:

Master/Detail form created
by the Data Form Wizard

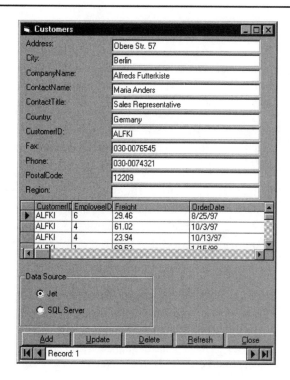

Building a Master/Detail form requires making a couple more choices in the wizard. You'll see the "Select Record Source" panel of the wizard twice, since you have to tell the wizard which records to use for the master part of the form and which records to use for the detail part of the form. When you've selected both record sources, the wizard will prompt you to select the joining fields so that it can keep the information synchronized.

The wizard creates a form that uses the OLE DB MSDataShape Provider to retrieve data from the data source. The MSDataShape Provider returns (not surprisingly) *data shapes,* which are most easily thought of as hierarchical record-sets. The simplest data shape has a parent recordset that includes a field in each row that is actually a pointer to a child recordset. When you retrieve the parent row, the child recordset is automatically constructed and made available.

I'll cover data shaping in detail in Chapter 10. For now, you might just want to take a peek at the CommandText property of the ADO Data control used on the sample form:

```
SHAPE(select
Address,City,CompanyName,ContactName,ContactTitle,
Country,CustomerID,Fax,Phone,PostalCode,Region
from Customers Order by CompanyName} AS ParentCMD
APPEND ({select CustomerID,EmployeeID,Freight,OrderDate,OrderID,
RequiredDate,ShipAddress,ShipCity,ShipCountry,
ShipName,ShippedDate,ShipPostalCode,ShipRegion,
ShipVia from Orders Order by OrderID } AS ChildCMD
RELATE CustomerID TO CustomerID) AS ChildCMD
```

Because this form uses the Data Shape provider, we also have to use a slightly different method for switching between Jet and SQL Server data sources. The Data Shape provider works by listing two providers in the OLE DB connection string, one for the Data Shape itself and one for the underlying data. Here's the code from our modified version of the form:

```
Private Sub optJet_Click()
    If optJet.Value Then
        With datPrimaryRS
            .ConnectionString = "PROVIDER=MSDataShape;" & _
            "Data PROVIDER=Microsoft.Jet.OLEDB.4.0;" & _
            "Data Source=C:\Program Files\ ➡
Microsoft Visual Studio\VB98\Nwind.mdb;"
            .Refresh
            Set grdDataGrid.DataSource = _
            .Recordset("ChildCMD").UnderlyingValue
        End With
    End If
End Sub

Private Sub optSQLServer_Click()
    If optSQLServer.Value Then
        With datPrimaryRS
            .ConnectionString = "PROVIDER=MSDataShape;" & _
```

```
                        "Data PROVIDER=MSDASQL;driver={SQL Server};" & _
                        "server=(local);uid=;pwd=;database=Northwind;"
                        .Refresh
                        Set grdDataGrid.DataSource = _
                        .Recordset("ChildCMD").UnderlyingValue
                    End With
                End If
            End Sub
```

The only new concept here is the UnderlyingValue property used to retrieve a child recordset from the Data Shape. Retrieving the UnderlyingValue of the field in the parent recordset that has the name of the child recordset returns a direct reference to that child recordset, which is suitable for use as a data source for the grid.

NOTE   Of course, you'll need to change the ConnectionString settings in this code if you haven't placed the Northwind database in its default location.

Programming the ADO Data Control

Now that you've seen several ways of using the ADO Data control on a form, it's time to look at what you can do with it programmatically. You had a taste of this when we looked at the wizard-generated code, and the important properties of the control were covered earlier in the chapter. Now let's take a more systematic look at the methods and events supported by the ADO Data control.

The Refresh Method

There's only one data-related method of the ADO Data control: the Refresh method. (The control also has some of the standard VB methods, such as Drag, Move, and Zorder, shared by many controls; those simple visual methods aren't covered in this book.)

The Refresh method of the ADO Data control essentially tells the control to throw away all the data it has loaded and get all its data anew from the underlying OLE DB provider. There are two reasons why you might want to use this method:

- The data in the database might actually have changed. This is the case in multiuser applications, and is the reason that the Data Form Wizard puts a Refresh button on the form.

- The properties of the control might have changed. This is the case where, for example, you switch a control from one database to another.

You need to call the Refresh method for these two cases, but you shouldn't call it any more than necessary, since each trip to the server for more data obviously consumes time and system resources.

Events

Although the ADO Data control shares several events with other controls, what we're interested in here are the data-related events. These include the following:

- EndOfRecordset

- Error

- WillMove

- MoveComplete

- WillChangeField

- FieldChangeComplete

- WillChangeRecord

- RecordChangeComplete

- WillChangeRecordset

- RecordsetChangeComplete

Except for the first two, these events fall neatly into "before" and "after" pairs. Let's look at each of them in more detail. The Events form in the sample project has message boxes attached to each event to allow you to see in detail when they occur.

You can review the code from this section in the frmEvents form in the Bound-Controls sample project. That form also contains additional code to prevent the WillMove and MoveComplete events from being fired before the form is fully loaded. If you try to do anything in these events before the form is fully loaded, you'll get data binding errors.

The EndOfRecordset event is called whenever the user navigates past the end of the recordset in either direction (that is, by going to the previous record from the first record or by going to the next record from the last record). This event occurs before the recordset is actually repositioned. The event procedure for this event has three arguments, as shown in this example:

```
Private Sub adodcNw_EndOfRecordset(fMoreData As Boolean, _
  adStatus As ADODB.EventStatusEnum, _
  ByVal pRecordset As ADODB.Recordset20)
    Dim intReply As Integer
    intReply = MsgBox("EndOfRecordset event. " & _
     "Do you want to see this event in the future?", _
     vbYesNo)
    If intReply = vbNo Then
        adStatus = adStatusUnwantedEvent
    End If
End Sub
```

The fMoreData argument is used by ADO. If you actually add more records to the recordset while in this event, you need to set this argument to True.

The adStatus argument is both passed in by ADO and used on its return. This argument will be adStatusOK if the move was successful, or adStatusCantDeny if the move was successful and cannot be cancelled. In addition, you can set this argument to adStatusUnwantedEvent to prevent this event from firing in the future. In cancelable events such as WillMove, you can set this argument to adCancel to tell ADO not to permit the action that caused the event to fire in the first place.

The pRecordset argument contains the actual recordset that's being manipulated. You can use this argument or the ADO Data control's Recordset property interchangeably, if you want to work with the underlying data.

The Error event is triggered whenever an OLE DB or ADO error occurs that's not directly caused by your own Visual Basic code. For example, if you change a record and move to another record using the ADO Data control (which would automatically save your changes), but the underlying database record is locked by another user, it will raise the Error event. This event comes with a bunch of arguments, nearly all of which just pass information on from the underlying error:

```
Private Sub adodcNwind_Error(ByVal ErrorNumber As Long, _
  Description As String, ByVal Scode As Long, _
  ByVal Source As String, ByVal HelpFile As String, _
  ByVal HelpContext As Long, fCancelDisplay As Boolean)
    Dim intReply As Integer
    intReply = MsgBox("An ADO Error has occured. " & _
      "The error number is " & ErrorNumber & ". The " & _
      "error description is """ & Description & """. " & _
      "The " & _
      "error code on the server is " & Scode & ". The " & _
      "source of the error is """ & Source & """. " & _
      "Do you wish " & _
      "to display the default message?", vbYesNo)
    If intReply = vbNo Then
        fCancelDisplay = True
    End If
End Sub
```

Note that if you do not set the fCancelDisplay argument to True during your procedure, the ADO Data control will proceed to display its own message.

The WillMove and MoveComplete events are triggered by moving through the recordset. You'll see the WillMove event before any move, whether it be moving to the first record, the last record, or any other record. You can cancel the Will-Move event, but even if you do, you'll still get the MoveComplete event. The MoveComplete event is fired whenever you either successfully move to another record or cancel a move in the WillMove event. Here's some code from the frmEvents sample form:

```
Private Sub adodcNwind_MoveComplete( _
  ByVal adReason As ADODB.EventReasonEnum, _
  ByVal pError As ADODB.Error, _
  adStatus As ADODB.EventStatusEnum, _
  ByVal pRecordset As ADODB.Recordset20)
    MsgBox "MoveComplete"
  If Not mfLoaded Then
      Exit Sub
```

```
        End If
        adodcNwind.Caption = _
        adodcNwind.Recordset.AbsolutePosition & " of " & _
        adodcNwind.Recordset.RecordCount
    End Sub

    Private Sub adodcNwind_WillMove( _
     ByVal adReason As ADODB.EventReasonEnum, _
     adStatus As ADODB.EventStatusEnum, _
     ByVal pRecordset As ADODB.Recordset20)
        Dim intReply As Integer
        If Not mfLoaded Then
            Exit Sub
        End If
        intReply = MsgBox("Cancel WillMove?", vbYesNo)
        If intReply = vbYes Then
            adStatus = adStatusCancel
        End If
    End Sub
```

You'll find that if you cancel the WillMove event, you still get the MoveComplete event, and then you get an Error event telling you that the operation was cancelled. An easy way to test this with the frmEvents form is to simply use the ADO Data control to move to the next record once the form has loaded.

The WillChangeField and FieldChangeComplete events bracket any change you make to the data in any field that's being retrieved via this data control. Here are the definitions for those two events, taken from the frmEvents form in the BoundControls sample project:

```
    Private Sub adodcNwind_WillChangeField( _
     ByVal cFields As Long, _
     Fields As Variant, _
     adStatus As ADODB.EventStatusEnum, _
     ByVal pRecordset As ADODB.Recordset20)
        Dim intReply As Integer
        intReply = MsgBox("Cancel WillChangeField?", vbYesNo)
        If intReply = vbYes Then
            adStatus = adStatusCancel
        End If
    End Sub
```

```
Private Sub adodcNwind_FieldChangeComplete( _
  ByVal cFields As Long, _
  Fields As Variant, _
  ByVal pError As ADODB.Error, _
  adStatus As ADODB.EventStatusEnum, _
  ByVal pRecordset As ADODB.Recordset20)
      MsgBox "FieldChangeComplete"
End Sub
```

In these events, the cFields argument tells you how many fields have changes pending, and the Fields argument is an array of those Field objects. These events can be triggered by anything that sets the Value of a field, whether that's typing directly into a bound control or altering a field's value through code.

The WillChangeRecord and RecordChangeComplete events fire any time you're making a change to a record (including when you make a change to a field, so you'll typically see the WillChangeField and WillChangeRecord events occur together). Here are their event procedures:

```
Private Sub adodcNwind_WillChangeRecord( _
  ByVal adReason As ADODB.EventReasonEnum, _
  ByVal cRecords As Long, _
  adStatus As ADODB.EventStatusEnum, _
  ByVal pRecordset As ADODB.Recordset20)
      Dim intReply As Integer
      intReply = MsgBox( _
        "Cancel WillChangeRecord?", vbYesNo)
      If intReply = vbYes Then
          adStatus = adStatusCancel
      End If
End Sub

Private Sub adodcNwind_RecordChangeComplete( _
  ByVal adReason As ADODB.EventReasonEnum, _
  ByVal cRecords As Long, _
  ByVal pError As ADODB.Error, _
  adStatus As ADODB.EventStatusEnum, _
  ByVal pRecordset As ADODB.Recordset20)
      MsgBox "RecordChangeComplete"
End Sub
```

In these events, the EventReasonEnum argument tells you why the event was fired. It can be one of these values:

- adRsnAddNew if a record was added
- adRsnDelete if a record was deleted
- adRsnUpdate if a call to the Update method generated this event
- adRsnUndoUpdate if an Update was undone
- adRsnUndoAddNew if an Add New operation was undone
- adRsnUndoDelete if a Delete operation was undone
- adRsnFirstChange if a field in the record was changed for the first time

In these events, the cRecords argument is set to the number of records with pending changes. The passed recordset is filtered to hold only the records with pending changes (and it causes an error to try to change the Filter property of the recordset within one of these events).

The WillChangeRecordset and RecordsetChangeComplete events bracket changes to the overall recordset contents:

```
Private Sub adodcNwind_WillChangeRecordset( _
ByVal adReason As ADODB.EventReasonEnum, _
adStatus As ADODB.EventStatusEnum, _
ByVal pRecordset As ADODB.Recordset20)
    Dim intReply As Integer
    intReply = MsgBox( _
     "Cancel WillChangeRecordset?", vbYesNo)
    If intReply = vbYes Then
        adStatus = adStatusCancel
    End If
End Sub

Private Sub adodcNwind_RecordsetChangeComplete( _
ByVal adReason As ADODB.EventReasonEnum, _
ByVal pError As ADODB.Error, _
adStatus As ADODB.EventStatusEnum, _
ByVal pRecordset As ADODB.Recordset20)
    MsgBox "RecordsetChangeComplete"
End Sub
```

In these events, the adReason argument again tells you why the event was fired, but it takes on a different set of values:

- adRsnRequery if the Requery method was called

- adRsnResynch if the Resync method was called

- adRsnClose if the recordset was closed

WARNING
A final word of caution: Although these events pass you a copy of the ADO Data control's recordset, the copy passed is an ADO 2 recordset. What this means is that you can't use any of the new ADO 2.1 or 2.5 methods or properties on this copy of the recordset.

NOTE
Given the problems with the ADO Data control events detailed above, you may want to consider just using straight ADO Recordset events in your applications. You can read more about this technique in Chapter 8.

The Hierarchical FlexGrid Control

The final data-bound control that I'll cover in this chapter is the Hierarchical Flex-Grid control. This control, new to Visual Basic 6, is designed to show multiple resultsets from a SHAPE command in a single read-only format. I'll cover the multiple-recordset capability in Chapter 6, when we use the Data Environment to build connections with this capability. But right now you already know enough to get an attractive display of a resultset that contains data from more than one table.

The Data Form Wizard will create forms using the Hierarchical FlexGrid, but these forms will display only a single table. For creating forms, then, you'll probably find the regular grid form to be more useful.

A Sample Hierarchical FlexGrid Form

Figure 5.10 shows a form using the Hierarchical FlexGrid control. (Like the other forms in this chapter, it's in the BoundControls sample project.) This form displays information from a single view based on the Northwind Customers, Orders, Order Details, and Products tables. Although the form does not allow data editing, it is moderately interactive: it allows the user to drag columns to rearrange them. If the user drags a column, the hierarchy and sorting are automatically reworked.

Although this form appears to display a hierarchical recordset, it's actually displaying a single recordset based on a view. The illusion of hierarchy comes about because the Hierarchical FlexGrid in this case is set to merge adjacent cells in the same column (for instance, the cells in the Company Name column) that contain the same value.

FIGURE 5.10:

Example Hierarchical Flex-Grid form

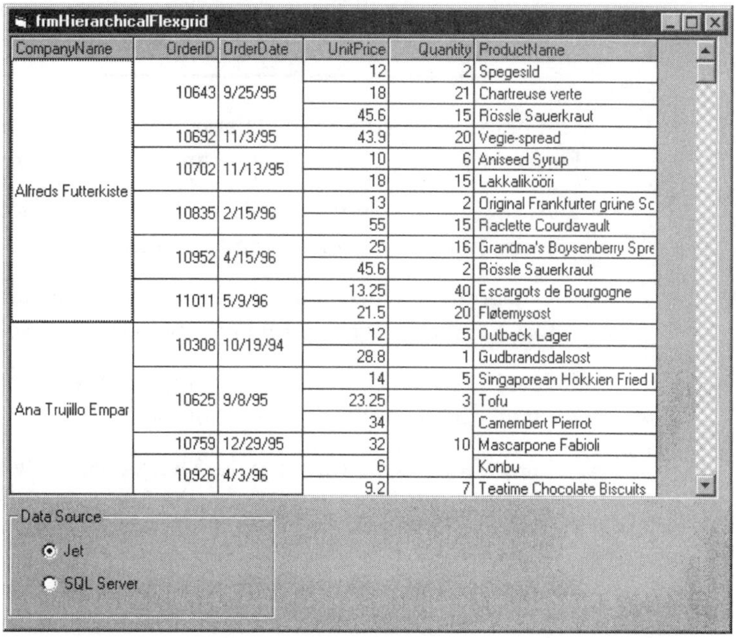

This form involves two controls, an ADO Data control and a Hierarchical Flex-Grid control. The ADO Data control has its Visible property set to False, since the entire resultset is visible at one time in the grid.

The ADO Data control has its connection set to use the same Data Link file that the rest of the forms in this chapter rely on. The CommandType property is set to adCmdText and the CommandText property to:

```
SELECT Customers.CompanyName, Orders.OrderID,
    Orders.OrderDate, [Order Details].UnitPrice,
    [Order Details].Quantity, Products.ProductName
FROM ((((Customers INNER JOIN
    Orders ON
    Customers.CustomerID = Orders.CustomerID) INNER JOIN
    [Order Details] ON
    Orders.OrderID = [Order Details].OrderID) INNER JOIN
    Products ON [Order Details].ProductID = Products.ProductID)
```

NOTE   If you're not great with SQL syntax, remember that you can use the Query Designer in the Data View to build views like this graphically, and then copy the SQL statement into the property that needs it. If you build a SQL statement for SQL Server and want to use it on Jet, you'll need to insert the parentheses to group the FROM clauses one at a time, as shown in this example.

Most of the properties of the Hierarchical FlexGrid are at their default settings in this example. The properties that are not default are:

- AllowUserResizing, which is set to flexResizeBoth. This allows the user to resize both rows and columns by clicking and dragging with the mouse.

- DataSource, which is set to adodcNwind, the name of the ADO Data control, to bind the grid automatically to the data source.

- FixedCols, which is set to 0 to suppress the blank selection column that normally displays at the left edge of the grid.

- MergeCells, which is set to flexMergeFree to allow the control to merge adjacent cells that have the same value. This is the setting that makes the grid display the "outline" look.

This form is designed to sort the data on the Hierarchical FlexGrid control. It does so by taking advantage of the built-in sorting capabilities of the control:

```
Public Sub SortGrid()
    With MSHFlexGrid1
        .Col = 0
        .ColSel = .Cols - 1
```

```
        .Sort = 1
    End With
End Sub
```

Setting the Col property tells the grid which column to begin the sort with; setting the ColSel property tells it the column to end the sort with (columns in the grid have a zero-based numbering). Setting the Sort property to 1 triggers a left-to-right ascending sort, in this case on the CompanyName column.

There's also code behind this form to enable the column dragging:

```
Private Sub MSHFlexGrid1_MouseDown(Button As Integer, _
  Shift As Integer, x As Single, y As Single)
    With MSHFlexGrid1
        .Tag = ""
        If .MouseRow <> 0 Then
            Exit Sub
        End If
        .Tag = Str(.MouseCol)
        .MousePointer = vbSizeWE
    End With
End Sub

Private Sub MSHFlexGrid1_MouseUp(Button As Integer, _
  Shift As Integer, x As Single, y As Single)
    With MSHFlexGrid1
        .MousePointer = vbDefault
        If .Tag = "" Then
            Exit Sub
        End If
        .Redraw = False
        .ColPosition(Val(.Tag)) = .MouseCol
        SortGrid
        .Redraw = True
    End With
End Sub
```

When the user clicks the primary mouse button, the MouseDown code first checks to see whether they're on the header row of the grid. If they are, the Tag property of the grid is set to the column that's being dragged and the mouse pointer is set to a two-headed arrow. In the corresponding MouseUp event, if the Tag property has a value then we know it's time to rearrange and resort the data. Setting the Redraw property to False keeps the grid from showing changes until we're done. Setting the ColPosition property of the dragged column to the new mouse position moves that column, and calling the SortGrid procedure re-sorts the data.

As you can see, it's possible to get a good deal of functionality with little coding from this control. With Visual Basic 6, we're finally seeing fulfillment of the promise of ActiveX controls as insertable components with complex user interface behavior.

So far, all the forms we've worked with have depended on a single resultset (with the exception of the Master/Detail form, which used a SHAPE command to construct a single hierarchical recordset). Now it's time to look at the new Data Environment Designer, which allows easy construction of much more complex database connections and enables your code to respond to ADO events.

CHAPTER

SIX

6

Rapid Data Access with the Data Environment

- Creating Connections

- Using Command Objects in the Data Environment

- Data Environment Options and Operations

- Binding Forms to the Data Environment

- Using ADO Events in the Data Environment

- Using the Data Environment in Code

Early versions of Visual Basic used only forms and modules to create programs. One of the major advances of Visual Basic since then has been the introduction of additional designers. A Visual Basic designer provides a way to manipulate an object and its code within Visual Basic projects—for example, forms are handled by the Forms Designer.

One of the new designers in Visual Basic 6 is the Data Environment Designer (DED). This designer creates and manipulates Data Environment objects, which represent ADO connections and commands. A single Data Environment can contain multiple connections and multiple commands within those connections. You can also attach code to events of objects contained within the Data Environment, just as you can to events of forms within the Forms Designer.

To create a new Data Environment, choose Project ➤ Add Data Environment from the Visual Basic menus, or choose the Data Environment button on the New Object drop-down button on the Visual Basic standard toolbar. This will create, by default, Data Environment1, containing a Connection object named Connection1.

Creating Connections

When you create a new Data Environment, it isn't connected to any particular data source, since Visual Basic doesn't know what you want to do with it. But there is a blank Connection object within the Data Environment just waiting to be connected.

Like any other object within a designer, Connection objects within the Data Environment Designer have properties that show in the Visual Basic properties window. You can dictate which data source a Connection object will use by setting these properties:

- Attributes

- CommandTimeout

- ConnectionSource (this property holds an OLE DB connection string)

- ConnectionTimeout

- CursorLocation (by default, Data Environment connections use client-side cursors)

However, there's an easier way to hook up a connection than composing the OLE DB connection string by hand. Right-click the Connection object within the designer and select Properties, or click the Connection object within the designer and click the Properties button on the designer's toolbar. Either action will open the familiar Data Link Properties dialog box that we first saw in Chapter 4 to allow you to use the stock OLE DB dialog box for connecting to an OLE DB provider.

Of course, you don't have to accept the default name for the Connection object (and probably shouldn't, since more descriptive names are easier to grasp in code). You can assign a name to the object by changing the Name property directly in the object's property sheet, by slowly double-clicking the object and typing a new name, or by right-clicking the object and choosing Rename to specify your own name for the connection.

You may have noticed that the Connection properties above don't include properties necessary for controlling ADO security. That's because Connection objects in the Data Environment have two sets of security properties, one for design time and one for run time. If you use the Categorized tab of the Visual Basic property window, it's easy to see these two sets of properties. There are four Design Authentication properties:

DesignPassword   Holds the password to use at design time.

DesignPromptBehavior   Specifies when to prompt the user for logon information and can be set to adPromptAlways, adPromptComplete, adPromptCompleteRequired, or adPromptNever. These correspond to values of the Prompt property (which is not a standard property but is found as a property in the provider-related Properties collection) on the underlying ADO Connection object, which I covered in Chapter 3.

DesignSaveAuthentication   Tells the designer whether to save the values of DesignPassword and DesignUserName in the files that hold the Data Environment Connection object's definition. By default, this property is set to False.

DesignUserName   Holds the username to use at design time.

There are also four Runtime Authentication properties that exactly parallel the Design Authentication properties:

RunPassword   Holds the password to use at run time.

RunPromptBehavior   Can be set to adPromptAlways, adPromptComplete, adPromptCompleteRequired, or adPromptNever.

RunSaveAuthentication   Tells the designer whether to save the values of RunPassword and RunUserName in the files that hold the Data Environment Connection object's definition. By default, this property is set to False.

RunUserName   Holds the username to use at run time.

WARNING   If you set DesignSaveAuthentication or RunSaveAuthentication to True, then the user names and passwords you've entered are available in plain text to anyone who has access to your Visual Basic source code files.

You're not limited to a single connection within a Data Environment. You can create additional connections by right-clicking the root node in the Data Environment and choosing Add Connection or by clicking the Add Connection button on the Data Environment Designer toolbar. Either action will create another Connection object with a serialized name within the designer. In addition to appearing in the Data Environment, all Data Environment connections appear in the Data View window.

It's possible for the information in a connection to change while you're working with it. For example, someone might add new stored procedures to the database, or delete existing tables, or eliminate the user you've specified for retrieving design information. To bring a connection up to date, right-click it and choose Refresh, or select it and click the Refresh button on the Data Environment toolbar. This will refresh all the locally stored metadata about the connection and rebuild the Data Environment's internal lists of objects from the data source.

Using Command Objects in the Data Environment

The fact that you can persist a connection with an OLE DB provider via ADO, together with the code attached to it, is moderately interesting. But connections alone won't get you data. For that, you need Command objects. Command objects in the Data Environment are wrappers around ADO Command objects. In this section, you'll learn how to create Command objects and see what you can do with them in the Data Environment.

Creating Command Objects

To create a Command object within a Data Environment, select the Connection or Command object that will be the parent of this Command object and click the Add Command button on the Data Environment toolbar, or right-click the parent object and choose Add Command (if the parent is a connection) or Add Child Command (if the parent is a command). Any of these procedures will create a new, blank Command object, just waiting to be connected to data. Once again, you should immediately rename the Command object to something more intuitive than the default Command1.

There are three basic properties that determine what data a Command object will retrieve:

ConnectionName   Is the name of the Connection object that should be used to hook up this Command object. This will be automatically filled in with the parent Connection when you create the new Command object.

CommandType   Corresponds to the ADO CommandType property. You can set this to adCmdText (for SQL statements), adCmdTable (for tables), or adCmdStoredProc (for stored procedures).

CommandText   Corresponds to the ADO CommandText property. It will contain the SQL statement, table name, or stored procedure name that this command should use to retrieve data. If you're entering CommandText directly in the Visual Basic properties window, you have to enter names exactly. However, if you create a Command object, right-click it, and choose Properties, you'll find that you can select a table, view, synonym, or stored procedure name from a combo box in the object's property pages.

When you assign these three properties, the Command object node in the Data Environment Designer will automatically retrieve information on the schema of the resultset that it represents and create child Field objects in the TreeView. At this time the Command also retrieves parameter information, if it's based on a stored procedure. Figure 6.1 shows what a Data Environment looks like after creating a simple table-based Command object. Note that the status bar in the Data Environment describes the highlighted node of the TreeView.

FIGURE 6.1:

A Data Environment with a
single command

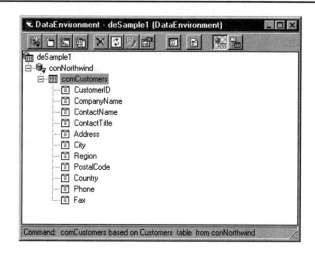

FIGURE 6.1:

A Data Environment with a single command

Command objects also have a set of advanced properties that echo the ADO Command properties:

CacheSize   Sets the number of records that should be cached locally (defaults to 100).

CallSyntax   Specifies the exact string that ADO should send to the data source to execute the command. For example, if you base a command on a stored procedure named CustOrderHist in a SQL Server database, this property will contain {? = CALL dbo.CustOrderHist(?)}, which is the ODBC syntax for calling a stored procedure. Unless your data source uses wildly nonstandard syntax for stored procedures, you won't need to alter this property's value.

CommandTimeout   Sets the number of seconds to wait for data to be returned when the Command is executed (defaults to 30).

CursorLocation   Can be set to adUseClient (for client-side cursors, the default) or adUseServer (for server-side cursors).

CursorType   Can be set to adOpenStatic (the default), adOpenDynamic, adOpenKeyset, or adOpenForwardOnly.

GrandTotalName   Applies only to grand total aggregate Commands. These are discussed later in the chapter.

LockType   Can be set to adLockReadOnly (the default), adLock-Pessimistic, adLockOptimistic, or adLockBatchOptimistic. Note that by default you won't be able to edit records retrieved by this Command.

MaxRecords   Sets the maximum number of records that should be retrieved from the data provider. By default this is zero, which means that there is no limit on the number of records.

Prepared   Can be set to True to save a compiled version of the Command for faster execution. If the provider doesn't support compiled commands, you'll receive an error when you try to set this property to True.

Since many developers use stored procedures for all data access in client-server environments, there's also a shortcut for creating Command objects based on stored procedures. Select a Connection object and click the Insert Stored Procedures button on the Data Environment toolbar, or right-click the Connection object and choose Insert Stored Procedures. The Data Environment will display the Insert Stored Procedures dialog box shown in Figure 6.2. Select as many stored procedures as you like by moving them from the Available list box to the Add list box and then click Insert. The Data Environment will automatically insert a Command object for each of the stored procedures you've chosen. You can repeat this operation later if you want to add additional Command objects based on other stored procedures. Depending on the source of the Command objects, the Data Environment will display different icons—the icon for a SQL statement, for instance, will be different from that for a stored procedure.

FIGURE 6.2:

Insert Stored Procedures
dialog box

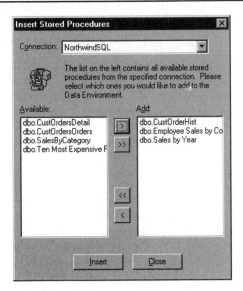

If you've got a Data View connection to the database you want to work with, there's an even easier way to create a Data Environment Command object. Simply expand the Data View until you can see the object you'd like to use as the source for the Data Environment Command object (for example, a table or stored procedure). Then drag that object from the Data View window and drop it in the Data Environment window. If there's already a Data Environment Connection pointing to the same data source, the Data Environment will create a Command for this Connection and automatically hook it up to the object you dragged and dropped. If there's no matching Connection object, the Data Environment will create both the Connection and the Command.

Working with Command Objects

Now that you've created a Command object, what's next? You can perform a variety of operations with the object directly within the Data Environment. These include examining the properties of the Command, setting properties for the Field objects contained in this Command, refreshing the Command from the underlying data source, debugging it (if the Command is based on a stored procedure), and designing it (if the Command is based on a SQL string).

To see the properties of a Command object, right-click the object and choose Properties, or select the object and click the Properties button on the Data Environment toolbar. Either action will open the property sheet for the object. This property sheet has six tabs:

General   Lets you choose the data that you want the Command connected to (see Figure 6.3). When you choose an object type from the Database Object list, the Object Name list will automatically be refreshed to indicate which objects of that type are available via the selected Connection. If you choose SQL Statement, the SQL Builder button will launch the Visual Database Tools Query Builder to let you create a SQL statement on the fly.

FIGURE 6.3:

General tab of a Command
object's property sheet

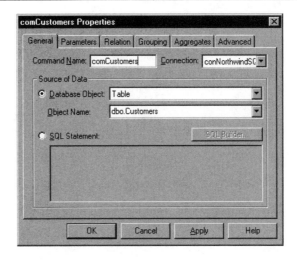

Parameters   Lets you examine the properties of any parameters your
Command contains. Naturally, this only makes sense for Commands
based on stored procedures. I'll cover the use of parameterized stored procedures later in this chapter.

Relation, Grouping, and Aggregates   Are used to relate parent and child
Commands. You'll see this in the section on Command object hierarchies
below.

Advanced   Provides you with one-stop access to the advanced properties
of the Command object (see Figure 6.4). One nice thing about using this
method, instead of the Visual Basic property window, to set these properties
is that it won't let you change things that don't make sense. For example, to
choose a type of cursor other than static, you must use a server-side cursor.

FIGURE 6.4:

Advanced tab of a Command object's property sheet

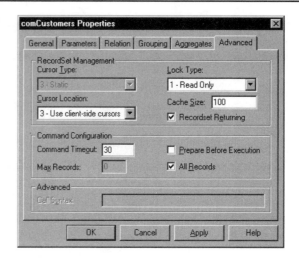

To set properties for a Field object underneath a Command object, right-click the Field object and select Properties, or select the object and click the Properties button on the Data Environment toolbar. This will open the property sheet for the Field object. The property sheet will show you the datatype and size of the field. It also lets you set two properties used when basing form controls on this field: the type of control to use and the caption that should be placed beside the field. You'll learn more about creating forms based on Command objects later in the chapter.

To refresh a Command object, right-click the object and select Refresh, or select the object and click the Refresh button on the Data Environment toolbar. The Data Environment will warn you that any user-defined information stored with the fields of this Command object will be lost and let you abort the process at this point (it does this whether there is any such information or not). If you choose to continue, all the metadata about the object is fetched anew from the data source. This includes information about the Command itself (for example, the current definition of a stored procedure, which might have changed since the command was created) as well as all the Field and Parameter information stored beneath it.

To debug a Command object based on a stored procedure, right-click the object and select Debug. This will load the stored procedure into the T-SQL Debugger. (The Debug option will be unavailable if the Command object is not based on a stored procedure.) Details on debugging stored procedures using the T-SQL Debugger are covered in Chapter 4.

To design a Command object based on a SQL statement, right-click the object and choose Design (again, this option will be unavailable if the Command object is not based on a SQL statement) or select it and click the Design button on the Data Environment toolbar. This will load the text of the SQL statement into the Visual Database Tools Query Designer, as discussed in Chapter 4.

Command Object Hierarchies

Were it limited to single Commands, the Data Environment wouldn't offer much advantage over the Data Form Wizard we saw in Chapter 5. However, there's much more to the Data Environment than just a wrapper for ADO Command objects. For starters, there's an easy way to design hierarchical recordsets using the Data Environment. The Data Environment implements the notion of a Command hierarchy—a set of Command objects with particular relations that correspond to an ADO Shape Command. While I won't cover data shaping in detail until Chapter 10, here is a good place to learn what the Data Environment can do for you in this regard.

Later in this chapter, you'll see how to bind the information from Command hierarchies to controls on a form. You can either use a single Hierarchical Flex-Grid control to hold the entire hierarchy, or bind individual recordsets and fields to individual controls on a form. But first, you need to understand what sorts of recordsets you can create.

Command hierarchies can represent three basic kinds of information:

- Relation hierarchies

- Grouping hierarchies

- Aggregates

A relation hierarchy contains information from a set of tables that are related in a traditional one-to-many relationship. For example, Figure 6.5 shows the frmRelationalHierarchy form in the DataEnvironmentSample project. This form uses the Hierarchical FlexGrid control to display information from the Customers, Orders, and Order Details tables. Note that the grid allows you to use the + and – signs to expand and contract detail information from the three tables. It draws on three Command objects, each based on a SQL statement.

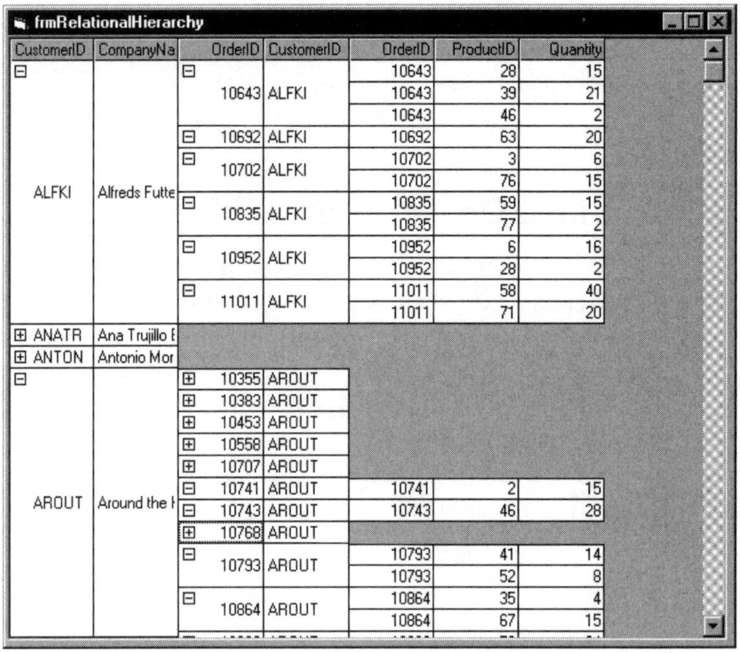

FIGURE 6.5:

Relation hierarchy on
a form

To create a relation hierarchy, first create a Connection object, and then create a Command object based on a SQL statement such as

```
SELECT CustomerID, CompanyName FROM Customers
```

The next step is to create a child Command object beneath the first Command object. You can do this by right-clicking the parent Command object and selecting Add Child Command, or by selecting the parent Command object and clicking the Add Child Command button on the Data Environment toolbar. The Data Environment will insert a new Command object in the TreeView display beneath the parent Command object. Display the properties for the child command and assign it a SQL statement such as

```
SELECT OrderID, CustomerID FROM Orders
```

Then select the Relation tab on the property sheet for the child Command object. You need to choose a pair of fields (in this case, the CustomerID field in each statement) and click the Add button to tell the Data Environment how the two tables are related. Figure 6.6 shows the Relation tab for this particular case.

FIGURE 6.6:

Relating two Command
objects

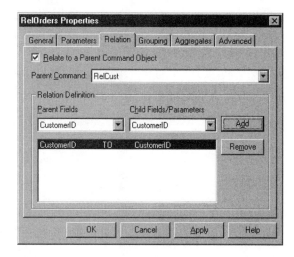

You can repeat the same process to create a child Command of the Orders Command object that draws information from the OrderDetails table based on a SQL statement such as

```
SELECT OrderID, ProductID, Quantity FROM [Order Details]
```

Once again, you must navigate to the Relations tab to specify how this Command is related to its parent.

That's all you have to do to create a relation hierarchy. To produce a quick browse form like the one shown in Figure 6.5, just right-drag the top level Command object from the hierarchy to an empty form and choose Hierarchical Flex-Grid from the context menu that appears when you drop the object.

A grouping hierarchy lets you take a single Command object and split it up so that some of the fields are used to group other fields. Figure 6.7 shows the result of displaying a grouping hierarchy on frmGroupingHierarchy in the DataEnvironmentSample sample project. Here you can see a list of product categories and expand or collapse the categories to show their constituent products.

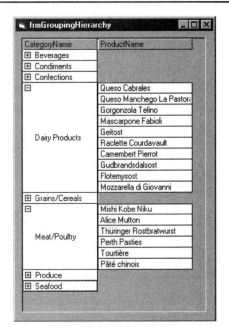

To create this particular form, start with a Command object based on the SQL statement

```
SELECT Categories.CategoryName, Products.ProductName
FROM Products
INNER JOIN Categories
ON Products.CategoryID = Categories.CategoryID
```

You can convert this Command into a grouping hierarchy by opening its property sheet and setting appropriate properties on the Grouping tab. To do this, first check the Group Command Object check box to tell the Data Environment that this Command will be grouped. Then enter a name for the grouping Command that will be created from this Command—for example, byCategory. Select the fields that you want to use for grouping and move them from the Fields In Command list box to the Fields Used For Grouping list box. Figure 6.8 shows the completed tab on the property sheet.

In the Data Environment window, the grouped hierarchy is displayed as a single Command object. However, instead of fields, this object has two child folders, one containing the summary fields that the Command is grouped by and one containing the detail fields that are shown for each record.

An aggregate lets you add a calculated total to a grouped Command. (While you can create aggregates on ungrouped Commands, they won't be displayed and aren't very useful.) Figure 6.9 shows the frmAggregate form in the DataEnvironmentSample sample project. Here the TotalOrders column is an aggregate that displays the total of the orders for the listed company.

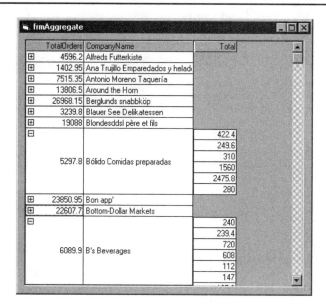

This form started with a Command object based on the SQL statement

```
SELECT Customers.CompanyName,
[Order Details].UnitPrice * [OrderDetails].Quantity
AS Total
FROM Customers INNER JOIN Orders
ON Customers.CustomerID = Orders.CustomerID
INNER JOIN [Order Details]
ON Orders.OrderID = [Order Details].OrderID
```

I then used the Grouping tab in the property sheet for the Command to set up a grouping Command named byCompany that groups on the CompanyName field. The last step was to fill in the necessary information on the Aggregates tab, shown in Figure 6.10:

Name   Is the name (and default column caption) to use for the calculated field.

Function   Dictates how the field should be calculated. You can choose between Any (which selects a random value from the available choices), Average, Count, Maximum, Minimum, Standard Deviation, and Sum.

Aggregate On combo   Tells which level of grouping to calculate the total across. In this particular instance, the aggregate is on a group-by-group basis.

Field combo   Lets you pick the field that should be aggregated.

FIGURE 6.10:

Defining an aggregate Command

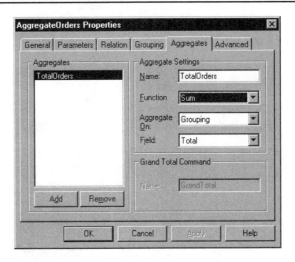

When you create a Command hierarchy (of any of the three types I discussed in this section), the Data Environment adds an additional menu item to the shortcut menu for the top-level Command, Hierarchy Info. This menu item brings up a simple dialog box that will display either the SHAPE statement that the Data Environment has automatically generated or the hierarchy of ADO objects involved in the command.

With practice, you can tell one type of hierarchical command from another just by looking at them in the Data Environment. Figure 6.11 shows the three Command hierarchies discussed in this section:

- The relation hierarchy is displayed as a series of SQL Command objects, with child Commands being subordinate to their parent Commands.

- The grouping hierarchy is displayed as a single Command object with folders dividing the grouping fields from the detail fields.

- The aggregate field is shown with a special +/- field symbol.

FIGURE 6.11:

Command hierarchies in the Data Environment

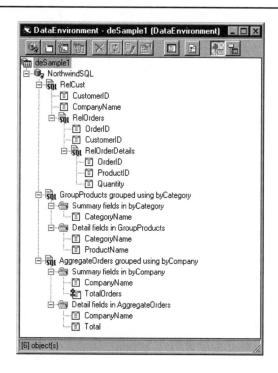

Data Environment Options and Operations

While most of the operation of the Data Environment is completely automatic, there are a few options you can set by hand. These fall into two categories. General options control the overall behavior of the Data Environment. Field Mapping options are useful when you want to create forms by using drag-and-drop from the Data Environment, which I'll cover in the next section.

General Options

You can set the general options for the Data Environment by right-clicking the root node in the Data Environment Designer and choosing Options, or by clicking the Options button on the Data Environment toolbar. This will open a dialog box with six check boxes. These options (and the control type options discussed next) are set once and apply to all Data Environments within your project. Changes take effect as soon as you close the dialog box.

Show Properties Immediately After Object Creation   By default, this option is off. Turning it on is helpful if you're creating many Command and Connection objects from scratch, since it saves having to separately open the property sheet for each object.

Prompt Before Deleting Object   By default, this option is on. Turn it off if you'd rather not get a warning when deleting objects from your Data Environment.

Show Status Bar   By default, this option is on, and it causes the status bar to appear at the bottom of the Data Environment.

Show System Objects   By default, this option is off. If you turn it on, any system objects that are part of Commands in this Data Environment will be displayed.

Disable Warnings   By default, this option is off. If you turn it on, it suppresses warning messages when you're doing something that the Data Environment thinks is wrong—for example, saving a Command object that has no CommandText.

Prompt Before Executing Command   By default, this option is on. To retrieve metadata from SQL commands or stored procedures, the Data Environment may need to execute the command on the server. Leaving this box checked will ensure that the Data Environment warns you before it does so—probably the better choice, since executing commands could have drastic side effects such as modifying or deleting data.

Associating Control Types with Data

As you'll see in the next section, one of the most powerful features of the Data Environment is the ability to create data-based forms and reports with simple drag-and-drop operations. The Data Environment Designer ships with a set of default associations between datatypes and fields, but you can change these associations on several levels.

If you like, you can set a control type to be used specifically with a particular Field object within a particular Command object. To do this, open the property sheet for the Field object and select the control you'd like to use from the combo box in the Field Mapping section. This combo box shows all the ActiveX controls registered on your computer, as well as the intrinsic Visual Basic controls. (It's likely to contain quite a number of controls that are inappropriate, so choose with care.) The Data Environment will happily try to create whatever control you choose, defaulting back to creating a text box if, for whatever reason, the control you've chosen can't be created on a Visual Basic form.

If the Field Mapping for a particular control remains set to <Use Default>, the Data Environment next looks to see whether you've specified a control type for the exact datatype of the underlying field in the data source. You can examine these mappings by choosing the Field Mapping tab of the Data Environment Options dialog box. To see specific datatypes in the list presented by this dialog box, you need to check the Show All Data Types check box. Once again, you can choose control types from a combo box listing all controls registered on your computer.

Finally, if there is no Field Mapping for a particular datatype, the Data Environment uses the control type specified for the datatype category. The Data Environment groups datatypes into categories and specifies a default control for each category. For example, the adChar and adWChar datatypes are grouped in the Text category and displayed by default with a TextBox control.

There are also two special entries on the Data Environment options list of datatypes:

Caption   Is used to determine the type of control to create for the captions of other controls. This property is used only if you have the Drag And Drop Field Captions check box checked.

Multiple   Is used to determine the type of control to use if you drag and drop an entire Command object. That is, this control is used for each field from the Command object when you drop the Command object rather than dropping individual fields.

Table 6.1 shows the default field mappings that the Data Environment is installed with.

T A B L E 6 . 1 : Default Field Mappings in the Data Environment

Category	Datatype	Control
Binary		TextBox
	adBinary	<Use default>
	adLongVarBinary	<Use default>
	adVarBinary	<Use default>
Boolean		CheckBox
	adBoolean	<Use default>
Caption		Label
	Caption	<Use default>
Currency		TextBox
	adCurrency	<Use default>
Date		TextBox
	adDate	<Use default>
	adDBDate	<Use default>
Empty		TextBox
	adEmpty	<Use default>

Continued on next page

TABLE 6.1 CONTINUED: Default Field Mappings in the Data Environment

Category	Datatype	Control
	adNull	\<Use default\>
Integer		TextBox
	adBigInt	\<Use default\>
	adInteger	\<Use default\>
	adSmallInt	\<Use default\>
	adTinyInt	\<Use default\>
	adUnsignedBigInt	\<Use default\>
	adUnsignedInt	\<Use default\>
	adUnsignedSmallInt	\<Use default\>
	adUnsignedTinyInt	\<Use default\>
Long		TextBox
	adDecimal	\<Use default\>
	adDouble	\<Use default\>
	adNumeric	\<Use default\>
	adSingle	\<Use default\>
	adVarNumeric	\<Use default\>
Memo		TextBox
	adLongVarChar	\<Use default\>
	adLongVarWChar	\<Use default\>
	adVarChar	\<Use default\>
	adWVarChar	\<Use default\>
Multiple		TextBox
	Multiple	\<Use default\>
Other		TextBox

Continued on next page

TABLE 6.1 CONTINUED: Default Field Mappings in the Data Environment

Category	Datatype	Control
	adBSTR	<Use default>
	adError	<Use default>
	adGUID	<Use default>
	adIDispatch	<Use default>
	adIUnknown	<Use default>
	adUserDefined	<Use default>
Text		TextBox
	adChar	<Use default>
	adWChar	<Use default>
Time		TextBox
	adDBTime	<Use default>
	adDBTimeStamp	<Use default>
Variant		TextBox
	adVariant	<Use default>

Miscellaneous Data Environment Options

You can also adjust some of the options that control the look of the TreeView of objects within the Data Environment. The Data Environment offers two arrangements of its TreeView and lets you suppress the display of Field objects.

By default, the Data Environment displays a TreeView with Command objects as children of their parent Connection objects. If you prefer, you can choose an alternate display with Connections and Commands in separate folders within the TreeView. To display items grouped by folder, right-click the root node and select Arrange By Object, or click the Arrange By Objects button on the Data Environment toolbar. To display items in the default hierarchy, right-click the root node and select Arrange By Connection, or click the Arrange By Connections button on the Data Environment toolbar.

You can also choose to suppress the display of Field objects in the TreeView. This is most useful when you want a sense of the overall structure of the Data Environment and don't need to work with the properties of individual fields. To display or hide fields, right-click the root node in the TreeView and select Show Fields. This is a toggle menu item, and there is no toolbar equivalent.

Binding Forms to the Data Environment

Once you've created Connection and Command objects to retrieve the data you're interested in, the next step is to display that data to the user somehow. Visual Basic 6 supports binding data from one class to another, and you can bind objects from the Data Environment to user interface objects such as forms and Data Reports. I'll cover Data Reports in the next chapter, but first it's time to take a look at binding data from the Data Environment to a form.

Creating Bound Forms

Binding a control on a form to a Data Environment is nearly the same process as binding a control to a Data control—except that there's no Data control involved. Figure 6.12 shows the frmSimpleBound form from the DataEnvironmentSample sample project. This form uses data binding to retrieve data from the Northwind database via a Data Environment.

FIGURE 6.12:

Form bound to a Data Environment

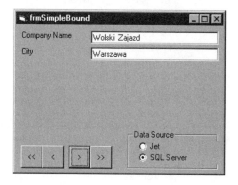

Four properties control the binding of controls to fields from a Data Environment:

DataSource   Holds the name of the Data Environment itself.

DataMember   Holds the name of the Command object within the Data Environment that contains the field that the control will be bound to.

DataField   Holds the name of the field that the control will be bound to.

DataFormat (optional)   Lets you add data formatting to get a nicer display of information. You can set this property to General (the default), Number, Currency, Date, Time, Percentage, Scientific, Boolean, Checkbox, Picture, or Custom.

Of course, since there's no Data control involved, there's no way for the user to navigate between records. To work around this problem, the sample form includes four command buttons to build its own navigation control. In addition, it's got code to switch between Jet and SQL Server databases:

```
Private deCurrent As Object

Private Sub cmdFirst_Click()
    deCurrent.rsCustomers.MoveFirst
End Sub

Private Sub cmdLast_Click()
    deCurrent.rsCustomers.MoveLast
End Sub

Private Sub cmdNext_Click()
    With deCurrent.rsCustomers
        .MoveNext
        If .EOF Then
            .MoveLast
        End If
    End With
End Sub

Private Sub cmdPrevious_Click()
    With deCurrent.rsCustomers
        .MovePrevious
        If .BOF Then
            .MoveFirst
```

```
        End If
    End With
End Sub

Private Sub Form_Load()
    Set deCurrent = deNorthwindJet
End Sub

Private Sub optJet_Click()
    Set txtCompanyName.DataSource = deNorthwindJet
    Set txtCity.DataSource = deNorthwindJet
    Set deCurrent = deNorthwindJet
End Sub

Private Sub optSQLServer_Click()
    Set txtCompanyName.DataSource = deNorthwindSQL
    Set txtCity.DataSource = deNorthwindSQL
    Set deCurrent = deNorthwindSQL
End Sub
```

Here deCurrent is an object reference to the Data Environment. The optJet_Click and optSQLServer_Click procedures control whether this variable is pointing to the Jet or SQL Server Data Environments in the sample project.

If you inspect the sample project, you'll find that there is nothing named rsCustomers in either one of these Data Environments. Where, then, does this object come from? The answer is that the Data Environment automatically creates an ADO Recordset object corresponding to each Command object within the Data Environment. In order to avoid ambiguity between the Command and Recordset objects, it automatically prepends "rs" to the Recordset object's name.

Using Drag-and-Drop

Obviously, building bound forms by setting individual control properties would be just as tedious with the Data Environment as with the ADO Data control. That's why the Data Environment Designer and the Forms Designer work together to enable drag-and-drop form design. If you arrange a form and a Data

Environment in the Visual Basic workspace so that you can see them both, you can perform these drag-and-drop operations:

- If you drag a Command and drop it on a form, you'll get a data entry control for each field in the Command, and a label for each control (assuming you have the Data Environment Field Mapping options set to create labels).

- If you drag a single field and drop it on a form, you'll get a data entry control for just that field, as well as a label.

- If you right-drag a Command and drop it on a form, you'll get the choice of binding the Command to a regular DataGrid control, a Hierarchical Flex-Grid control, or a group of bound controls. (This is how the sample forms in the Command Hierarchy section earlier in this chapter were built.)

- If you drag a Command that's at the top of a relation hierarchy and drop it on a form, you'll get individual Data controls for the parent Command and a Hierarchical FlexGrid control for the child Command.

- If you drag a Command that's at the bottom of a relation hierarchy and drop it on a form, you'll get individual Data controls for that Command only.

In all these cases, the drag-and-drop operation creates the controls only. You'll still need to add code if you want to allow the user to navigate through the records. You can use the code from the simple bound form in the previous section for this purpose.

Using Parameterized Stored Procedures

If you drag a Command based on a parameterized stored procedure to a form and open the form, you'll find that it does not display any data. This is because the Data Environment opens the recordset before you have any chance to supply a value for the parameter, so of course there are no records in it. In order for you to retrieve data this way, you'll need to first close the empty recordset, then supply a value for the parameter, then rebind the new recordset to the controls. Here's some code from frmParameter in the DataEnvironmentSample sample project that does this:

```
Private Sub cmdExecute_Click()
    With deNorthwindSQL
        If .rsdbo_CustOrderHist.State = _
        adStateOpen Then
            .rsdbo_CustOrderHist.Close
```

```
            End If
            .dbo_CustOrderHist txtCustomerID
            If .rsdbo_CustOrderHist.RecordCount > 0 Then
                Set txtProductName.DataSource = deNorthwindSQL
                Set txtTotal.DataSource = deNorthwindSQL
                cmdFirst.Enabled = True
                cmdLast.Enabled = True
                cmdPrevious.Enabled = True
                cmdNext.Enabled = True
            Else
                txtProductName.Text = ""
                txtTotal.Text = ""
                cmdFirst.Enabled = False
                cmdLast.Enabled = False
                cmdPrevious.Enabled = False
                cmdNext.Enabled = False
            End If
        End With
    End Sub
```

Note the distinction between `deNorthwindSQL.dbo_CustOrderHist` and `deNorthwindSQL.rsdbo_CustOrderHist`. The former refers to the Command object in the Data Environment hierarchy, and the latter refers to the recordset based on that Command object. Command objects based on stored procedures can be treated as methods within your Visual Basic code. The arguments to the method, of course, are the parameter values you wish to supply.

Also note the block of code that checks to see whether the recordset is already open and, if it is, closes it. If you try to recreate an open recordset, you'll get an error, but you'll also get an error if you try to close an already closed recordset. This code block avoids both of those errors.

Using ADO Events in the Data Environment

So far in this chapter I've exclusively used the Data Environment as a visual designer for ADO Connections and Commands. But there's another level to the Data Environment Designer. Like a form, a Data Environment actually consists of a visual piece plus a class module. In this case, the visual piece goes away at run time, but the class module remains and gets instantiated whenever a client (such as a form or a Data Report) uses data from the Data Environment. And, like a form, a Data Environment supports events.

In fact, there are three sets of events you can use from the Data Environment:

- Data Environment events

- Connection events

- Recordset events

I'll review each of these in turn in the next section of this chapter. The frmEvents form in the DataEnvironmentSample sample project (shown in Figure 6.13) allows you to experiment with events on a simple form bound to a Data Environment with a single command. When you launch the sample, the Data Environment begins writing rows to the ListView as events occur, so you can see what's going on in which order.

FIGURE 6.13:

The Events sample in action

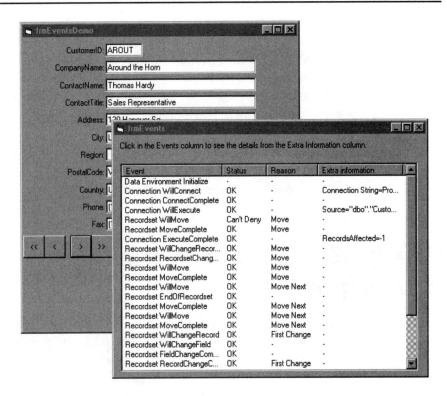

Data Environment Events

The Data Environment itself only supports the two standard class module events, Initialize and Terminate:

```
Private Sub DataEnvironment_Initialize()
Private Sub DataEnvironment_Terminate()
```

The Initialize event is the first event that happens when any client component uses the Data Environment to retrieve data. The Terminate event is the last event that happens when the Data Environment is shut down.

Connection Events

Connection objects in the Data Environment support nine events:

- The connection events WillConnect, ConnectComplete, InfoMessage, and Disconnect

- The execution events WillExecute and ExecuteComplete

- The transaction events BeginTransComplete, CommitTransComplete, and RollBackTransComplete

Generally, the first connection event is the WillConnect event, which has this signature:

```
Private Sub <ConnectionName>_WillConnect( _
ConnectionString As String, _
UserID As String, _
Password As String, _
Options As Long, _
adStatus As ADODB.EventStatusEnum, _
ByVal pConnection As ADODB.Connection)
```

This event happens when ADO is about to use the OLE DB provider to connect to the data, but before that connection is actually made. The ConnectionString, UserID, Password, and Options arguments are passed straight through from the corresponding properties in the Data Environment. The adStatus argument will be equal to adStatusOK when this event is called. You can set this argument within the body of the event procedure. If you set it to adStatusCancel, then the connection will not happen (and the ConnectComplete event will be called with adStatus set to adStatusCancel). If you set it to adStatusUnwantedEvent, then your program will not retrieve any further notifications of WillConnect events on this object during this session. The pConnection argument contains the ADO Connection that's about to be initialized.

You can set the adStatus argument of *any* Data Environment event procedure to adStatusUnwantedEvent to suppress further firing of that event.

During the connection process, you may receive one or more InfoMessage events:

```
Private Sub <ConnectionName>_InfoMessage( _
  ByVal pError As ADODB.Error, _
  adStatus As ADODB.EventStatusEnum, _
  ByVal pConnection As ADODB.Connection)
```

This event will occur only if the OLE DB Provider posts any warnings during the connection process. If it does, the pError argument will be an ADO Error object containing the warning. The adStatus argument will always be set to adStatusOK when this event occurs.

The ConnectComplete event occurs when ADO has successfully completed a connection to the underlying data source via OLE DB:

```
Private Sub <ConnectionName>_ConnectComplete( _
  ByVal pError As ADODB.Error, _
  adStatus As ADODB.EventStatusEnum, _
  ByVal pConnection As ADODB.Connection)
```

Here adStatus will be adStatusOK if all went well, adStatusCancel if the Will-Connect event was cancelled, and adStatusErrorsOccurred if something went wrong. In the latter case, pError will be an ADO Error object containing information on what went wrong. The pConnection argument, of course, holds the Connection itself.

The Disconnect event happens when ADO disconnects from the data source:

```
Private Sub <ConnectionName>_Disconnect( _
  adStatus As ADODB.EventStatusEnum, _
  ByVal pConnection As ADODB.Connection)
```

In this case, adStatus will always be adStatusOK, and the pConnection argument holds the now-closed connection.

The WillExecute event happens whenever a Command object is about to be executed. This is most often when you open a recordset, though you can use Visual Basic code to execute commands that don't return recordsets. The signature is:

```
Private Sub <ConnectionName>_WillExecute( _
Source As String, _
CursorType As ADODB.CursorTypeEnum, _
LockType As ADODB.LockTypeEnum, _
Options As Long, _
adStatus As ADODB.EventStatusEnum, _
ByVal pCommand As ADODB.Command, _
ByVal pRecordset As ADODB.Recordset20, _
ByVal pConnection As ADODB.Connection)
```

The Source argument holds the name of the command, while CursorType, LockType, and Options dictate the type of ADO recordset that will be opened. If you like, you can alter any of these arguments within the event procedure. If you want to cancel the event (and therefore the recordset), you can do so by setting adStatus to adCancel. The pCommand, pRecordset, and pConnection arguments are respectively pointers to the ADO Command, Recordset, and Connection objects involved in the operation.

WARNING   As with the event procedures for the ADO Data control that you saw in Chapter 5, you need to manually edit the definition of any event procedures for a Connection that include a Recordset argument to change the type of the argument to ADODB.Recordset20.

The ExecuteComplete event occurs, of course, after a command is done executing:

```
Private Sub <ConnectionName>_ExecuteComplete( _
ByVal RecordsAffected As Long, _
ByVal pError As ADODB.Error, _
adStatus As ADODB.EventStatusEnum, _
ByVal pCommand As ADODB.Command, _
ByVal pRecordset As ADODB.Recordset20, _
ByVal pConnection As ADODB.Connection)
```

The RecordsAffected argument specifies how many records the execution changed, if any. If no records are changed (for example, when a recordset is first opened), this is set to –1. If there was any error, pError will tell you what the error was. The other arguments are the same as for the WillExecute event except, of course, that you can't cancel an ExecuteComplete event.

The BeginTransComplete, CommitTransComplete, and RollbackTransComplete events are called after completion of the corresponding transaction methods:

```
Private Sub <ConnectionName>_BeginTransComplete( _
ByVal TransactionLevel As Long, _
ByVal pError As ADODB.Error, _
adStatus As ADODB.EventStatusEnum, _
ByVal pConnection As ADODB.Connection)
Private Sub <ConnectionName>_CommitTransComplete( _
ByVal pError As ADODB.Error, _
adStatus As ADODB.EventStatusEnum, _
ByVal pConnection As ADODB.Connection)
Private Sub <ConnectionName>_RollbackTransComplete( _
ByVal pError As ADODB.Error, _
adStatus As ADODB.EventStatusEnum, _
ByVal pConnection As ADODB.Connection)
```

These events give you an easy way to check whether transactional processing is going as planned. They each set adStatus to adStatusOK if all is well and adStatusErrorsOccurred if something is wrong. In the latter case, pError points to an ADO Error object with details on the problem. The pConnection argument passes in the Connection that's hosting the transactional operations. The TransactionLevel argument to BeginTransComplete tells you the current nesting depth of transactions.

Recordset Events

Command objects in the Data Environment don't directly support events. However, the ADO recordsets based on those objects do expose eleven events to the Data Environment Designer:

- The record fetch events FetchComplete and FetchProgress
- The movement events WillMove, MoveComplete, and EndOfRecordset
- The field change events WillChangeField and FieldChangeComplete
- The record change events WillChangeRecord and RecordChangeComplete
- The recordset change events WillChangeRecordset and RecordsetChangeComplete

The FetchComplete and FetchProgress events are called during lengthy asynchronous record retrievals.

```
Private Sub <RecordsetName>_FetchComplete( _
ByVal pError As ADODB.Error, _
adStatus As ADODB.EventStatusEnum, _
ByVal pRecordset As ADODB.Recordset20)
Private Sub <RecordsetName>_FetchProgress( _
ByVal Progress As Long, _
ByVal MaxProgress As Long, _
adStatus As ADODB.EventStatusEnum, _
ByVal pRecordset As ADODB.Recordset20)
```

You won't actually see these two events unless you explicitly open a recordset asynchronously in code, by setting asynchronous operation in the Open method. If you do this, the FetchProgress event is fired once every time the cache is loaded up with records from the data source. The Progress argument tells you how many records have been retrieved, and the MaxProgress argument tells you how many records the command expects to receive when it's done. The FetchComplete method is fired when there is no more data to fetch on an asynchronous connection.

The WillMove and MoveComplete events bracket all movement through the recordset:

```
Private Sub <RecordsetName>_WillMove( _
ByVal adReason As ADODB.EventReasonEnum, _
adStatus As ADODB.EventStatusEnum, _
ByVal pRecordset As ADODB.Recordset20)
Private Sub <RecordsetName>_MoveComplete( _
ByVal adReason As ADODB.EventReasonEnum, _
ByVal pError As ADODB.Error, _
adStatus As ADODB.EventStatusEnum, _
ByVal pRecordset As ADODB.Recordset20)
```

The WillMove event is called before the recordset is actually repositioned, and the MoveComplete event is called after the new record is the current record. For both events, the adReason argument tells you why the event has been fired. Table 6.2 lists all the possible values of this argument and shows which values can occur in which events. You can cancel the WillMove event but not the MoveComplete event. If the WillMove event can't be cancelled, the adStatus argument will be adStatusCantDeny; otherwise, it will be adStatusOK. If the MoveComplete is successful, it will have an adStatus argument of adStatusOK; otherwise, it will be adStatusErrorsOccurred and the pError argument will contain an ADO Error object with the details.

TABLE 6.2: ADO EventReasonEnum Values

Value	Reason	WillMove/ Move-Complete	WillChange-Record/Record-Change-Complete	WillChange Recordset/ Recordset-Change-Complete
adRsnAddNew	New record added	No	Yes	No
adRsnClose	Recordset closed	No	No	Yes
adRsnDelete	Record deleted	No	Yes	No
adRsnFirstChange	Any field in the recordset was changed for the first time	No	Yes	No
adRsnMove	Move to a bookmark	Yes	No	No
adRsnMoveFirst	Move to first record	Yes	No	No
adRsnMoveLast	Move to last record	Yes	No	No
adRsnMoveNext	Move to next record	Yes	No	No
adRsnMove-Previous	Move to previous record	Yes	No	No
adRsnRequery	Requery of the data source	Yes	No	Yes
adRsnResynch	Synchronize a disconnected recordset	No	No	Yes
adRsnUndo-AddNew	Undo of an Add New	No	Yes	No
adRsnUndoDelete	Undo of a Delete	No	Yes	No
adRsnUndoUpdate	Undo of an update	No	Yes	No
adRsnUpdate	Record updated	No	Yes	No

The EndOfRecordset event is fired when you attempt to move past the current end of the recordset:

```
Private Sub <RecordsetName>_EndOfRecordset( _
fMoreData As Boolean, _
adStatus As ADODB.EventStatusEnum, _
ByVal pRecordset As ADODB.Recordset20)
```

Here, of course, the pRecordset argument is a pointer to the current recordset, and the adStatus argument will be either adStatusOK or adStatusCantDeny, depending on whether the movement can be cancelled. If you like, you can add more records to the recordset within this event procedure. If you do this, you must set the fMoreData argument to True.

The WillChangeField and FieldChangeComplete events flank any change to a field within a recordset:

```
Private Sub <RecordsetName>_WillChangeField( _
ByVal cFields As Long, _
ByVal Fields As Variant, _
adStatus As ADODB.EventStatusEnum, _
ByVal pRecordset As ADODB.Recordset20)
Private Sub <RecordsetName>_FieldChangeComplete( _
ByVal cFields As Long, _
ByVal Fields As Variant, _
ByVal pError As ADODB.Error, _
adStatus As ADODB.EventStatusEnum, _
ByVal pRecordset As ADODB.Recordset20)
```

In both of these events, the Fields argument is an array of ADO Field objects contained in a Variant. The cFields argument tells you how many Field objects are in this array, and the pRecordset argument is a pointer to the recordset being changed. In the WillChangeField event, the adStatus argument will be adStatus-OK or adStatusCantDeny. If it's adStatusOK, you can set it to adCancel to cancel the change and roll back the changes. In the FieldChangeComplete event, adStatus will be adStatusOK if the change succeeded, or adStatusErrorsOccurred if it failed. In the latter case, you can check the pError argument, which points to an ADO Error object, to determine what went wrong. These events fire when you set the Value property of a field, which you do automatically when you change data in a bound control and then move to another control or another record.

The WillChangeRecord and RecordChangeComplete events surround every change to an individual record in the recordset:

```
Private Sub <RecordsetName>_WillChangeRecord( _
ByVal adReason As ADODB.EventReasonEnum, _
ByVal cRecords As Long, _
adStatus As ADODB.EventStatusEnum, _
ByVal pRecordset As ADODB.Recordset20)
Private Sub <RecordsetName>_RecordChangeComplete( _
ByVal adReason As ADODB.EventReasonEnum, _
ByVal cRecords As Long, _
ByVal pError As ADODB.Error, _
adStatus As ADODB.EventStatusEnum, _
ByVal pRecordset As ADODB.Recordset20)
```

In both of these events, the cRecords argument tells you how many records are being changed (which could be more than one if you're doing a batch update). The pRecordset argument is a pointer to the recordset being changed. In the WillChangeRecord event, the adStatus argument will be adStatusOK or adStatusCantDeny. If it's adStatusOK, you can set it to adCancel to cancel the change and roll back the changes. In the RecordChangeComplete event, adStatus will be adStatusOK if the change succeeded, or adStatusErrorsOccurred if it failed. In the latter case, you can check the pError argument, which points to an ADO Error object, to determine what went wrong. These events fire when you update a record in the recordset, usually by moving to another record on a bound form.

The WillChangeRecordset and RecordsetChangeComplete provide before and after notification of changes to the entire recordset as the result of Open or Requery operations:

```
Private Sub <RecordsetName>_WillChangeRecordset( _
ByVal adReason As ADODB.EventReasonEnum, _
adStatus As ADODB.EventStatusEnum, _
ByVal pRecordset As ADODB.Recordset20)
Private Sub <RecordsetName>_RecordsetChangeComplete( _
ByVal adReason As ADODB.EventReasonEnum, _
ByVal pError As ADODB.Error, _
adStatus As ADODB.EventStatusEnum, _
ByVal pRecordset As ADODB.Recordset20)
```

The pRecordset argument is a pointer to the recordset being changed. In the WillChangeRecordset event, the adStatus argument will be adStatusOK or adStatusCantDeny. If it's adStatusOK, you can set it to adCancel to cancel the change and roll back the changes. In the RecordsetChangeComplete event, adStatus will be adStatusOK if the change succeeded, or adStatusErrorsOccurred if it failed. In the latter case, you can check the pError argument, which points to an ADO Error object, to determine what went wrong.

Using the Data Environment in Code

The frmCars form in the DataEnvironmentSample sample project demonstrates the use of stored procedures to manipulate data via the Data Environment. For efficiency, many developers prefer to use stored procedures for all data manipulation. This database contains three stored procedures, one each to insert, update, and delete records in a simple table:

```
CREATE PROCEDURE InsertCar
    @caryear char(4),
    @carMake varchar(50)
    @carModel varchar(50) AS
    INSERT INTO tblCars (Year, Make, Model)
    VALUES (@caryear, @carMake, @carModel)
CREATE PROCEDURE UpdateCar
    @carID int,
    @caryear char(4),
    @carMake varchar(50)
    @carModel varchar(50) AS
    UPDATE tblCars
    SET Year=@caryear, Make=@carMake, Model=@CarModel
    WHERE ID=@carID
CREATE PROCEDURE DeleteCar
    @carID int AS
    DELETE FROM tblCars
    WHERE ID=@carID
```

NOTE The Cars database is not one of the standard SQL Server databases. If you want to experiment with this sample, you'll need to create it on your server. The sample project includes a script file, `cars.sql`, that will recreate this database on a SQL 7 server. To use the script file, launch SQL Query Analyzer, open this file, and click the Run button.

Figure 6.14 shows the sample form that manipulates data in the tblCars table. Note that although this form uses a Hierarchical FlexGrid for data display (which is, as you know, read only), it also provides a separate data-entry and editing area as well as buttons to add a new record, update an existing record, or delete an existing record.

FIGURE 6.14:

Sample form using stored procedures

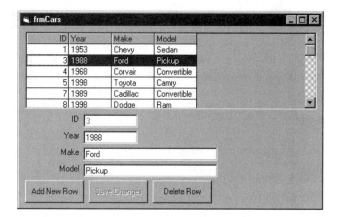

Most of the code behind this form is "bookkeeping" code, devoted to making sure that the correct buttons stay enabled and the correct data gets moved around. When the user selects a row in the Hierarchical FlexGrid, it automatically transfers the information from that row to the four text boxes:

```
Private Sub hfgCars_SelChange()
    txtID.Text = hfgCars.TextArray(( _
      hfgCars.Row * hfgCars.Cols) + 0)
    txtYear.Text = hfgCars.TextArray(( _
      hfgCars.Row * hfgCars.Cols) + 1)
    txtMake.Text = hfgCars.TextArray(( _
      hfgCars.Row * hfgCars.Cols) + 2)
    txtModel.Text = hfgCars.TextArray(( _
      hfgCars.Row * hfgCars.Cols) + 3)
    txtID.Enabled = False
    cmdUpdate.Enabled = False
    cmdDelete.Enabled = True
End Sub
```

The TextArray method of the Hierarchical FlexGrid control provides access to the data in the control without needing to set the Row and Col properties to the cell that you're interested in (which has the side effect of moving the focus). It takes as its single argument an index calculated by multiplying the desired row by the number of columns in the control and then adding the desired column.

When the user decides to add a new row, the code simply clears the Data Entry controls and sets a module-level flag:

```
Private Sub cmdAddNew_Click()
    txtID.Enabled = False
    txtYear.Enabled = True
    txtMake.Enabled = True
    txtModel.Enabled = True
    txtID.Text = "<Identity>"
    txtYear.Text = ""
    txtMake.Text = ""
    txtModel.Text = ""
    txtYear.SetFocus
    fAddNew = True
    cmdUpdate.Enabled = True
    cmdAddNew.Enabled = False
    cmdDelete.Enabled = False
End Sub
```

The user is then free to type in whatever new information they like. Alternatively, typing without clicking the Add New Row button disables that button until the user saves the changes. Clicking the Save Changes button does the real work:

```
Private Sub cmdUpdate_Click()
    If fAddNew Then
        deCars.InsertCar txtYear, txtMake, txtModel
        fAddNew = False
        txtID.Text = ""
        txtYear.Text = ""
        txtMake.Text = ""
        txtModel.Text = ""
        hfgCars.Row = hfgCars.Rows - 1
    Else
        deCars.UpdateCar txtID, txtYear, txtMake, txtModel
    End If
    deCars.rstblCars.Requery
    Set hfgCars.DataSource = deCars
    cmdUpdate.Enabled = False
```

```
        cmdAddNew.Enabled = True
        If deCars.rstblCars.RecordCount > 0 Then
            hfgCars.Col = 0
            hfgCars.ColSel = 3
            cmdDelete.Enabled = True
        End If
    End Sub
```

There are two paths through this code, depending on whether the user was adding or editing a row. In the case of new rows, the code calls the InsertCar stored procedure in the database by executing the InsertCar method of the Data Environment object that's connected to that database. The parameters of the stored procedure just become the arguments to the method. Similarly, in the case of existing rows, the UpdateCar stored procedure is called. The only real difference is that the latter method takes four arguments instead of three, since it has to tell the database which row to update.

With either method, the changes in the table are not automatically reflected in the Hierarchical FlexGrid control. To display the changes, the code first requeries the underlying recordset from the tblCars Command in the Data Environment, and then resets the DataSource property of the Hierarchical FlexGrid control to tell it to pick up changes from the newly requeried recordset.

Deleting a record is also simple. The code calls the DeleteCar method of the Data Environment:

```
    Private Sub cmdDelete_Click()
        Dim intRet As Integer
        intRet = MsgBox("Are you sure?", vbYesNo)
        If intRet = vbYes Then
            deCars.DeleteCar txtID
        End If
        deCars.rstblCars.Requery
        Set hfgCars.DataSource = deCars
        If deCars.rstblCars.RecordCount > 0 Then
            hfgCars.Col = 0
            hfgCars.ColSel = 3
            cmdDelete.Enabled = True
        End If
    End Sub
```

Of course, the Hierarchical FlexGrid control needs to be refreshed in this case as well. Also, if there are any records remaining, this code ensures that the entire new current row is selected in the grid.

CHAPTER
SEVEN

7

Creating Data Reports

- Anatomy of a Data Report

- Creating Data Reports

- Properties on Data Reports

- Summarizing Data on Data Reports

- Using Data Reports

- Data Reports in Code

Visual Basic developers have always had to struggle a bit when creating printed summaries of database tables. For years, the choice has been between using third-party packages, including Crystal Reports (which ships with Visual Basic), and using COM Automation to create Microsoft Access reports. There were drawbacks to each of these strategies, most notably in additional overhead. Visual Basic 6 adds a new tool to the report designer's workbench: the Data Report.

Data Reports are banded reports (that is, they contain "bands" of information that can be repeated multiple times) that can be bound directly to data sources, either via the Data Environment or directly through code. In this chapter, you'll learn how to create and manipulate Data Reports and see how you can use them to create a permanent record of the data you've retrieved via ADO.

Figure 7.1 shows a typical Data Report (the drSalesDetail Data Report from the DataReports sample project) at run time. Note that some information is repeated, such as the label that says "Order ID," while other information is unique, such as the ID number of each order. The actual appearance of the Data Report at run time depends on the data in the data source when the Data Report is displayed, printed, or exported. The "shape" of the Data Report is determined at design time.

FIGURE 7.1:

Typical Data Report at run time

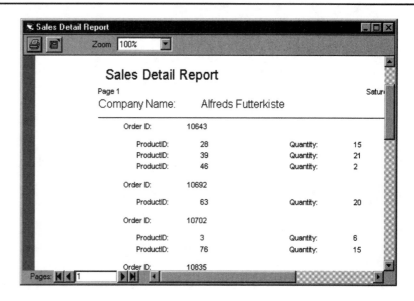

Anatomy of a Data Report

Just like forms, Data Reports have a different appearance at design time than they do at run time. Figure 7.2 shows the same Data Report as Figure 7.1, but this time it's open in the Data Report Designer. As you can see, the report consists of a series of bands, each of which can be repeated one or more times (or even no times at all, depending on the data that the report is attached to).

FIGURE 7.2:

The Data Report Designer

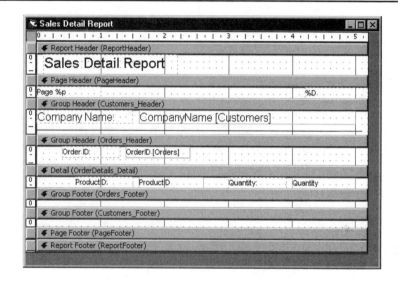

This particular Data Report is based on a hierarchical set of Command objects (Customers, Orders, and Order Details) in a Data Environment that uses the SQL Server Northwind database as its data source. The bands in the Data Report mimic the structure of the relational hierarchy, along with a few extra bands thrown in:

- The Report Header is displayed once at the top of the entire report.

- The Page Header is displayed at the top of each page.

- The Group Header (Customers_Header) is displayed once for each row returned by the Customers Command.

- The Group Header (Orders_Header) is displayed once for each row returned by the Orders Command.

- The Detail (OrderDetails_Detail) is displayed once for each row returned by the Order Details Command. (The Detail band corresponds to the lowest level in the relational hierarchy.)

- The Group Footer (Orders_Footer) is displayed once for each row returned by the Orders Command.

- The Group Footer (Customers_Footer) is displayed once for each row returned by the Customers Command.

- The Page Footer is displayed at the bottom of each page.

- The Report Footer is displayed once at the bottom of the entire report.

Note that some of these bands, such as the Page Footer, are empty. Nothing will be displayed for an empty band. You'll also see that the structure is symmetrical, with each Header eventually matched by a corresponding Footer. The most general information is at the top and bottom of the designer; the most specific information (the Detail section) is at the center. The Headers and Footers surround the detail section like the layers of an onion. The overall structure should be very familiar to users of other reporting products such as Microsoft Access or Crystal Reports.

Creating Data Reports

Now that you've got some idea what a Data Report looks like, it's time to see how to create one. In this section, you'll see that Data Reports are intimately linked to Data Environments and that you can create controls on a Data Report by dragging and dropping objects from the Data Environment. You can also use a special set of controls (displayed on a reserved tab of the Visual Basic Toolbox) to create controls from scratch. These controls include calculated fields and special controls destined for use in headers and footers.

Using Drag-and-Drop from the Data Environment

The simplest possible Data Report starts with a single Command in a Data Environment. Suppose you have a Data Environment that contains a Command object connected to the Product table in the Jet version of the Northwind database. The first step of creating a Data Report to display information retrieved by this Command object is to create the Data Report itself. You can do this by choosing the

Project ≻ Add Data Report menu item in Visual Basic, or by choosing the Data Report item on the New Object drop-down toolbar button. Either way, you'll get a blank Data Report, open in the Data Report Designer. By default, it will have five sections:

- Report Header

- Page Header

- Detail

- Page Footer

- Report Footer

There's not much use for a Data Report without data. To connect the Data Report to the data, of course, you use the properties of the Data Report. (You'll need to set these properties directly in the Visual Basic Properties window, since Data Reports don't have a property sheet.) Besides naming the Data Report something sensible—such as drProducts, in this case—you need to set two properties to make the data connection:

- The DataSource property should be set to the name of the Data Environment that connects to the data you want to display on this report.

- The DataMember property should be set to the name of the Command object in the Data Environment that contains the top (in this case, only) grouping level for the Data Report.

Once you've set these two properties, you need to refresh the Data Report so that it will display the correct headers and footers. To do this, right-click anywhere in the Data Report Designer and choose Retrieve Structure. Visual Basic will warn you that this will pretty well destroy the existing report and ask for permission to proceed. If you're just creating the report, it's safe to respond Yes to this warning. This will insert additional Header and Footer sections as necessary and assign the correct names to all the Headers and Footers and the Detail section.

WARNING For any operation that requires access to the data source (such as refreshing the structure of the Data Report), you'll need to have the Data Environment open in its designer as well.

To continue, you'll need to arrange objects in the Visual Basic design space so that you can see both the Data Report and the Data Environment in their respective designers. Then you can drag either fields or entire Command objects from the Data Environment and drop them on the Data Report. If you drag and drop a field, the Data Report Designer will create a RptTextBox control bound to that field and a RptLabel control with the name of that field to use as a caption. If you drag and drop a Command, the designer will create RptTextBox and RptLabel controls for each field in the Command and arrange them vertically on the report. (You'll learn about the RptTextBox and RptLabel controls in the next section.)

Controls within the Data Report Designer can be manipulated just like controls in the Form Designer. That is, you can move and resize them with the mouse, or change their properties in the Properties window. (However, the items on the Format menu are grayed out and unavailable when you're working with Data Report controls.) You can even drag controls from section to section. However, there's a limit on dragging controls between sections, as well as to creating controls in the first place: a control can only be placed on a section at or below its place in the relational hierarchy. For example, if you have a hierarchy based on Categories and Products, with Categories as the parent Command, you can place objects from the Categories Command in any section, but objects from the Products Command can only be placed in the Detail section.

WARNING   The Data Report Designer doesn't support multidimensional hierarchies. That is, suppose you have a Data Environment containing a Command based on Orders that has child Commands based on both Employees and Order Details. If you base a Data Report on the Orders Command, only one of its children (the one that is alphabetically first) will be available on the Data Report. The only way to use the other child Command is to create an entirely separate hierarchy that contains only that child Command.

Using the Data Report Toolbox

You can also create controls on a Data Report by using the controls in the Data Report Toolbox. This is a tab in the regular Visual Basic Toolbox that's created the first time that you open the Toolbox while a Data Report is open in Design View. Although this tab looks just like any other Toolbox tab, Data Report controls can only be used on Data Reports. You'll find that you can't drag them to other tabs in the Toolbox, and you can't drag controls from other tabs to the DataReport tab.

For all practical purposes, the DataReport tab is a completely separate Toolbox that just happens to be displayed in the same window as the regular Toolbox.

The Data Report Toolbox contains seven icons, shown in Figure 7.3. From top to bottom, these are:

Pointer   This works just like the Pointer in the regular Toolbox, but only on Data Reports.

RptLabel   This control holds static text on a Data Report and is similar to a regular Label control.

RptTextBox   This control holds dynamic, bound text on a Data Report and is similar to a regular TextBox control.

RptImage   This control holds static images on a Data Report and is similar to a regular Image control.

RptLine   This control can be used to draw lines on a Data Report and is similar to a regular Line control.

RptShape   This control can be used to draw circles, squares, ellipses, and rectangles on a Data Report and is similar to a regular Shape control.

RptFunction   This control can be used to create special text boxes displaying summary information on a Data Report. It has no analog in the regular Forms Toolbox. You'll learn more about the RptFunction control later in the chapter.

FIGURE 7.3:

The Data Report Toolbox

The only bound control available in the Data Report Designer is the RptTextBox control. You might think that a RptImage control could display bound data from fields containing image data, but you'd be wrong. If your database contains information that won't display properly in a text box, there's no good way to show that information on a Data Report. The best you can do is show the binary information in the field, which is usually not very helpful.

Creating RptLabel, RptImage, RptLine, and RptShape controls is very similar to creating their Form Designer analogs. The only major difference is that these controls may have somewhat fewer properties. (I'll cover report control properties later in this chapter.) Creating a RptTextBox control is the same as creating a regular TextBox control except that you'll need to set the three data properties:

DataMember   Holds the name of the Command object in the Data Environment that this RptTextBox control's data comes from.

DataField   Holds the name of the field in the Command object in the Data Environment that this RptTextBox control's data comes from.

DataFormat   Holds an optional format name for displaying the data with formatting.

The Data Report Designer does its best to help you select the DataField and DataMember properties for a RptTextBox control that you create by hand. If you drop such a control in the top level of a Data Report based on a hierarchy, the DataField property will display a combo box with choices based only on the top Command in the corresponding relational hierarchy. If you select a value for the DataField property in such a case, it will fill in the proper DataMember for you. If you drop a RptTextBox control into a lower section, then the DataMember property will also display a combo box letting you choose from any table at or above that level, and the DataField combo box will be adjusted accordingly.

In most cases, unless you have very limited screen real estate, you'll find it more convenient to create bound fields by simple drag-and-drop operations, rather than by using the Data Report Toolbox.

Using Calculated Fields

Sometimes you'll want to display derived information on a Data Report. For example, the drSalesDetails2 Data Report from the DataReports sample shows the total of each line in the detail section of the Order. This total is calculated by multiplying the quantity by the unit price for each row in the Order Details table.

In some report designers (such as the one provided with Microsoft Access), you can create such calculated controls directly in the designer. The Data Report Designer, unfortunately, is not sophisticated enough to support this functionality. If you inspect the design of the Sales Details Report 2, you'll discover that it's based on the Customers2 hierarchy within the deNorthwindSQL Data Environment. At the lowest level of this hierarchy there's a Command object based on a SQL statement:

```
SELECT OrderID, ProductID,
Quantity * UnitPrice AS LineTotal
FROM [Order Details]
```

In other words, the calculation is embedded directly in the Command, rather than being calculated in any way by the report. This is generally the only way to place calculated fields on a Data Report. However, you can use the RptFunction control to create an aggregate calculation in the Data Report Designer. You'll learn more about this technique later in the chapter.

Special Header and Footer Controls

In addition to bound information and static information (such as the label for a field), you can also place some special variable controls on a Data Report. Typically these controls are most useful in Headers and Footers. You can insert these controls by right-clicking in a section and choosing Insert Control, followed by the type of control you wish to insert. Table 7.1 lists all the special controls that are supported by the Data Report Designer.

You can also create these special controls by inserting a RptLabel control and using a code, starting with a percent sign, where you'd like the variable information filled in. These codes are also listed in Table 7.1. To use a percent sign in the caption of a RptLabel control, you must double it to %%.

TABLE 7.1: Special Controls for Data Reports

Control (Menu choice)	Code
Current Page Number	%p
Total Number of Pages	%P
Current Date (Short Format)	%d

Continued on next page

TABLE 7.1 CONTINUED: Special Controls for Data Reports

Control (Menu choice)	Code
Current Date (Long Format)	%D
Current Time (Short Format)	%t
Current Time (Long Format)	%T
Report Title	%i

Properties on Data Reports

Like just about everything else in Visual Basic, Data Reports and their components have properties that you can set in the Visual Basic Properties window or (in some cases) from code. In this section I'll summarize the properties that are available for customizing Data Reports.

Data Report Properties

Some properties of Data Reports are similar to those of forms. Others are completely new. Here's the list:

Name   Contains the name of the report.

BorderStyle   Can be set to vbBSNone, vbFixedSingle, vbSizable (the default), vbFixedDouble, vbFixedDialog, vbFixedToolWindow, or vbSizableToolWindow. These properties control the type of border shown on the Data Report window when it's displayed in preview mode at run time.

BottomMargin, LeftMargin, RightMargin, and **TopMargin**   Specify in twips (the default is 1440) how much white space should be left around the report when it's printed.

Caption   Specifies the window title for the Data Report when it's displayed in preview mode.

ControlBox, Icon, MaxButton, and **MinButton**   Set the display of the window widgets when the Data Report is displayed in preview mode.

DataMember   Contains the name of the top Command object used by the report.

DataSource   Contains the name of the Data Environment used by the report.

Enabled   Specifies whether the Data Report should respond to run-time events.

Font   Specifies the default font to be used on the report. This font can be overridden on a section or control basis.

GridX and **GridY**   Specify the granularity of the control placement grid at design time.

Height, Left, StartupPosition, Top, and **Width**   Specify the size and location of the window that will display the report at run time.

MouseIcon and **MousePointer**   Set a mouse pointer to use when the report is displayed in preview mode at run time.

Palette and **PaletteMode**   Control the display of any graphics on the Data Report.

ReportWidth   Specifies the width of every section on the report, in the designer, in twips. (Each section has its own Height property.)

RightToLeft   Controls text display on BiDirectional language systems.

ShowInTaskbar   Is set to True if you'd like the report to have its own button in the Windows Taskbar.

Tag   Is present, as it is on every other Visual Basic object, to hold arbitrary designer-specified data.

Title   Is used to label the report when it's printed or exported to HTML.

Visible   Controls whether the report can be seen on screen when it's previewed. You'll probably want to leave this set to its default value of True.

Section Properties

By contrast, Sections on Data Reports have very few properties:

Name   Identifies the section. This property is originally assigned by the Data Report Designer when you retrieve the structure for the Data Report, but you can change it if you like.

ForcePageBreak   Tells the designer whether this section should cause any special action when the Data Report is previewed or printed. By default, it's set to rptPageBreakNone. You can also choose rptPageBreakBefore to ensure that this section starts the top of a new page every time it's processed, rptPageBreakAfter to have this section be the last thing on a page, or rptPageBreakBeforeAndAfter to combine both of these effects.

Height   Controls the vertical distance the section takes up. Of course, you can also adjust this by dragging the report section baselines within the designer.

KeepTogether   Is used to keep important information on the same page. If you set this property to True, and the section will not fit on the current page, then printing or previewing the Data Report will start a new page at this point.

Visible   Controls whether this section will be displayed at run time.

Control Properties

For the most part, properties for RptLabel, RptTextBox, RptImage, RptLine, and RptShape controls are exactly the same as for the Label, TextBox, Image, Line, and Shape controls that you're already familiar with. I won't review these basic properties, such as BackColor and RightToLeft, here. But there are a few properties of the RptTextBox control that are unique. You've already seen several of these properties, but I'll repeat them here for reference:

DataMember   Holds the name of the Command object in the Data Environment that this RptTextBox control's data comes from.

DataField   Holds the name of the field in the Command object in the Data Environment that this RptTextBox control's data comes from.

DataFormat   Holds an optional format name for displaying the data with formatting.

CanGrow   Tells the Data Report whether it can allocate additional space to this control at run time. If you set this property to True, and the data for the control is larger than will fit in the design time size of the control, then the Height property of the control will be increased to hold the additional data.

NOTE   Unlike the report designer in Microsoft Access, the Data Report Designer does not implement a CanGrow property on Sections. You need only change the control property to allow this behavior and the section will grow to fit the control.

Summarizing Data on Data Reports

It's often convenient to have summary data presented on reports. For example, on a sales report, you might want to see both the details of individual sales and the total of all sales for the month. The Data Report Designer allows you to create summary information by using a special control (the RptFunction control) or by using a grouping or aggregate hierarchy within the Data Environment that the report is bound to. In this section, you'll see how to use both of these techniques.

Using the Function Control

The RptFunction control has no exact analog in the regular Visual Basic controls. It looks like a regular text box at run time, but it has the unique ability to summarize information from the Data Report. Figure 7.4 shows the last page of the drSalesDetails2 Data Report from the DataReports sample. The Line Total for each line of the report is based on a calculated field in the SQL statement that the Command object is based on, as you learned earlier in the chapter. However, the Order total, Customer total, and Grand total controls are RptFunction controls. As you can see, these controls give an aggregate sum for information above them in the Data Report.

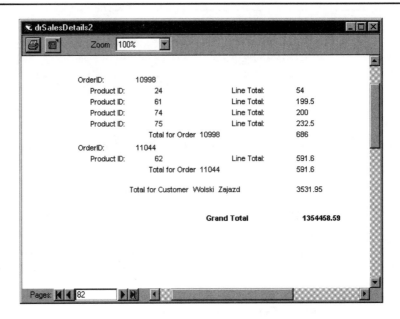

To use the RptFunction control, select it in the Data Report Toolbox and draw it on the Data Report, just as you would any other text box. However, you can only place this control in a Footer section of the report. The Data Report Designer enforces this limitation and won't allow you to place a RptFunction control in a Header or Detail section.

In addition to the DataField, DataMember, and DataFormat properties that it shares with the RptTextbox control, the RptFunction control supports a Function-Type property. You can set this to one of eight values:

- rptFuncSum (the default) to add values together

- rptFuncAve to average values

- rptFuncMin to choose the smallest value

- rptFuncMax to choose the largest value

- rptFuncRCnt to count the number of rows

- rptFuncVCnt to count the number of non-null distinct values

- rptFuncSDEV to calculate standard deviation

- rptFuncSERR to calculate standard error

Whatever function you choose is applied over the entire scope of the Footer section that contains the control. For example, if you place a RptFunction control in the Orders Footer and set its FunctionType property to rptFuncMax, it will display the maximum value of the field for each order. If you place the identical control in the Report Footer, it will display the maximum value from the entire report.

Using Grouping and Aggregate Hierarchies

In Chapter 6, you learned to create Data Environments containing grouping and aggregate hierarchies. The Data Report Designer uses these hierarchies to display grouped information. Figure 7.5 shows a portion of the drGrouping Data Report in the DataReports sample. This particular report is based on a Command object that retrieves information from the Customers table and that is grouped by Country.

FIGURE 7.5:

Grouping Data Report

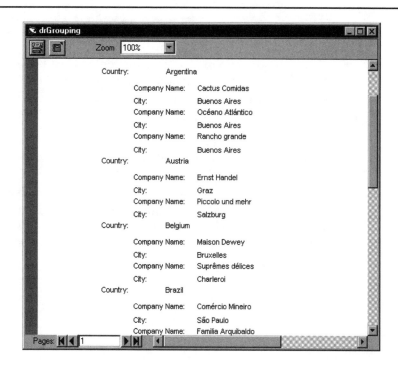

Grouping reports are just beyond the limit of what the Data Report Designer can do for you automatically. In order to create such a report, you need to first create a Data Environment Command object that uses grouping (see Chapter 6 if you need a refresher on this). When you do this, of course, the Data Environment Designer displays the grouping and detail fields separately. For example, if you open the deNorthwindJet Data Environment in the DataReports sample, you'll find that there's a Command object named "Customers grouped using Customers_ Grouping." This object has subfolders labeled "Summary fields in Customers_Grouping" and "Detail fields in Customers."

The first trick is that none of these choices appears explicitly for the DataMember property of a Data Report. Once you've chosen this Data Environment as the DataSource, you'll find that the choices for DataMember include Customers and Customers_Grouping. These are the actual names of the saved Command objects. For a grouping report, of course, you need to choose the Customers_Grouping command object.

The other thing you need to know is how to create a new Header and Footer pair on the Data Report. Even after assigning Customers_Grouping as the Data-Member and retrieving the structure for the Data Report, there won't be any Header or Footer corresponding to the grouping fields (in this case, to the Country field). To insert a new Header and Footer pair, right-click anywhere in the Data Report and choose Insert Group Header/Footer.

If your report contains only a Detail section, you'll automatically get a Header above the Detail and a Footer below the Detail. If your report already contains Headers and Footers, you'll see a dialog box similar to the one in Figure 7.6. This dialog box allows you to select the level of grouping that you'd like the new Header and Footer to control. You can either drag and drop the New Group Header and New Group Footer controls to the appropriate position or use the arrow controls to move them up and down. Moving these controls up results in a more encompassing grouping.

FIGURE 7.6:

Creating a New Group
Header/Footer pair

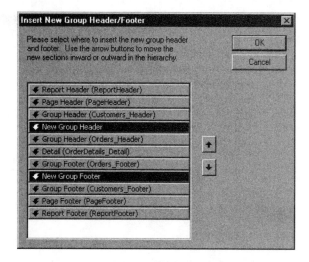

By the way, if you ever create a Header and Footer pair by accident, or the Data Report Designer automatically creates one that you don't want, just right-click in the offending section and choose Delete Group Header/Footer.

After you've created the new sections, you can complete the grouping report by using the same drag-and-drop actions that you would for any other Data Report. You'll find that the fields from the grouping folder in the Data Environment can be dragged to the Header, Footer, or Detail section, while the fields from the detail folder in the Data Environment can only be dragged to the Detail section on the Data Report.

You can also base a Data Report on an aggregate Command object within the Data Environment Designer. Figure 7.7 shows part of the drAggregate Data Report in the DataReports sample project.

FIGURE 7.7:

Aggregate Data Report

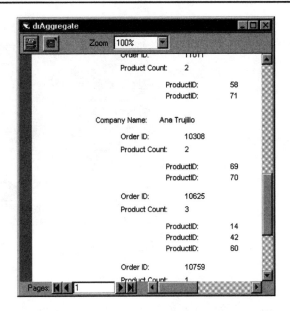

To create such a report, you need to first create a Data Environment containing an aggregate field. This particular report is based on a Command hierarchy containing commands for Customers, Orders, and OrderDetails. The Orders Command includes an aggregate field, ProductCount, which counts the products in the Order Details table for each order.

Creating a Data Report including this field is straightforward. You just hook up a blank Data Report to this Command hierarchy using the DataMember property of the Data Report, and drag and drop fields as you always would. You'll find that the aggregate field can be dropped in any section except for Page or Report Headers or Footers. Thus, in the case of this example, the ProductCount aggregate field is in the Orders_Header section.

Aggregate fields and the RptFunction control perform the same task of aggregating some piece of information across an entire section. There are two differences between them:

- Since aggregate fields are precalculated by the Data Environment, they can be placed in Header sections. RptFunction controls, in contrast, can be placed only in Footer sections, since their value isn't known until the entire section has been processed.

- There are differences in the functions available. In particular, aggregate fields can use the Any function to pick a random value, which is not available to RptFunction controls. On the other hand, RptFunction controls can summarize by Value Count or Standard Error, neither of which is available in an aggregate field.

Using Data Reports

Once you've created a Data Report, what can you do with it? There are four basic operations that you can perform on Data Reports:

- Print Preview
- Print
- Export to Text
- Export to HTML

In this section, I'll cover each of these operations in turn.

Print Preview

To show a Data Report on screen, you place it into print preview mode at run time. You do this by calling the Show method of the Data Report:

```
<DataReportName>.Show([Modal], [OwnerForm])
```

The Modal and OwnerForm arguments work the same way for Data Reports as they do for regular Visual Basic forms. That is, by default Data Reports are not modal, but you may set the Modal argument to vbModal to make them modal instead. By default, the window in which a Data Report is displayed is owned by the desktop. You can also specify that it is owned by a particular Visual Basic form. This has the effect of keeping the report on top of the form.

When you display a Data Report in print preview mode, the toolbar in the Data Report's window contains three controls:

- The Print button, of course, will print the report.
- The Export button allows you to export the report to a number of file formats.

- The Zoom box allows you to select the magnification of the report on screen. You can set this to 100%, 75%, 50%, 25%, 10%, or Fit, which makes sure the entire report can be seen in the window.

WARNING   Before you can display a Data Report on screen, you must have a printer installed.

Print

To print a Data Report, you call the report's PrintReport method:

```
<DataReportName>.PrintReport([ShowDialog As Boolean=False], _
[Range As PageRangeConstants=rptRangeAllPages], _
[PageFrom],[PageTo]) As Long
```

The ShowDialog argument controls whether you'd like the report to go straight to the printer or prompt the user for details. If this argument is omitted (the default), the report is printed immediately, on the default printer, and all pages are printed. If you set ShowDialog to True, then Visual Basic will display the Print dialog box shown in Figure 7.8, allowing the user to choose a non-default printer and select the pages and number of copies to print.

FIGURE 7.8:

The Data Report Print dialog box

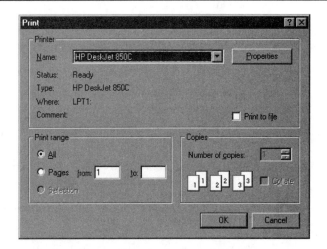

The Range argument can be set to rptRangeAllPages to print the entire report, or rptRangeFromTo to print selected pages. Either way, entire pages are printed, even if only part of the page shows on screen.

The PageFrom and PageTo arguments let you specify the first and last pages for the print job, if you've chosen rptRangeFromTo as the Range argument.

The PrintReport method returns a unique identifier that can be used for asynchronous event processing. You'll learn about this later in the chapter.

If the user chooses the Print button on a Data Report that's open in print preview mode, they'll always be presented with the Print dialog box.

WARNING   If you use Intellisense in Visual Basic, you'll also see a PrintForm method in the list of available methods for the Data Report. This shows up only because Data Reports are based on forms. For all practical purposes, you can ignore this method.

Export

Data Reports can be exported programmatically or interactively by the user. In Visual Basic code, you can call the ExportReport method:

```
<DataReportName>.ExportReport([FormatIndex],[FileName], _
[Overwrite As Boolean=True], _
[ShowDialog As Boolean=False], _
[Range As PageRangeConstants=rptRangeAllPages], _
[PageFrom],[PageTo]) As Long
```

The FormatIndex argument specifies one of four built-in export formats: rptFmtHTML for export to HTML, rptFmtUnicodeHTML for export to HTML with the Unicode character set, rptFmtText for export to text, or rptFmtUnicode-Text for export to text with the Unicode character set.

The FileName argument specifies the file to be created by the ExportReport method.

The OverWrite argument tells the method whether to overwrite an existing file.

The ShowDialog argument determines whether or not the Export dialog box, seen in Figure 7.9, will be displayed to the user.

FIGURE 7.9:

The Export dialog box for a
Data Report

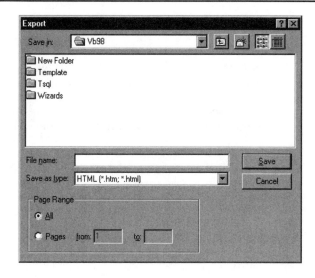

The Range argument can be set to rptRangeAllPages to export the entire report,
or rptRangeFromTo to export selected pages. Either way, entire pages will be
exported, even if only part of the page shows on screen.

The PageFrom and PageTo arguments let you specify the first and last pages to
be exported, if you've chosen rptRangeFromTo as the value for the Range argument.

The Export method returns a unique identifier that can be used for asynchronous event processing. You'll learn about this later in the chapter.

If the user chooses the Export button on a Data Report that's open in print preview mode, they'll always be presented with the Export dialog box.

WARNING   The pages specified to the ExportReport method won't necessarily match the
pages seen in the print preview mode, since the ExportReport method uses the
exported fonts to calculate page breaks.

Figure 7.10 shows how the drGrouping Data Report from the DataReports sample project looks when exported to text and HTML formats.

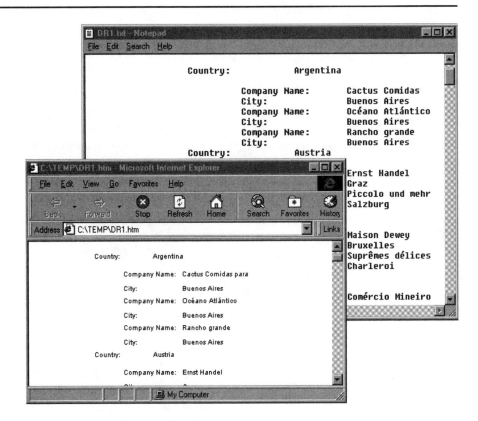

Data Reports in Code

You've already seen the important methods and properties of Data Reports. To wrap up the chapter, you'll learn about the events that Data Reports support, and see how you can bind a Data Report directly in code.

Data Report Events

The Data Report object supports these nine events:

- Initialize and Terminate
- Activate and Deactivate

- ProcessingTimeout

- AsyncProgress

- Error

- Resize and QueryClose

The frmEvents form in the DataReports sample project, shown in Figure 7.11, will let you experiment with these events. This form instantiates the drSalesDetail Data Report; the Data Report contains code in each event procedure that writes information back to this form.

FIGURE 7.11:

Events from a Data Report

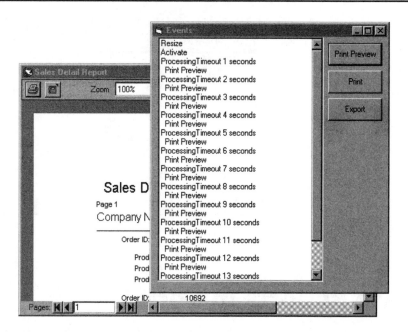

The Initialize and Terminate events are the standard class module events. Since a Data Report consists of a user interface and a class module (just like a form), it supports these events:

```
Private Sub DataReport_Initialize()
Private Sub DataReport_Terminate()
```

The Initialize occurs as soon as the report is created, and the Terminate occurs when the report is closed and all references to it are released.

The Activate and Deactivate events track whether the Data Report is the active window:

```
Private Sub DataReport_Activate()
Private Sub DataReport_Deactivate()
```

The Activate event is fired whenever the Data Report becomes the active window, and the Deactivate event is fired whenever the focus moves to another window.

The ProcessingTimeout event occurs during synchronous processing:

```
Private Sub DataReport_ProcessingTimeout( _
ByVal Seconds As Long, Cancel As Boolean, _
ByVal JobType As MSDataReportLib.AsyncTypeConstants, _
ByVal Cookie As Long)
```

When you use the Show method to display a report on screen, there are two steps involved in the processing. First, ADO has to process the query from the Data Environment to the data provider. You can't get into the middle of this process from the Data Report; you just have to wait for it to finish. After that, the Data Report has to work out how to display the data on screen. This process is synchronous—that is, the Show method blocks other Visual Basic code from executing. However, during this synchronous process, the ProcessingTimeout event will be fired approximately once per second. The Seconds argument will tell you how many seconds have passed since control returned to the Data Report. If you like, you can set the Cancel argument to True to cancel the remaining processing.

This event also occurs when you are printing or exporting a Data Report. You can check the JobType argument to determine what exactly is going on. JobType will have one of three values:

- rptAsyncPreview if you're in the Show method

- rptAsyncPrint if you're in the Print method, or the user has clicked the Print button

- rptAsyncExport if you're in the Export method, or the user has clicked the Export button.

WARNING   Don't get fooled by the constant names. ProcessingTimeout is a synchronous event despite using the rptAsync constants.

The Cookie argument contains the return value from the ExportReport or Print-Report method, if one of those methods was used to start the process. You can use this argument to determine which of several concurrent processes triggered this event.

The AsyncProgress event fires about once per second during asynchronous processing:

```
Private Sub DataReport_AsyncProgress( _
ByVal JobType As MSDataReportLib.AsyncTypeConstants, _
ByVal Cookie As Long, _
ByVal PageCompleted As Long, _
ByVal TotalPages As Long)
```

When you (or your user) print or export a Data Report, there are three steps involved. First, ADO has to process the query from the Data Environment to the data provider. You can't get into the middle of this process from the Data Report; you just have to wait for it to finish. After that, the Data Report has to work out how to display the data on screen. This process is synchronous. Finally, the Data Report triggers the print or export process. These processes are asynchronous—that is, other Visual Basic code will continue executing while the print or export is finished. However, the AsyncProgress event will be triggered about once per second, so you can keep track of what's going on.

The JobType and Cookie arguments allow you to track which process triggered the event, just as they do in the ProcessingTimeout event. You can't track the number of seconds processing has taken (unless you maintain your own timer), but you can use the PageCompleted and TotalPages arguments to tell how far the process has proceeded. Since printing and exporting are actually handled by external libraries, you can't cancel these events.

WARNING   Don't count on ProcessingTimeout and AsyncProgress events to happen precisely once per second. If your system is heavily loaded, some of these events might be skipped. In particular, if you're checking for a length of time in the Processing-Timeout event, be sure to check for greater than rather than equal time.

The Error event is triggered whenever an error occurs that's not in Visual Basic code:

```
Private Sub DataReport_Error( _
ByVal JobType As MSDataReportLib.AsyncTypeConstants, _
```

```
ByVal Cookie As Long, _
ByVal ErrObj As MSDataReportLib.RptError, _
ShowError As Boolean)
```

Once again, the JobType and Cookie arguments allow you to determine which process triggered the error. The ErrObj argument contains the details of the error. If you process the error yourself, you'll want to set the ShowError argument to False to suppress the default error display.

WARNING   If you're printing or exporting, not every error will trigger this event. For example, if there's no printer driver installed, you will receive an Error event. However, if there's a printer installed but it's out of paper, you won't receive an error. That's because the "out of paper" error belongs to the asynchronous print process, not to Visual Basic itself.

Finally, the Resize and QueryClose events are identical to their counterparts from forms:

```
Private Sub DataReport_Resize()
Private Sub DataReport_QueryClose( _
 Cancel As Integer, CloseMode As Integer)
```

The Resize event is fired whenever the Data Report is in preview mode and the user resizes the window. (This event does *not* fire when the user changes the zoom factor of the Data Report.)

The QueryClose event is fired whenever the Data Report preview window is about to be closed. The CloseMode argument is set to a value that indicates what's closing the window:

- vbFormControlMenu if the user closed the Data Report manually

- vbFormCode if the Data Report is closed from code

- vbAppWindows if the current Windows session is ending

- vbAppTaskManager if the Windows Task Manager is closing the application

If you like, you can attempt to cancel the closing by setting the Cancel argument to True.

Binding Data Reports Directly

Although it's easy to create Data Reports via drag-and-drop and leave them bound to their original Data Environment, you can also bind Data Reports to an ADO Recordset object directly in code. For example, the Rebind sample in the DataReports sample project first displays a simple Data Report and then changes it from a Jet database to a SQL database.

Here's the code that does the rebinding:

```
Private Sub cmdRebind_Click()
    Dim intI As Integer
    drProducts.Show
    MsgBox "Click OK to rebind the Datareport"
    With drProducts
        Set .DataSource = Nothing
        .DataMember = ""
        Set .DataSource = deNorthwindSQL.rsProducts
        On Error Resume Next
        With .Sections("Products_Detail").Controls
        For intI = 1 To .Count
            .Item(intI).DataMember = ""
        Next intI
        End With
        On Error GoTo 0
        .Show
    End With
End Sub
```

To bind a Data Report at run time, you of course need to change its data properties. Here we've chosen to set the DataSource property of the Data Report to an ADO Recordset created by a Data Environment. However, you can actually use any ADO Recordset as the data source for a Data Report (as long as the recordset contains the proper fields!). This gives you wide flexibility to display the results of ad hoc queries.

You might think that you also need to set the DataMember properties to field names; in fact, for the report itself and for top-level controls, you need to set this property to an empty string. If the Data Report is hierarchical, controls in lower levels of detail do need to have their DataMember property set to the name of the field to be displayed.

Note also that this code uses a For Next loop rather than a For Each loop to enumerate the controls in the detail section. The Data Report Controls collection does not support the NewEnum method that's necessary for using a For Each loop.

By now, you've seen most of what can be done with ADO by using Visual Basic's built-in designers and rapid development tools, including the Data View, Data Environment, and Data Report objects. But there's always more to be done beyond using the built-in tools. In the next chapter, you'll start learning the cutting-edge operations that you can perform using ADO directly from Visual Basic code.

8

Fine-Tuning ADO through Visual Basic Code

- Basic Operations

- Working with Persisted Recordsets

- Advanced Operations

As you've seen, Visual Basic 6.0 empowers you to use ADO in many ways without writing much code. You can explore data sources with the Data View, create data entry and inquiry forms using bound controls, and connect to complex hierarchies of data using the Data Environment. You can even present information in a form suitable for printing by using the Data Report. But at some point, you'll find that you've exhausted the built-in user interface resources. At that point, you'll need to roll up your figurative sleeves and start writing code. In this chapter, you'll learn how to perform some of the most essential data-related tasks using ADO from Visual Basic code. In the remainder of the book, I'll dig into some more-advanced code operations, including data shaping, using ADO on the Internet, and even creating your own data sources.

Basic Operations

There are some basic operations that any data access library needs to support. Of course, ADO easily allows you to perform all these operations, including:

- Connecting to a data source

- Running a stored procedure

- Creating a recordset

- Sorting and finding information in a recordset

- Adding, deleting, and updating records

In this section, you'll learn to perform these basic operations using ADO from your Visual Basic applications. For the most part, ADO makes these operations simple and straightforward, but there are some pitfalls that you need to watch out for.

Connecting to Data Sources

Not surprisingly, you use the Connection object to connect to a data source. After all, that's what a Connection object represents: a connection to a single data source. All data operations in ADO involve instantiating a Connection object, either explicitly or implicitly. When you create a Connection object and later associate that object with a recordset, you're using an explicit connection. When you simply open a recordset, supplying a connection string when you do so, you're using an implicit connection. ADO still creates a Connection object in the latter case, but it's strictly internal to ADO's own workings.

You can control the behavior of the Connection object to some extent by setting properties before you call the object's Open method. The properties of interest are:

- ConnectionString
- ConnectionTimeout
- Mode
- CursorLocation
- DefaultDatabase
- IsolationLevel
- Provider

The ConnectionString property can be used to specify a data source or to supply other information making up an ADO connection string. Although I've been using connection strings throughout this book, this is the first place that I've needed to create one without using the Visual Basic IDE. I'll discuss the format used for connection strings in the next section of this chapter. Although you can specify the ConnectionString property before calling the Open method, it's usually just as convenient to supply it as an argument to that method. If you're working as part of a development team, you might want to consider setting the properties explicitly to make the code more maintainable.

The ConnectionTimeout property tells ADO how many seconds it should wait for a data source to respond. By default, this is set to 15. If you're connecting across a busy network or the Internet, you may need to increase this timeout value. You can only change the value of this property before you've called the Open method on the Connection object.

You can use the Mode property to ask for particular permissions when you open a connection. If the requested permissions can't be set, you'll get an error when you call the Open method. By default, the Mode of a Connection object is adModeUnknown. Usually it makes more sense to set this property on a Record or a Stream object, rather than on a connection as a whole, to preserve flexibility in your code.

The CursorLocation property can be set to adUseServer to use the cursors supplied by the OLE DB provider for the connection, or to adUseClient to use the client-side cursor library. For advanced functionality you may need to use the client-side library, although this will add additional overhead.

You can use the DefaultDatabase property to specify which database on a server a particular Connection should use for data operations. Alternatively, you can specify this as a part of the connection string. For example, if you're using the SQL Server provider, you can either set the DefaultDatabase property or put the name of the default database in as the Initial Catalog argument in the connection string. The advantage of using the DefaultDatabase property is that it's provider independent. Any objects that use this Connection object will inherit its default database.

The IsolationLevel property controls the effect that one transaction has on other transactions. Table 8.1 shows the possible settings for this property. You normally won't need to alter the IsolationLevel property.

TABLE 8.1: IsolationLevel Property Values

Constant	Effect
adXactUnspecified	Value returned when the provider is unable to determine the current isolation level.
adXactChaos	Prohibits overwriting pending changes from more highly isolated transactions. This is the default setting.
adXactBrowse	Allows you to view, but not change, uncommitted changes from other transactions.
adXactReadUncommitted	Same as adXactBrowse.
adXactCursorStability	Allows you to view changes from other transactions only after they've been committed.
adXactReadCommitted	Same as adXactCursorStability.
adXactRepeatableRead	Allows requerying a recordset to include changes pending from other transactions.
adXactIsolated	Forces all transactions to be isolated from other transactions. You should choose this value for the strictest transactional processing.
adXactSerializable	Same as adXactIsolated.

The Provider property allows you to specify an OLE DB Provider before opening the connection. It's usually more convenient to include this as the Provider argument in the connection string.

I discussed using the Connection object's Open method in Chapter 3. Now it's time to dig in a little further. The syntax of the Open method is as follows:

```
Connection.Open ConnectionString, UserID, Password, Options
```

Depending on how you write your code, you might supply all, some, or none of the four arguments to the method. One way or another, you must supply a connection string, either by filling in the ConnectionString argument in the Open method or by setting the connection's ConnectionString property before calling the Open method.

Usually, you'll supply the UserID and Password as part of the connection string. However, in cases where that information is supplied by the user, you might find it more convenient to use the arguments to the Open method. For example, you'll find this code in frmOpen in the ADOCode sample project:

```
Private Sub cmdConnect_Click()
    ' Connect using ID and password supplied
    ' by the user interface
    Dim cnn As ADODB.Connection

    On Error GoTo HandleErr

    Set cnn = New ADODB.Connection
    cnn.Open "Provider=SQLOLEDB.1;" & _
      "Server=(local);Initial Catalog=pubs", _
      txtUserID, txtPassword

    MsgBox "Connection Succeeded"
    cnn.Close

ExitHere:
    Exit Sub

HandleErr:
    MsgBox "Error " & Err.Number & ": " & _
      Err.Description
    Resume ExitHere
End Sub
```

As you can see, by using the UserID and Password arguments you can avoid either hard-coding security information or manipulating the connection string to insert these values. If you specify UserID and Password both in the connection string and as separate arguments, the arguments override any values set in the connection string.

The last argument to the Open method specifies whether the connection should be opened synchronously. You can use the constants adConnectUnspecified for a synchronous connection (the default, so you needn't bother to specify a value at all in this case) or adAsyncConnect for an asynchronous connection. Chapter 3 shows how to use ADO events to monitor the progress of an asynchronous connection.

You should also be familiar with the Close method of the Connection object. This method disconnects the Connection object from the data source without destroying the object itself. While the object is in this state, you can change the connection string or other properties, and then execute the Open method again to reconnect with new information. When you're completely done with a Connection object, you can either set it equal to Nothing or just let it go out of scope to reclaim the memory it's using.

Connection Strings

You'll recall from Chapter 3 that an OLE DB connection string has this format:

```
Provider=value;File Name=value;Remote Provider=value; ➥
Remote Server=value; URL=value;
```

- The Provider argument specifies the name of the OLE DB provider to use. Table 8.2 shows the possible values that this argument can have for the providers that are shipped with the Microsoft Data Access Components.

- The File Name value specifies a file containing connection information—for example, an ODBC file data source. If you use the File Name argument, you must omit the Provider argument.

- The Remote Provider value specifies the name of a provider to use on the server when opening a client-side connection. This option applies to Remote Data Service (RDS) connections only. See Chapter 11 for more information on RDS.

- The Remote Server value specifies the name of a server to retrieve data from when using RDS.

- The URL value specifies the connection string as a URL rather than as an ODBC-style string.

All these arguments are optional. You can include additional arguments in the ConnectionString property, in which case they are passed to the OLE DB provider without any alteration by ADO.

NOTE   You can specify a provider by a name with or without a version number. For example, SQLOLEDB.1 refers to a particular release of the SQL Server provider, while SQLOLEDB refers to the most recent release of the driver installed on the computer where the code is running. If you use versioned names, you don't have to worry about retesting your code when a provider is updated (though you also can't take advantage of any of the new features of the provider).

TABLE 8.2: OLE DB Provider Names

Provider	Value
Microsoft.Jet.OLEDB.3.51	Microsoft Jet 3.51 OLE DB Provider
Microsoft.Jet.OLEDB.4	Microsoft Jet 4 OLE DB Provider
DTSPackageDSO.1	Microsoft OLE DB Provider for DTS Packages
MSDAIPP.DSO	Microsoft OLE DB Provider for Internet Publishing
MSDASQL.1	Microsoft OLE DB Provider for ODBC Drivers
MSOLAP.1	Microsoft OLE DB Provider for OLAP Services
MSDAORA.1	Microsoft OLE DB Provider for Oracle
SQLOLEDB.1	Microsoft OLE DB Provider for SQL Server
MS Remote.1	MS Remote
MSDataShape.1	MSDataShape
MSIDX	Microsoft OLE DB Provider for Microsoft Indexing Services
ADSDSOObject	Microsoft OLE DB Provider for Microsoft Active Directory Service
MSPersist	Microsoft OLE DB Persistence Provider

Although you normally can connect to a data source using just the provider name, User ID, and password, if you examine connection strings built using the Data Link Properties dialog box you'll find that they're usually much more complex than that. This is because any argument that's not understood by ADO itself is automatically passed to the underlying OLE DB driver for interpretation, and most OLE DB drivers understand a wide variety of arguments.

For an exhaustive listing of the arguments understood by any given provider, you'll need to consult that provider's documentation. For the providers supplied by Microsoft, you'll find that documentation in the Platform SDK, available as part of the Microsoft Developer Network Library. Table 8.3 lists some of the most common and useful arguments for the Jet, SQL Server, and Oracle providers that are used in the examples in this book.

TABLE 8.3: Sample Connection String Arguments

Provider	Argument	Description
Jet	Data Source	Name of the Jet database to connect to.
Jet	Jet OLEDB:System Database	Name of the system database to use when verifying username and password.
SQL Server	Integrated Security	Set to the literal value "SSPI" to use Windows NT login security.
SQL Server	Data Source	Name of the SQL Server to connect to.
SQL Server	Server	Name of the SQL Server to connect to.
SQL Server	Initial Catalog	Name of the SQL Server database to connect to.
Oracle	Data Source	Name of the Oracle server to connect to.

Running Stored Procedures

As you saw in Chapter 3, you can use the Command object to execute statements on a connection. In this section you'll learn how to use a Command object to execute a stored procedure in a SQL Server database.

Stored procedures are collections of SQL statements that are saved in a database. Some databases also precompile these statements for faster execution. These procedures can take input parameters and return output parameters. For example, in the Northwind SQL Server database there's a stored procedure named SalesByCategory. Here's the SQL that creates that stored procedure:

```
CREATE PROCEDURE SalesByCategory
    @CategoryName nvarchar(15),
    @OrdYear nvarchar(4) = '1998'
AS
IF @OrdYear != '1996'
 AND @OrdYear != '1997'
 AND @OrdYear != '1998'
BEGIN
    SELECT @OrdYear = '1998'
END
SELECT ProductName,
    TotalPurchase=ROUND(SUM(CONVERT(decimal(14,2), OD.Quantity *
(1-OD.Discount) * OD.UnitPrice)), 0)
FROM [Order Details] OD, Orders O, Products P, Categories C
WHERE OD.OrderID = O.OrderID
    AND OD.ProductID = P.ProductID
    AND P.CategoryID = C.CategoryID
    AND C.CategoryName = @CategoryName
    AND SUBSTRING(CONVERT(
    nvarchar(22), O.OrderDate, 111), 1, 4) = @OrdYear
GROUP BY ProductName
ORDER BY ProductName
```

Here, @CategoryName and @OrdYear are a pair of input parameters to the stored procedure, both defined as being of the nvarchar datatype. The stored procedure uses these parameters to filter a recordset of order information. The recordset becomes the return value of the stored procedure.

Retrieving a recordset from a stored procedure is a three-step process:

1. Create a command object and connect it to a data source.

2. Supply values for any input parameters.

3. Use the command object's Execute method to retrieve the data.

As an example, consider this code from frmStoredProcedure in the ADOCode sample project:

```
Private Sub cmdGo_Click()
    ' Fill a listbox with the results
    ' of a stored procedure
```

```
Dim cnn As New ADODB.Connection
Dim cmd As New ADODB.Command
Dim prm As ADODB.Parameter
Dim rst As ADODB.Recordset
Dim fld As ADODB.Field

Dim strTemp As String

' Connect to the data source and the SP
cnn.Open "Provider=SQLOLEDB.1;" & _
  "Data Source=(local);Initial Catalog=" & _
  "Northwind;Integrated Security=SSPI"
With cmd
    .ActiveConnection = cnn
    .CommandText = "SalesByCategory"
    .CommandType = adCmdStoredProc
    .Parameters.Refresh
End With

' Now walk through the Parameters, filling
' in the input parameters
For Each prm In cmd.Parameters
    If (prm.Direction = adParamInput) Or _
      (prm.Direction = adParamInputOutput) Then
        prm.Value = InputBox(prm.Name, _
          "Enter parameter value")
    End If
Next prm

' Retrieve and display the records
Set rst = cmd.Execute
For Each fld In rst.Fields
    strTemp = strTemp & fld.Name & vbTab
Next fld
lboResults.AddItem strTemp
Do Until rst.EOF
    strTemp = ""
    For Each fld In rst.Fields
        strTemp = strTemp & fld.Value & vbTab
    Next fld
```

```
        lboResults.AddItem strTemp
        rst.MoveNext
    Loop

End Sub
```

This code starts by connecting to the Northwind database on the local SQL Server, using Windows NT security. (As always, if your environment is different, you may have to modify the connection string.) Then it creates a Command object and loads it with the SalesByCategory stored procedure. Setting the CommandType property of the Command object to adCmdStoredProc is optional, but the code will execute faster if you tell ADO that this is a stored procedure, rather than make ADO figure that out by itself.

The call to the Refresh method of the Command object's Parameters collection tells ADO to query the data source and find out what parameters are required by this stored procedure. Once the Parameters collection is populated, the code walks through it one parameter at a time and prompts the user for values for all input parameters.

Finally, the Execute method of the Command object is used to send the parameter values to the data source and fill in the recordset with the returned data.

While this method works, it's not the most efficient way to execute a stored procedure. The bottleneck is the Refresh method of the Parameters collection. This method can require multiple round-trips of information between the client and the server to do its job. If you already know the details of the stored procedure, you can avoid using the Refresh method by creating your own parameters. This method is also demonstrated in frmStoredProcedure in the ADOCode sample project:

```
Private Sub cmdCreateParameters_Click()
    ' Fill a listbox with the results
    ' of a stored procedure. Create all
    ' necessary parameters on the client.

    Dim cnn As New ADODB.Connection
    Dim cmd As New ADODB.Command
    Dim prm As ADODB.Parameter
    Dim rst As ADODB.Recordset
    Dim fld As ADODB.Field

    Dim strTemp As String
```

```
' Connect to the data source and the SP
cnn.Open "Provider=SQLOLEDB.1;" & _
 "Data Source=(local);Initial Catalog=" & _
 "Northwind;Integrated Security=SSPI"
With cmd
    .ActiveConnection = cnn
    .CommandText = "SalesByCategory"
    .CommandType = adCmdStoredProc
End With

' Create the necessary parameters, using
' the values supplied through the UI
Set prm = cmd.CreateParameter( _
 "@CategoryName", _
 adVarWChar, adParamInput, 15, _
 txtCategoryName.Text)
cmd.Parameters.Append prm
Set prm = cmd.CreateParameter( _
 "@OrdYear", _
 adVarWChar, adParamInput, 4, _
 txtOrdYear.Text)
cmd.Parameters.Append prm

' Retrieve and display the records
Set rst = cmd.Execute
For Each fld In rst.Fields
    strTemp = strTemp & fld.Name & vbTab
Next fld
lboResults2.AddItem strTemp
Do Until rst.EOF
    strTemp = ""
    For Each fld In rst.Fields
        strTemp = strTemp & fld.Value & vbTab
    Next fld
    lboResults2.AddItem strTemp
    rst.MoveNext
Loop

End Sub
```

The difference between this and the previous procedure is in the method used to populate the Parameters collection of the Command object. This procedure uses the CreateParameter method of the Command object:

```
Command.CreateParameter Name, Type, Direction, Size, Value
```

- The Name argument must match the name that the underlying data source is expecting for the parameter.

- The Type argument specifies a datatype for the parameter. These datatypes are expressed by constants supplied by ADO. Because ADO uses a single set of constants for all data sources, you might have trouble determining the appropriate constant to use in some cases. The simplest solution to this problem is to first use the Parameters.Refresh method to get the parameter from the server and then examine the Type property of the returned parameter. Once you know what this type is, you can create your own matching parameter in the future.

- The Direction argument is a constant that tells ADO whether this is an input or an output parameter (or both).

- The Size argument specifies the size of the parameter. You do not need to specify a Size for fixed-length datatypes such as integer or datetime. On the other hand, with some datatypes you might need to set additional properties. For floating-point parameters, for example, you need to explicitly set the Precision and NumericScale properties.

- The Value argument specifies the actual value to use for the parameter. Make sure to specify Null for the value if there's a chance you won't be passing a value to the stored procedure; otherwise the stored procedure will think there's no data for the parameter and raise an error.

All these arguments are optional when you're calling the CreateParameter method. You can create parameters and then set the properties afterwards if you prefer not to do the entire operation in one line of code.

WARNING   Note that newly created Parameter objects are not appended to the Parameters collection by default! You must remember to call the Command object's Parameters collection's Append method, or your newly created Parameter won't be attached to the Command. ADO is deliberately designed this way to allow you to create additional provider-specific properties before appending the Parameter, if that's ever necessary.

In general, if you're writing code that will always call the same stored procedure, it's worth your while to explicitly code the parameters using the CreateParameter method. You should save the Parameters.Refresh method for situations where you don't know in advance what the Parameters collection should contain.

Retrieving Data

To retrieve data in ADO, you use the Recordset object (or, sometimes, the Record or Stream objects). I covered the basics of the Recordset's Open method in Chapter 3. To refresh your memory, the syntax of this method is:

```
Recordset.Open Source, ActiveConnection, CursorType, ➥
LockType, Options
```

All these arguments are optional, because they can all be supplied by setting properties of the Recordset object before calling the Open method. For example, you can omit the LockType argument here if you have already set the LockType property of the Recordset object, or if you're happy with the default read-only locking.

The Source argument specifies where the records should be retrieved from. Because Providers are so flexible, there are a lot of possibilities for the Source argument. It can be

- a Command object that returns records

- a SQL statement

- a table name

- a stored procedure name

- the name of a file containing a persisted recordset

- the name of a Stream object containing a persisted recordset

- a URL that specifies a file or other location with data

Not all these options, of course, are valid for all providers.

The ActiveConnection argument specifies the ADO connection to use. This can be either a Connection object that you've already opened or a connection string. In the latter case, ADO creates a connection "behind the scenes" specifically for this recordset to use.

The CursorType and LockType arguments correspond to the cursor type and lock type parameters discussed in the previous section.

The Options argument supplies additional information to the provider. Generally, you can omit this argument, but some Open methods may be faster if you include it. Valid Options include:

- adCmdUnknown, which is the default and supplies no additional information to the provider.

- adCmdText, which tells the provider that the CommandText property is a textual definition of a stored procedure.

- adCmdTable, which tells the provider that the CommandText property is the name of a table.

- adCmdStoredProc, which tells the provider that the CommandText property is the name of a stored procedure.

- adCmdFile, which tells the provider that the CommandText property is the name of a file.

- adCmdTableDirect, which tells the provider that the CommandText property is the name of a table that should be opened using low-level calls. Most providers don't support this.

- adCmdURLBind, which tells the provider that the CommandText is a URL.

- adAsyncExecute, which tells the provider that the command should be executed asynchronously.

- adAsyncFetch, which tells the provider that the cache should be filled synchronously, and then additional rows fetched asynchronously.

- adAsyncFetchNonBlocking, which tells the provider to fetch records asynchronously if it can be done without blocking the main thread of execution.

For examples of recordset operations, see the frmRecordset form in the ADOCode sample project. Perhaps the simplest way to open a recordset is to just supply the name of a table in the data source as the source of the recordset:

```
Private Sub cmdTable_Click()
    ' Open a recordset based on a table
    Dim rst As New ADODB.Recordset
    Screen.MousePointer = vbHourglass
    rst.Open "Customers", _
```

```
        "Provider=Microsoft.Jet.OLEDB.4.0;" & _
        "Data Source=C:\Program Files\" & _
        "Microsoft Visual Studio\VB98\Nwind.mdb", _
        adOpenKeyset, adLockOptimistic
    Screen.MousePointer = vbDefault
    MsgBox rst.RecordCount & " records retrieved"
End Sub
```

In this case, the entire table is opened as a recordset. If you're using ADO to retrieve data in a client-server or three-tier setting, this probably isn't the best thing to do. A general rule of client-server processing is to retrieve only the data that you actually need at the moment. You can do this by supplying a SQL statement to be resolved by the data source. In this case, only the requested records will be returned:

```
Private Sub cmdStatement_Click()
    ' Open a recordset based on a SQL statement
    Dim rst As New ADODB.Recordset
    Screen.MousePointer = vbHourglass
    rst.Open "SELECT * FROM authors " & _
        "WHERE au_lname = 'Ringer'", _
        "Provider=SQLOLEDB.1;" & _
        "Data Source=(local);" & _
        "Initial Catalog=pubs;" & _
        "User ID=sa", _
        adOpenStatic, adLockPessimistic
    Screen.MousePointer = vbDefault
    MsgBox rst.RecordCount & " records retrieved"
End Sub
```

Alternatively, you can open a recordset on a view instead of a table. This allows you to define a persistent set of joins and restrictions directly on the server:

```
Private Sub cmdView_Click()
    ' Open a recordset based on a View
    Dim rst As New ADODB.Recordset
    Dim intRecords As Integer
    Screen.MousePointer = vbHourglass
    rst.Open "SALES", _
        "Provider=MSDAORA.1;" & _
        "Data Source=CASTOR;" & _
        "User ID=DEMO;" & _
        "Password=DEMO"
```

```
    Do Until rst.EOF
        intRecords = intRecords + 1
        rst.MoveNext
    Loop
    Screen.MousePointer = vbDefault
    MsgBox intRecords & " records retrieved" & _
      "; RecordCount is " & rst.RecordCount
End Sub
```

Note the loop used in this example to count the records returned. That's because the RecordCount property isn't always accurate. You'll find that:

- If the provider doesn't support counting records, the RecordCount property will be equal to –1.

- If the provider supports approximate positioning or bookmarks, the RecordCount will be accurate.

- If the provider (or cursor type) doesn't support approximate positioning or bookmarks, the RecordCount won't be accurate until you've retrieved every record in the recordset.

- Forward-only cursors will always return –1 for the RecordCount, even after all the records have been retrieved.

Finding and Sorting Data

Given a set of records, there are some common tasks. For example, you might want to find a particular record, or the first record meeting some criterion. Or you might want to sort the recordset. In this section, I'll review the basics of finding and sorting data in ADO recordsets.

How you find a record depends on the type of recordset. A few OLE DB providers (notably the Microsoft Jet Provider) support a special type of recordset, the direct table recordset. Such recordsets (opened with the adCmdTableDirect option) can use an indexed search to find data. Other recordsets must use a slower sequential search.

Finding Data in a Direct Table Recordset

If you've created a direct table access Recordset object, some providers allow you to use the fast Seek method to locate specific rows. (Attempting to use the Seek method with any other recordset results in a runtime error.) You must take two specific steps to use the Seek method to find data:

1. Set the recordset's Index property to the name of an index on the underlying table. This tells ADO which index you'd like it to search through. If you want to use the primary key for searching, you must know the name of the primary key. (It's usually PrimaryKey, unless your application has changed it.)

2. Use the Seek method to find the value you want. The Seek method works from a search operator and one or more values to search for. The search operator must be one of the intrinsic constants shown in Table 8.4. If the index is on a single column, you supply a value to search for in that column. If the index is on multiple columns, you should supply one search value for each column, using the Visual Basic Array() function to create an array from these values.

> **WARNING** Currently, the only provider shipped as part of MDAC that supports Index and Seek is the Jet provider.

TABLE 8.4: Seek Options

Seek Option	Meaning
adSeekAfterEQ	Seek the key equal to the value supplied, or, if there is no such key, the first key after the point where the match would have occurred.
adSeekAfter	Seek the first key after the point where a match occurs or would occur.
adSeekBeforeEQ	Seek the key equal to the value supplied, or, if there is no such key, the first key before the point where the match would have occurred.
adSeekBefore	Seek the first key before the point where a match occurs or would occur.
adSeekFirstEQ	Seek the first key equal to the value supplied.
adSeekAfterEQ	Seek the last key equal to the value supplied.

You'll find an example of using the Seek method in the frmRecordset form in the ADOCode sample project:

```
Private Sub cmdSeek_Click()
    ' Find a record using the Seek method
```

```
' This requires a direct table recordset
Dim rst As New ADODB.Recordset
Dim strSeek As String

Screen.MousePointer = vbHourglass
rst.Open "Customers", _
 "Provider=Microsoft.Jet.OLEDB.4.0;" & _
 "Data Source=" & App.Path & "\ADOCode.MDB", _
 adOpenDynamic, adLockOptimistic, _
 adCmdTableDirect
Screen.MousePointer = vbDefault

' Now set the index we want to seek on
rst.Index = "PrimaryKey"
' Get a value to seek for
strSeek = InputBox("Customer ID to Find:", _
 "Seek input", "FOLKO")

' Seek the record and report results
rst.Seek strSeek, adSeekAfterEQ
If rst.EOF Then
    MsgBox "No matching record found"
Else
    MsgBox "Found customer " & _
      rst("CompanyName")
End If
End Sub
```

Note that the procedure checks the EOF property of the recordset after invoking the Seek method. If the Seek fails, EOF will be set to True. This is the only way to tell whether the Seek method found a matching record.

WARNING   With the Jet 4 OLE DB provider, the Seek method will only work on recordsets created from Jet 4 databases (for example, databases created with Microsoft Access 2000). When in doubt, you can use the Supports method, discussed later in this chapter, to determine whether the Seek method will work at all.

Finding Data Using the Find Method

Most recordsets cannot use the Seek method for finding data. Fortunately, ADO provides a second method for finding records that's universally supported. This is the Find method of the recordset, which is implemented with a great deal of flexibility. It allows you to optimize the search so it has to look through the smallest number of rows to find the data it needs. Because you can use Find to continue searching with the next record, you won't need to start back at the beginning of the recordset to find subsequent matches. In addition, you can use loops to walk your way through the records because you can restart the search without going back to the first row. The biggest disadvantage to the Find method is that you can only search on a single criterion. For multiple criteria, you can use the Filter property instead.

The syntax for the Find method is:

```
Recordset.Find Criteria, SkipRows, SearchDirection, Start
```

All but the first parameter are optional.

- *Criteria* is a WHERE clause formatted as though in a SQL expression, without the word *WHERE*.

- *SkipRows* specifies the offset from the current row where the search should begin. It defaults to starting with the current row.

- *SearchDirection* can be adSearchForward (the default) or adSearchBackward.

- *Start* is an optional bookmark where the search should begin. The default is to begin with the current row.

For an example of the Find method, see the frmRecordset form in the ADOCode sample project:

```
Private Sub cmdFind_Click()
    ' Use the Find method to locate records
    Dim rst As New ADODB.Recordset
    Dim strCriteria As String

    Screen.MousePointer = vbHourglass
    rst.Open "SELECT * FROM authors", _
     "Provider=SQLOLEDB.1;" & _
     "Data Source=(local);" & _
     "Initial Catalog=pubs;" & _
     "User ID=sa", _
```

```
        adOpenStatic, adLockPessimistic
        Screen.MousePointer = vbDefault

        ' Find all the authors in California
        strCriteria = "State = 'CA'
        With rst
            .Find strCriteria
            Do While Not .EOF
                lboFound.AddItem rst("au_lname")
                ' Continue with the next record
                .Find strCriteria, 1
            Loop
        End With
    End Sub
```

Just as with the Find method, you must follow every call to a Find method with a check of the recordset's EOF property (or BOF property, if SearchDirection is adSearchBackward). If that property is True, there is no current row, and the Find method failed to find any matching records.

Note also the use of the SkipRows argument in the second call to the Find method in the sample code. By skipping a single row with each call, you can continue to find records starting at the point where the last search left off.

WARNING Find criteria treat null values differently from the way that some database engines (such as Jet) do. Because the ADO Find method does not understand the IsNull() or similar functions, the correct way to search for a Null using the Find method is with an expression such as "FieldName = Null" or "FieldName <> Null."

Sorting Recordsets

Unless you specify a sorting order for a recordset, the rows for that recordset might show up in any order. The order could depend on data from more than one table, and on the OLE DB provider that's supplying the original data. In any case, if you need a specific ordering, you must set up that ordering yourself. You can do this either with a SQL statement or with the Recordset object's Sort property.

Using a SQL ORDER BY Clause

You can create a Recordset object using a SQL statement including an ORDER BY clause. To do so, specify the SQL expression as the row source for the Recordset's Open method. For example, you could use this code fragment to create a recordset based on the Customers table, ordered by Company Name:

```
Dim rst As New ADODB.Recordset
    Screen.MousePointer = vbHourglass
    rst.Open "SELECT * FROM Customers " & _
     "ORDER BY CompanyName",
     "Provider=Microsoft.Jet.OLEDB.4.0;" & _
     "Data Source=C:\Program Files\" & _
     "Microsoft Visual Studio\VB98\Nwind.mdb", _
    adOpenKeyset, adLockOptimistic
```

Using the Sort Property

You can also set the Sort property of a recordset to change its sort order. The Sort property must be a string, in the same style as the ORDER BY clause of a SQL expression (that is, it's a comma-separated list of field names, optionally with ASC or DESC to indicate ascending or descending sorts).

Some OLE DB providers don't implement the necessary interfaces to allow sorting. If you're using a recordset from such a provider, you can still use the sort method, but only if you've created a client-side cursor.

For example, this code from the frmRecordset form in the ADOCode sample demonstrates how to change the sort order of a recordset from the Jet provider, even though the Jet provider itself doesn't support sorting:

```
Private Sub cmdSort_Click()
    ' Sort a recordset in descending order
    Dim rst As New ADODB.Recordset
    ' Fetch a recordset in native order
    Screen.MousePointer = vbHourglass
    rst.CursorLocation = adUseClient
    rst.Open "Customers", _
     "Provider=Microsoft.Jet.OLEDB.4.0;" & _
     "Data Source=C:\Program Files\" & _
     "Microsoft Visual Studio\VB98\Nwind.mdb", _
     adOpenKeyset, adLockOptimistic
    Screen.MousePointer = vbDefault
    lboFound.Clear
```

```
Do Until rst.EOF
    lboFound.AddItem rst.Fields("CompanyName")
    rst.MoveNext
Loop
' Now sort it on the CompanyName field
MsgBox "Click OK to sort descending"
rst.Sort = "CompanyName DESC"
lboFound.Clear
Do Until rst.EOF
    lboFound.AddItem rst.Fields("CompanyName")
    rst.MoveNext
Loop
End Sub
```

Note the use of the SQL DESC keyword to force a descending sort. The new sort takes effect as soon as the Sort property is set. In some cases, you may find that it's faster to simply open a new recordset based on a SQL statement with an ORDER BY clause than it is to use the Sort property.

Updating, Adding, and Deleting Data

Of course, almost any database application needs to be able to update, add, and delete data. ADO provides methods for accomplishing each of these tasks. The next few sections discuss the various data-manipulation methods that ADO supports. Of course, all these methods work on the Recordset object.

Changing Data in a Recordset

Changing data in a recordset is a three-step process:

1. Move to the row of the recordset containing the data.

2. Set new values for the fields that you want to change.

3. Use the Recordset object's Update method to save the new values.

You must explicitly call the Update method before you move to another row of the recordset, unless you're performing batch updates (see the next section for more information on batch updates). If you don't explicitly call the Update method, ADO calls it automatically when you move off a row and saves any pending changes to the record. You can also explicitly discard changes by calling the recordset's CancelUpdate method.

Batch Updates

If you use the client-side cursor library with a keyset or static cursor, you can also take advantage of ADO's ability to perform batch updates. That is, you can edit multiple records in a database, and then send all the updates to the underlying OLE DB provider to be stored in a single operation.

To use batch updates, simply change as many records as you please, and then call the UpdateBatch method. If you've used a client-side cursor, your changes will be cached on the client until you call the UpdateBatch method. At that time, all the changes will be sent to the server as a single operation.

If any of your changes can't be saved (for example, because another user has deleted the record), a runtime error occurs. In this case, you can use the Filter property with the adFilterAffectedRecords constant to filter the recordset down to only those records that had problems.

Adding New Rows to a Recordset

Adding new rows to a recordset is also a three-step process:

1. Call the AddNew method of the Recordset object to create a new row.

2. Fill in the Value property of any field you wish to assign a non-default value to.

3. Call the Update method to save the new row to the data source.

If you move off the row without calling Update, ADO helpfully calls the Update method for you (unless you've opened the recordset for batch updating). When you use the AddNew method, the new record becomes the current row as soon as you call the Update method.

Deleting Data from a Recordset

Deleting a record from a recordset is simple. You just move to the desired row and call the Delete method of the Recordset object.

You don't need to use the Update methods when deleting a row, unlike the case of adding a row. Once you delete it, it's gone—unless, of course, you wrapped the entire thing in a transaction. In that case, you can roll back the transaction to retrieve the deleted row.

After you delete a record, it is still the current record. The previous row is still the previous row, and the next row is still the next row. Use MoveNext to move to the next row, if that's where you'd like to be.

Data Manipulation Example

To see the Update, UpdateBatch, AddNew, and Delete methods in action, you can examine the frmRecordsetChanges form in the ADOCode sample project. This form, shown in Figure 8.1, allows you to invoke each of these four methods on a form-level Recordset object opened with a client-side cursor.

FIGURE 8.1:

The frmRecordsetChanges sample form

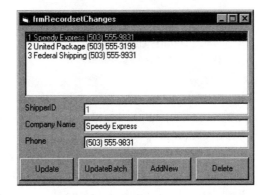

The form starts by opening a recordset as soon as the form itself is loaded:

```
Private Sub Form_Load()
    ' Initialize the recordset
    GetRecordset
End Sub

Private Sub GetRecordset()
    ' Get the current records from the server
    gfLoading = True
    ' If the recordset is open, close it.
    ' Otherwise, create it.
    If Not grst Is Nothing Then
        grst.Close
    Else
        Set grst = New ADODB.Recordset
    End If
```

```
        ' Use a client cursor to support batch updates
        grst.CursorLocation = adUseClient
        grst.Open "Shippers", _
         "Provider=SQLOLEDB.1;Server=(local);" & _
         "Initial Catalog=Northwind;User ID=sa", _
         adOpenDynamic, adLockOptimistic
        lboShippers.Clear
        ' Walk the recordset, displaying each record
        Do Until grst.EOF
            lboShippers.AddItem grst(0) & " " & _
             grst(1) & " " & grst(2)
            grst.MoveNext
        Loop
        gfLoading = False
        ' Highlight the first record
        lboShippers.ListIndex = 0
    End Sub
```

Once the recordset is loaded, this code moves through each record, concatenating all the fields and placing the concatenated strings in a list box. Note that the CursorLocation property of the recordset is set to adUseClient to support batch updating.

When a record is selected in the list box, the code uses the recordset's Find method to display the details of the appropriate record in the text boxes on the form:

```
    Private Sub lboShippers_Click()
        ' Find the record that's been selected and
        ' move its data to the textboxes
        Dim strCriteria As String

        strCriteria = "ShipperID = " & _
         Left(lboShippers.Text, 1)
        grst.MoveFirst
        grst.Find strCriteria
        If Not grst.EOF Then
            txtShipperID = grst.Fields("ShipperID")
            txtCompanyName = grst.Fields("CompanyName")
            txtPhone = grst.Fields("Phone")
        End If
    End Sub
```

Because the ShipperID field is an identity field, it can't be edited by the user. For this reason, the Enabled property of the txtShipperID text box is set to False. The other two text boxes have code attached to their Change events to push any changes from the user interface back to the recordset:

```
Private Sub txtCompanyName_Change()
    ' Save changes back to the recordset
    If Not gfLoading Then
        grst.Fields("CompanyName") = _
        txtCompanyName.Text
    End If
End Sub

Private Sub txtPhone_Change()
    ' Save changes back to the recordset
    If Not gfLoading Then
        grst.Fields("Phone") = _
        txtPhone.Text
    End If
End Sub
```

The command buttons on the form simply call the corresponding recordset methods:

```
Private Sub cmdAddnew_Click()
    ' Add a new record and clear the
    ' textboxes to accept the details
    grst.AddNew
    txtShipperID = ""
    txtCompanyName = ""
    txtPhone = ""
End Sub

Private Sub cmdDelete_Click()
    ' Delete the current record
    grst.Delete
    GetRecordset
End Sub

Private Sub cmdUpdate_Click()
    ' Update the current record
    grst.Update
    GetRecordset
```

```
End Sub

Private Sub cmdUpdateBatch_Click()
    ' Update all cached records
    grst.UpdateBatch
    GetRecordset
End Sub
```

The Supports Method

As you've seen throughout this chapter, not all recordsets are created equal. When you take into account the different ways that you can open recordsets, the various permutations of the CursorLocation, CursorType, LockType, and Options properties, and the different potential OLE DB providers that can be supplying the data, it can be difficult to be sure just which methods will work on which recordsets. Fortunately, ADO provides the Supports method, which allows you to query a recordset as to the functionality that it supports.

The Supports method returns True or False for specific options:

```
fReturn = rst.Supports(Option)
```

where Option is one of the intrinsic constants shown in Table 8.5.

TABLE 8.5: Constants for the Supports Method

Option	Returns True if...
adAddNew	You can use the AddNew method to add records to this recordset.
adApproxPosition	You can use the AbsolutePosition and AbsolutePage properties with this recordset.
adBookmark	You can use the Bookmark property with this recordset.
adDelete	You can use the Delete method to delete records from this recordset.
adFind	You can use the Find method to find records in this recordset.
adHoldRecords	You can change the recordset position without committing changes to the current record. This is necessary for batch updates.
adIndex	You can use the Index property to set an index for this recordset.
adMovePrevious	You can use MoveFirst and MovePrevious, or the Move method, to move backwards in this recordset.

Continued on next page

TABLE 8.5 CONTINUED: Constants for the Supports Method

Option	Returns True if...
adNotify	This recordset supports events.
adResync	You can use the Resync method to resynchronize this recordset with the underlying data.
adSeek	You can use the Seek method to find records in this recordset.
adUpdate	You can use the Update method to modify records in this recordset.
adUpdateBatch	You can use the UpdateBatch and CancelBatch methods on this recordset.

Working with Persisted Recordsets

If you're familiar with DAO or RDO, you might think of recordsets as entities that exist only in memory during the course of an application. ADO adds the ability to persist a recordset to a file on disk or to a Stream object. In fact, you can persist a recordset, later reopen it, edit it, reconnect it to the original data source, and save changes.

Saving a Recordset

To persist a recordset to disk for later use, you call its Save method:

```
rst.SaveDestination, PersistFormat
```

The Destination parameter is the full path and filename to the file that you wish to use to hold the contents of this recordset. The PersistFormat parameter is one of two intrinsic constants:

- adPersistADTG is the default. This saves the recordset in the Microsoft proprietary Advanced Data Tablegram format.

- adPersistXML can be specified to save the recordset as XML. If you save the recordset in XML format, you can open it directly in an advanced Web browser such as Internet Explorer 5.

ADTG files are smaller than XML files, so unless you need the advanced browser connection, stick to ADTG.

For an example of saving a recordset, see the frmPersist form in the ADOCode sample project. This procedure opens a recordset on the authors table from the SQL Server pubs database and saves it to an XML file:

```
Private Sub cmdSaveRecordset_Click()
    ' Save a recordset to disk
    Dim rst As New ADODB.Recordset
    Dim strFile As String
    ' Open the recordset from the database
    rst.CursorLocation = adUseClient
    rst.Open "SELECT * FROM authors", _
     "Provider=SQLOLEDB.1;" & _
     "Data Source=(local);" & _
     "Initial Catalog=pubs;" & _
     "User ID=sa", _
     adOpenStatic, adLockPessimistic
    ' Construct a file name
    strFile = App.Path & "\authors.xml"
    ' Destroy any existing file
    On Error Resume Next
    Kill strFile
    On Error GoTo 0
    ' Now save the recordset to disk
    rst.Save strFile, adPersistXML
    ' And remove it from memory
    rst.Close
    Set rst = Nothing
End Sub
```

Figure 8.2 shows the resulting XML file open in Internet Explorer 5. While XML is beyond the scope of this book, you can see that the XML encoding includes both schema and data information for the recordset.

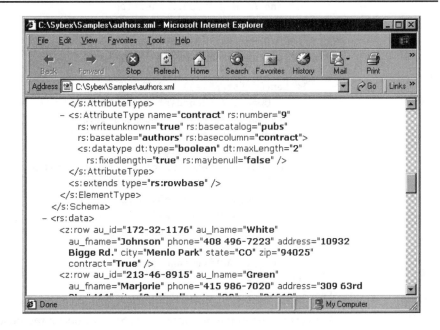

If you save a recordset and continue to work with it, updating records, your changes are written to the disk file whenever you call the Update method, until you call the recordset's Close method. When the Save method is invoked, the current record is reset to the first record in the recordset.

Some providers don't support the functionality necessary to save a recordset. If you have this problem, you can always set the CursorLocation property to adUseClient to create a client-side cursor.

Loading a Saved Recordset

To retrieve a saved recordset, you use the Open method of the recordset object. As the Source parameter, you supply the name of the disk file that contains the previously saved recordset. You don't have to create a Connection object when you reopen the recordset. Here's an example from the frmPersist form in the ADOCode sample database:

```
Private Sub cmdLoadRecordset_Click()
    ' Load a previously-saved recordset
    Dim rst As New ADODB.Recordset
```

```
Dim cnn As New ADODB.Connection
Dim strFile As String
' Construct a file name
strFile = App.Path & "\authors.xml"
' Make sure the file exists
If Len(Dir(strFile)) > 0 Then
    ' Open the recordset from the file
    rst.Open strFile, , adOpenStatic, _
     adLockPessimistic
    ' Show that we've got data
    MsgBox rst.RecordCount & " records found"
    ' Reconnect it to the database
    cnn.Open "Provider=SQLOLEDB.1;" & _
     "Data Source=(local);" & _
     "Initial Catalog=pubs;" & _
     "User ID=sa"
    Set rst.ActiveConnection = cnn
End If
End Sub
```

As you can see in the previous code, to reconnect a recordset to a database, you set the recordset's ActiveConnection property to a valid Connection object for the database. Once you've done this, you can update the recordset just like any other recordset.

WARNING   Cursor options are not persisted as part of a saved recordset. Be sure to specify the cursor type and locking type when you reopen a saved recordset. Otherwise, you'll get a default forward-only, read-only recordset.

Advanced Operations

ADO includes a number of methods to perform more complex data operations than those that you've already seen in this chapter. In the remainder of the chapter, you'll learn about two of these capabilities. First, I'll take a look at the use of asynchronous operations to avoid blocking program execution on slow connections. Next, I'll cover the use of batch updating, with emphasis on the things that you can do to deal with conflicts between client-side and server-side changes to your data.

Asynchronous Operations and ADO Events

With the rise of two-tier, three-tier, and intranet/Internet database applications, it's a fact of life that retrieving data can be a relatively slow operation. Fortunately, the designers of ADO recognized this fact and have implemented asynchronous operations to help out. Dealing with data asynchronously doesn't get the data back any faster, but it does mean that your entire application doesn't lock up during the time that ADO is performing an operation. In this section, I'll show you the three things you can do asynchronously in ADO:

- Make a connection

- Execute a command

- Retrieve a recordset

To perform any of these options asynchronously, you must be able to monitor the events of the associated object. That means that you'll need to declare your object with the Visual Basic WithEvents keyword, which in turn means that the object must be declared with module-level scope.

To perform an asynchronous connection, you must use the adAsyncConnect option when you execute the Connection object's Open method. For example, here's some code from the frmAsynchronous form in the ADOCode sample application:

```
Private WithEvents mcnn As ADODB.Connection

Private Sub Form_Load()
    txtConnectionString.Text = _
     "Provider=SQLOLEDB.1;" & _
     "Data Source=BIGREDBARN;" & _
     "Initial Catalog=Northwind;" & _
     "User ID=sa"
End Sub

Private Sub cmdConnect_Click()
    Set mcnn = New ADODB.Connection
    mcnn.ConnectionString = _
     txtConnectionString.Text
    mcnn.Open , , , adAsyncConnect
End Sub
```

```
Private Sub mcnn_ConnectComplete( _
 ByVal pError As ADODB.Error, _
 adStatus As ADODB.EventStatusEnum, _
 ByVal pConnection As ADODB.Connection)
    If adStatus = adStatusOK Then
        MsgBox "Connection is complete"
    Else
        MsgBox "Connection error: " & _
          pError.Description
    End If
End Sub

Private Sub mcnn_InfoMessage( _
 ByVal pError As ADODB.Error, _
 adStatus As ADODB.EventStatusEnum, _
 ByVal pConnection As ADODB.Connection)
    txtInfoMessage.Text = _
      pError.Description
End Sub
```

When you open the form, a text box on the user interface is filled in with a sample connection string (you'll need to modify this unless your SQL Server just happens to be named BIGREDBARN). Clicking the Connect button tells ADO to open a connection, using whatever string is currently displayed, and to make the connection asynchronously. If you like, you could perform other operations in code in this same procedure; they would not be blocked while waiting for the Open method to complete.

When the connection is made, or when ADO gives up trying to make the connection, the connection's ConnectComplete event is fired. Note that the name is somewhat misleading: this event will occur even if the connection is never completed, as soon as ADO decides there is a problem (try using the name of a nonexistent server or nonexistent database in your connection string to see this).

There's also an InfoMessage event. This event is specified to occur if the OLE DB provider emits a warning during the connection operation. You'll seldom if ever see this event with the Microsoft providers.

Both of these events supply the same three parameters: an Error object containing information on any error that occurred during the operation, a status value that contains further information on the events, and a pointer to the Connection object firing the event. The adStatus parameter can have five possible values in these and other events (not all of these values are sensible for all events):

- adStatusOK indicates that the operation was successful.

- adStatusErrorsOccurred indicates that the operation failed. In this case, you should examine the pError object or the pConnection.Errors collection for further information.

- adStatusCantDeny indicates that you tried to cancel an event that can't be cancelled. This value might be set by ADO after you've set the adStatus parameter in a previous occurrence of the event to adStatusCancel.

- adStatusCancel is a value that you can set within the event procedure. If you set the adStatus parameter to adStatusCancel, the event tells ADO to cancel the operation that caused the event in the first place.

- adStatusUnwantedEvent is another value that you can set within your event procedure code. By returning this value to ADO, you notify ADO that you don't want this event to continue firing for the duration of this operation.

To execute a command asynchronously, you simply execute it on a connection that's already been opened asynchronously. Here's an example from the frm Asynchronous form in the ADOCode sample project:

```
Private Sub cmdExecute_Click()
    ' Execute a command asynchronously
    Dim cmd As New ADODB.Command
    Dim rst As ADODB.Recordset
    cmd.CommandText = _
     txtCommandText.Text
    Set cmd.ActiveConnection = mcnn
    Set rst = cmd.Execute()
End Sub

Private Sub mcnn_WillExecute(Source As String, _
 CursorType As ADODB.CursorTypeEnum, _
 LockType As ADODB.LockTypeEnum, _
 Options As Long, _
 adStatus As ADODB.EventStatusEnum, _
 ByVal pCommand As ADODB.Command, _
 ByVal pRecordset As ADODB.Recordset, _
 ByVal pConnection As ADODB.Connection)
    MsgBox "About to execute " & Source
```

```
End Sub

Private Sub mcnn_ExecuteComplete( _
 ByVal RecordsAffected As Long, _
 ByVal pError As ADODB.Error, _
 adStatus As ADODB.EventStatusEnum, _
 ByVal pCommand As ADODB.Command, _
 ByVal pRecordset As ADODB.Recordset, _
 ByVal pConnection As ADODB.Connection)
    If adStatus = adStatusOK Then
        MsgBox "Command Executed"
    Else
        MsgBox "Command execution error: " & _
          pError.Description
    End If
End Sub
```

Once again, there are two events of interest here. The WillExecute event fires every time you try to execute a command on the connection whose events are being trapped. This is especially useful in situations where the user can submit ad hoc commands that you might want to examine before allowing. If you set the adStatus parameter in this event to adStatusCancel, the command won't be sent to the data source.

The ExecuteComplete event fires when the command is completed, either successfully or unsuccessfully. Again, you need to check the adStatus parameter to determine why the event was fired.

To open a recordset asynchronously, you specify the adAsyncFetch constant when you call the Recordset object's Open method. Here's an example from frmAsynchronous in the ADOCode sample project. It assumes you've already opened the connection to the database:

```
Private WithEvents mrst As ADODB.Recordset

Private Sub cmdOpen_Click()
    ' Open a recordset asynchronously
    Set mrst = New ADODB.Recordset
    mrst.ActiveConnection = mcnn
    mrst.CursorLocation = adUseClient
    mrst.CacheSize = 10
    mrst.Open txtSource.Text, , adOpenKeyset, , _
      adAsyncFetch
```

```
End Sub

Private Sub mrst_FetchComplete( _
 ByVal pError As ADODB.Error, _
 adStatus As ADODB.EventStatusEnum, _
 ByVal pRecordset As ADODB.Recordset)
    If adStatus = adStatusOK Then
        MsgBox "Fetch is complete"
    Else
        MsgBox "Recordset error: " & _
          pError.Description
    End If
End Sub

Private Sub mrst_FetchProgress( _
 ByVal Progress As Long, _
 ByVal MaxProgress As Long, _
 adStatus As ADODB.EventStatusEnum, _
 ByVal pRecordset As ADODB.Recordset)
    txtProgress = "Fetched " & Progress & _
      " of " & MaxProgress
End Sub
```

For an asynchronous fetch, you should use client-side cursors. You may also want to set the CacheSize property, as shown here, to specify the number of records to be retrieved at a time. The FetchProgress event will be fired as the records are being retrieved, and the FetchComplete event will be fired when all the records are retrieved.

The ADO documentation states that you must be using Visual Basic 6.0 or higher for FetchProgress and FetchComplete to fire. I've found that FetchProgress is unreliable even with Visual Basic 6.0.

Batch Updates and Conflicts

Batch updating, like most other programming techniques, has its good side and its bad side. On the good side, you can cache multiple changes on the client until you're ready to submit them to the server, and so cut down on potentially slow and expensive client-server round-trips. On the bad side, in a multiuser environment (which most multiple-tier environments are), the longer you cache changes the more chance that someone else will have changed a record that you were both working with.

ADO provides two methods to deal with record conflicts while batch updating. You can use the Resync method of the Recordset object to investigate changes on the server before submitting your changes. Alternatively, you can use the Filter method to determine which (if any) changes failed after calling the Batch-Update method. I'll work through both of these methods in the remainder of this chapter.

Using Resync to Detect Potential Conflicts

As you might guess, the Resync method is used to resynchronize client and server recordsets. The syntax is:

```
Recordset.Resync AffectRecords, ResyncValues
```

The AffectRecords argument takes one of four values:

- adAffectCurrent to resynchronize only the current record

- adAffectGroup to resynchronize all records matching the current Filter setting

- adAffectAll to resynchronize the entire recordset

- adAffectAllChapters to resynchronize multiple recordsets in a hierarchical recordset

The ResyncValues can be either adResyncAllValues (the default) or adResync-UnderlyingValues. If you choose adResyncAllValues, the client recordset is made to match the server recordset, and any pending updates are cancelled. This isn't what you'd want to do when checking the potential of update conflicts, of course. The alternative, adResyncUnderlyingValues, retrieves data from the server but stores it in the UnderlyingValue property instead of the Value property.

An example from the frmConflict form in the ADOCode sample project will help make this clear:

```
Private Sub cmdResync_Click()
    ' Open two recordsets, change both, and
    ' demonstrate the Resync method
    Dim rst1 As New ADODB.Recordset
    Dim rst2 As New ADODB.Recordset

    lboResults.Clear
```

```vb
' Retrieve the records on one connection
rst1.CursorLocation = adUseClient
rst1.Open "Customers", _
 "Provider=SQLOLEDB.1;Server=(local);" & _
 "Initial Catalog=Northwind;User ID=sa", _
 adOpenDynamic, adLockBatchOptimistic
rst1.MoveFirst

' And on another connection
rst2.CursorLocation = adUseClient
rst2.Open "Customers", _
 "Provider=SQLOLEDB.1;Server=(local);" & _
 "Initial Catalog=Northwind;User ID=sa", _
 adOpenDynamic, adLockBatchOptimistic
rst2.MoveFirst

' Change and commit from the first recordset
rst1.Fields("ContactTitle") = "SalesRep"
rst1.UpdateBatch
lboResults.AddItem _
 "Title changed to SalesRep on server"

' Now change the second recordset
rst2.Fields("ContactTitle") = "Representative"
lboResults.AddItem _
 "Title changed to Representative on client"

' Resync the changes
rst2.Resync adAffectAll, _
 adResyncUnderlyingValues

' And show the results
lboResults.AddItem _
 "Value = " & rst2.Fields("ContactTitle").Value
lboResults.AddItem _
 "Original Value = " & _
 rst2.Fields("ContactTitle").OriginalValue
lboResults.AddItem _
 "Underlying Value = " & _
 rst2.Fields("ContactTitle").UnderlyingValue

End Sub
```

This procedure starts by opening two recordsets on the same data. Since these recordsets are using implicit connections, they each get their own connection to the database, and it's perfectly possible to make independent changes on each recordset. Both recordsets are opened on the client with batch-optimistic locking, to enable batch updating.

First, the code makes a change to the first record in rst1 and uses the Update-Batch method to save this change back to the server. Then it makes a conflicting change to the same record in rst2. Rather than call the UpdateBatch method, though, the code calls the Resync method to investigate the properties of this field. If you run the code, you'll see results similar to these:

```
Value = Representative
Original Value = Sales Representative
Underlying Value = SalesRep
```

This tells you that, although the original value on the server was "Sales Representative," it's now "SalesRep," indicating that another user changed the record during the course of your edits. How you'd respond to this in code, of course, depends on the business logic that you're trying to implement. You might want to save your updates anyhow, or you might want to warn the user that there had been a change and perform a full Resync operation to reset to the values currently on the server.

Using Filter to Detect Actual Conflicts

As an alternative, you might just go ahead and call the UpdateBatch method after making whatever changes are necessary to your copy of the recordset. In this case, if there are any conflicts (records that have already been changed by another user), ADO will ignore those records in your changes, although it will save all the other changes. ADO will also raise an error for your Visual Basic code to intercept.

But then what? The best answer is to use the Filter property of the Recordset object to see exactly what records failed to update. To see this technique, you can examine frmConflict in the ADOCode sample project:

```
Private Sub cmdFilter_Click()
    ' Open two recordsets, change both, and
    ' demonstrate the Filter method
    Dim rst1 As New ADODB.Recordset
    Dim rst2 As New ADODB.Recordset

    On Error GoTo HandleErr
```

```
        lboResults.Clear

        ' Retrieve the records on one connection
        rst1.CursorLocation = adUseClient
        rst1.Open "Customers", _
         "Provider=SQLOLEDB.1;Server=(local);" & _
         "Initial Catalog=Northwind;User ID=sa", _
         adOpenDynamic, adLockBatchOptimistic
        rst1.MoveFirst

        ' And on another connection
        rst2.CursorLocation = adUseClient
        rst2.Open "Customers", _
         "Provider=SQLOLEDB.1;Server=(local);" & _
         "Initial Catalog=Northwind;User ID=sa", _
         adOpenDynamic, adLockBatchOptimistic
        rst2.MoveFirst

        ' Change and commit from the first recordset
        rst1.Fields("ContactTitle") = "SalesCritter"
        rst1.UpdateBatch
        lboResults.AddItem _
         "Title changed to SalesCritter on server"

        ' Now change the second recordset
        rst2.Fields("ContactTitle") = "New Rep"
        lboResults.AddItem _
         "Title changed to New Rep on client"

        ' Update the changes to the server
        rst2.UpdateBatch

ExitHere:
    Exit Sub

HandleErr:
    rst2.Filter = adFilterConflictingRecords
    lboResults.AddItem _
     "In error handler, " & rst2.RecordCount & _
     " record(s) conflicting"
    Resume ExitHere
End Sub
```

This code performs the same operations as the previous example, up to the point where the second recordset is changed. Then, instead of checking to see whether the changes can be saved, it simply calls the UpdateBatch method to try to save them. This will cause a runtime error, which will be thrown into the error-handling routine.

This routine sets the Filter property of the recordset in question to adFilterConflictingRecords. This tells ADO to rework the recordset, keeping only the records that didn't update successfully. You could then take necessary action, such as prompting the user or resyncing and then resaving changes.

The Filter property is designed for flexibility. Although this is the first time you've seen the filter property in this book, there are other ways that it can be useful. Table 8.6 shows the possible values that you can set for this property.

TABLE 8.6: Filter Property Values

Value	Meaning
Criterion string (such as "LastName = 'Butler'")	Filters the recordset to include only records matching the specified criterion.
Array of Bookmarks	Filters the recordset to include only records matching the supplied bookmarks.
" " (Zero-length string)	Removes any filters and returns all records to the recordset.
adFilterNone	Removes any filters and returns all records to the recordset.
adFilterPendingRecords	Filters the recordset to hold only records with changes that have not yet been sent to the server.
adFilterAffectedRecords	Filters the recordset to hold only records that were changed by the last call to the Delete, Resync, UpdateBatch, or CancelBatch method.
adFilterFetchedRecords	Filters the recordset to hold only the most recent records placed in the record cache.
adFilterConflictingRecords	Filters the recordset to hold only the records that failed to update in an UpdateBatch operation.

CHAPTER
NINE

Creating and Using Visual Basic Data Consumers

- ■ What Is a Data Consumer?

- ■ Data-Aware Classes

- ■ Data-Aware UserControls

- ■ Using the DataRepeater Control

Back in Chapter 5, you learned how to use bound controls with the ADO Data control to easily retrieve data from any OLE DB data provider. In previous versions of Visual Basic (through Visual Basic 5), that was pretty much the whole story when it came to data binding: you used a data control to provide data and intrinsic Visual Basic controls (text boxes, combo boxes, and so on) to show data, with data binding providing the connection between the two. But that was all that data binding was good for.

Visual Basic 6 extends the reach of data binding by allowing you to use it programmatically. You can create both data consumers and data sources and bind one to the other in code. Your own components can play either or both roles in the data binding relationship. In this chapter, you'll see how easy it is to create a data consumer. In Chapter 13, you'll learn how to create your own data sources as well.

What Is a Data Consumer?

A data consumer is any Visual Basic component that can accept data from a data source. In other words, it can be the target of a data binding relationship. Using Visual Basic 6, you can create objects and UserControls that function as data consumers. You do this by setting the DataBindingBehavior property of the class to an appropriate value:

- vbNone (the default) indicates that this class is not a data consumer.

- vbSimpleBound indicates that the class is a simple binding data consumer. A simple binding consumer is one that can be bound to a single data field. For example, the intrinsic TextBox control is simple bound.

- vbComplexBound indicates that the class is a complex binding data consumer. A complex binding consumer is one that can be bound to an entire row of data. For example, the Hierarchical FlexGrid control is complex bound. It might look like the control is bound to an entire recordset, but that's an illusion caused by it fetching multiple rows to display. Only one row is current at a time.

To use these new properties, you need to add some references to your Visual Basic project. A reference to the Microsoft Data Binding Collection is necessary for simple data binding, and a reference to the Microsoft Data Source Interfaces is necessary for complex data binding. If you choose the Data Project choice when you create a new Visual Basic project, these references are added automatically. If you need to add them by hand, just search for them in the References dialog box available from Project ➢ References.

In the following sections, you'll learn how to create both classes and data controls that can be bound.

Data-Aware Classes

You can create a class that's either simple bound or complex bound to data. By setting appropriate properties at run time, you can then bind an instance of such a class to any data source in your project.

Simple Binding with a Class

The first example is the easiest to understand. If you open the frmSimpleClass form in the DataConsumer sample, you'll find a form with an ADO Data control and a text box. As you use the navigation buttons on the ADO Data control to move through the underlying recordset (in this case, the Customers table from the Jet version of the Northwind database), the text box is continually updated to show the CompanyName field. This could be done just by binding the text box to the ADO Data control, but it's not. Rather, the text box is displaying information from an instance of the clsSimpleExample class, which is itself bound to the ADO Data control.

There's not much code in the class itself:

```
Private mstrName As String
Public Property Get Name() As String
    Name = mstrName
End Property
Public Property Let Name(NewName As String)
    mstrName = NewName
End Property
```

As you can see, this is just a class that exposes a single persistent read-write property named Name. The key, though, is something that doesn't show in code: the DataBindingBehavior property for the class is set to vbSimpleBound in the property sheet for the class.

The code behind the form makes use of the new BindingCollection object:

```
Private mobjBindingCollection As BindingCollection
Private mobjSimpleExample As clsSimpleExample

Private Sub Form_Load()
    ' Create the objects we need
    Set mobjBindingCollection = New BindingCollection
    Set mobjSimpleExample = New clsSimpleExample
    ' Tell the binding collection where to get data
    Set mobjBindingCollection.DataSource = _
    Me!AdodcCustomers
    ' And add a binding
    mobjBindingCollection.Add mobjSimpleExample, _
        "Name", "CompanyName"
End Sub

Private Sub AdodcCustomers_MoveComplete( _
 ByVal adReason As ADODB.EventReasonEnum, _
 ByVal pError As ADODB.Error, _
 adStatus As ADODB.EventStatusEnum, _
 ByVal pRecordset As ADODB.Recordset)
    Me!txtName = mobjSimpleExample.Name
End Sub
```

The BindingCollection object is the mechanism that Visual Basic uses to expose the internals of the data binding process. A BindingCollection object takes information from its DataSource property and supplies that information to all members of its internal collection of Binding objects. To add a new Binding object, you use the Add method of the BindingCollection:

```
BindingCollection.Add(Object As Object, _
  [PropertyName As String], _
  [DataField As String], _
  [DataFormat As IDataFormatDisp],
  [Key As String]) As Binding
```

Object   Represents any data consumer. In this example, this is an instance of the clsSimpleExample class.

PropertyName   Is the name of the property on the data consumer that should be bound. In this example, this is the Name property (the only property that clsSimpleExample exposes).

DataField   Is a field from the DataSource property of the BindingCollection object that you're working with. In this case, it's the CompanyName field.

DataFormat   Is an optional object that specifies a format for the display of the data.

Key   Is an optional key into the collection of Bindings. This is most useful if you have a single data source bound to multiple data consumers and wish to work with the properties of an individual consumer.

So, to recap:

1.   When you open the frmSimpleClass form, it creates an instance of the clsSimpleExample class and a new BindingCollection object.

2.   The form then specifies the location of its data by setting the DataSource property of the BindingCollection object to the ADO Data control that's sitting on the form.

3.   The class then gets hooked to the other side of the BindingCollection object by using that object's Add method to add a binding.

4.   Whenever you navigate to a new record using the ADO Data control, the control's MoveComplete event fires.

5.   In the event procedure for the MoveComplete event, the current value of the Name property of the class is retrieved and displayed in the text box on the form.

WARNING   Neither the intrinsic Visual Basic Data control nor the RDO-based Remote Data control can be bound programmatically—yet another reason to switch to ADO for data access.

Complex Binding with a Class

A class with complex data binding can bind to an entire recordset at once. For example, the frmComplexClass form in the DataConsumer sample project demonstrates binding an instance of a class to a recordset delivered by a Command object in a Data Environment.

The code in this case is a bit more complex (no surprise!) than that for the simple data binding case. Here's the class module:

```
Private WithEvents mrst As ADODB.Recordset

Public Property Get DataSource() As DataSource
    Set DataSource = mrst.DataSource
End Property
Public Property Set DataSource( _
 ByVal NewDataSource As DataSource)
    Set mrst.DataSource = NewDataSource
End Property

Public Property Get DataMember() As DataMember
    DataMember = mrst.DataMember
End Property
Public Property Let DataMember( _
 ByVal NewDataMember As DataMember)
    mrst.DataMember = NewDataMember
End Property

Public Property Get FirstFiveRows() As String
    Dim fld As ADODB.Field
    Dim strTemp As String
    Dim intI As Integer
    mrst.MoveFirst
    For Each fld In mrst.Fields
        strTemp = strTemp & fld.Name & vbTab
    Next fld
    strTemp = strTemp & vbCrLf
    For intI = 1 To 5
        For Each fld In mrst.Fields
            If fld.Type = adBinary Then
                strTemp = strTemp & _
                "<Long Binary>" & vbTab
```

```
            Else
                strTemp = strTemp & _
                CStr(fld.Value & "") & vbTab
            End If
        Next fld
        strTemp = strTemp & vbCrLf
        mrst.MoveNext
    Next intI
    FirstFiveRows = strTemp
End Property

Private Sub Class_Initialize()
    Set mrst = New ADODB.Recordset
End Sub
```

Classes that implement complex data binding must expose DataMember and DataSource properties, just like any other data consumer that can bind to an entire recordset (for example, a grid control). The DataMember and DataSource datatypes are provided by the Microsoft Data Source Interfaces type library. Of course, the DataBindingBehavior property of this class is set to vbComplexBound.

This class functions by maintaining an internal, hidden ADO recordset that will be populated by the data source that the class instance is bound to. When you set the DataMember and DataSource properties (in that order), this recordset is automatically initialized from the specified data source.

In the case of the DataConsumer sample, those properties are set when the form is loaded, and serve to connect the instance of the class to a Data Environment command that draws its data from the SQL Server version of the Northwind database:

```
Private mobjComplexExample As clsComplexExample
Private Sub Form_Load()
    ChangeTabs Me!Text1, 14
    Set mobjComplexExample = New clsComplexExample
    With mobjComplexExample
        .DataMember = "Orders"
        Set .DataSource = deNorthwindSQL
    End With
    Text1 = mobjComplexExample.FirstFiveRows
End Sub
```

The FirstFiveRows method of the class demonstrates the ability to retrieve data from the recordset.

NOTE

Note that the DataMember property is scalar. That is, it does not require the Set keyword.

Data-Aware UserControls

While data-aware classes are interesting, you're more likely to want data-aware UserControls in a real application. The most typical use of bound data is to build up a user interface on a form, and of course UserControls are the perfect tool to encapsulate a combination of user interface elements and functionality. In this section, you'll see how to build UserControls that can bind to a field or a recordset.

Simple Binding with a UserControl

You might think that simple binding with a UserControl would be as easy as adding a DataField property to the UserControl and properly delegating it . . . but you'd be wrong. The Visual Basic developers chose to hide the details of setting up a DataField property by adding this property to the Extender object, which is used to supply stock properties for all UserControls (for example, the Top property is an Extender property). What this means to you is that setting up simple binding is a matter of making proper settings in several different places. The good news is that once you learn how to set it up, it works.

The frmSimpleControl form in the DataConsumer sample project demonstrates a simple bound UserControl. You'll find the control itself saved as SimpleControl in the DataConsumerControls project. In this case, the interface of the control supplies a text box and a tabstrip. The bound data shows up in the text box, and the tabstrip is set to the first letter of the data. (In the sample, clicking a different letter doesn't do anything, though obviously you could extend it to, for example, search for records starting with that letter.) Figure 9.1 shows the frmSimpleControl form in action, reading records from the Jet version of the Northwind Traders database.

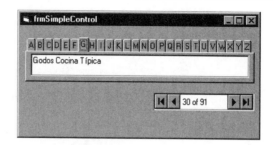

Here are the essential steps for making the constituent text box in the UserControl available for simple data binding:

1. Create a new UserControl and set its DataBindingBehavior property to vbSimpleBound.

2. Place a TextBox control within the UserControl.

3. If you haven't already done so, use the Add-In Manager to load the ActiveX Control Interface Wizard.

4. Using the ActiveX Control Interface Wizard, add a Text property to the UserControl. Map this property to the Text property of the constituent TextBox control.

5. With the UserControl selected, choose Tools ➤ Procedure Attributes. Select the Text procedure and click the Advanced button. Select the check boxes for Property Is Data Bound, This Property Binds To DataField, and Property Will Call CanPropertyChange Before Changing. Figure 9.2 shows how this dialog box should look for the property that you want to be bound for the UserControl.

6. Write code to save the value of the Text property whenever it's changed, whether it's changed by setting the property programmatically or by the user typing a new value into the constituent text box:

```
Private Sub txtData_Change()
    Me.Text = txtData.Text
End Sub
Public Property Let Text(ByVal New_Text As String)
    If CanPropertyChange("Text") Then
        txtData.Text() = New_Text
        PropertyChanged "Text"
    End If
End Property
```

FIGURE 9.2:

Setting the Data Binding
properties for a User
Control

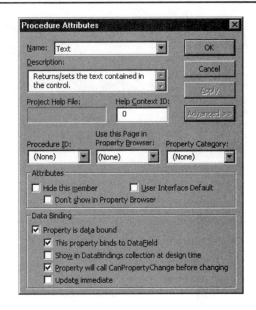

If you've worked with UserControls in the past, you'll know that the Property-Changed method is used to notify the control's container that a new value for some property needs to be saved. However, that's not quite what's going on here. The Visual Basic development team chose to overload this method, using it for a second purpose: If the property is bound, calling the PropertyChanged method tells the data source that there's changed data ready to write back to the database.

The CanPropertyChange method, in theory, is used to check whether or not the data source is read only. Although it should return False if the data is read only, in Visual Basic 6 it always returns True. Fortunately, Visual Basic 6 won't raise an error if you call PropertyChanged on a read-only data source. You could leave the check of CanPropertyChange out of your code entirely, but it's insurance for some future version when it will actually work as advertised.

Multiple Simple Bindings in the Same UserControl

You may also find that you need to bind multiple fields to a single UserControl. This is the case, for example, when you're building a composite control to enforce a uniform user interface for certain data across multiple applications. In this case, you'll need to use a DataBindings collection, but UserControls are set up to let you do this without writing any code.

The frmMultipleControl form in the DataConsumer sample project demonstrates this technique, using the MultipleControl UserControl from the DataConsumerControls project. As with the previous example, the DataBindingBehavior property of the control is set to vbSimpleBound. However, with this control, there are three text boxes on the user interface, each tied to a separate property of the control: Address, City, and Country.

Within the control itself, there's delegation code to handle all three of these properties, as well as to manage the PropertyChanged notifications when someone changes any value:

```
Public Property Get Address() As String
    Address = txtAddress.Text
End Property
Public Property Let Address(ByVal New_Address As String)
    If CanPropertyChange("Address") Then
        txtAddress.Text() = New_Address
        PropertyChanged "Address"
    End If
End Property

Public Property Get City() As String
    City = txtCity.Text
End Property
Public Property Let City(ByVal New_City As String)
    If CanPropertyChange("City") Then
        txtCity.Text() = New_City
        PropertyChanged "City"
    End If
End Property

Public Property Get Country() As String
    Country = txtCountry.Text
End Property
Public Property Let Country(ByVal New_Country As String)
    If CanPropertyChange("Country") Then
        txtCountry.Text() = New_Country
        PropertyChanged "Country"
    End If
```

```
End Property

Private Sub txtAddress_Change()
    Me.Address = txtAddress.Text
End Sub

Private Sub txtCity_Change()
    Me.City = txtCity.Text
End Sub

Private Sub txtCountry_Change()
    Me.Country = txtCountry.Text
End Sub
```

As with the single-field control, you use the Tools ➢ Procedure Attributes menu to set the data binding properties of the control. For each of the three properties, select the Property Is Data Bound, Show In DataBindings Collection At Design Time, and Property Will Call CanPropertyChange Before Changing check boxes. For one of the properties (it doesn't matter which one), you need to also select the This Property Binds To DataField check box. This will become the default bound property for the control. More importantly, though, Visual Basic won't assign a DataSource property to the control if you miss this step.

By setting the properties to appear in the DataBindings collection at design time, you can avoid having to write any code to populate that collection at run time. Instead, when you site an instance of the control on a form, you can click the ellipsis button in the control's DataBindings property in the properties window to open the Data Bindings dialog box. This dialog box, shown in Figure 9.3, lets you assign data properties to each of the control's bound properties.

FIGURE 9.3:

The Data Bindings
dialog box

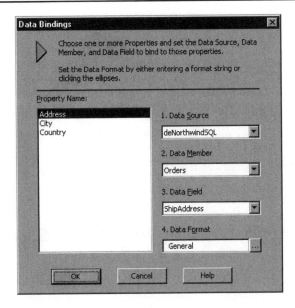

The frmMultipleControl form in the DataConsumer sample project uses a Data Environment to retrieve its data from the SQL Server version of the Northwind sample database. You'll find code behind the form that allows the command buttons to navigate through the recordset returned by the Orders command within this Data Environment:

```
Private Sub cmdFirst_Click()
    deNorthwindSQL.rsOrders.MoveFirst
End Sub

Private Sub cmdLast_Click()
    deNorthwindSQL.rsOrders.MoveLast
End Sub

Private Sub cmdNext_Click()
    With deNorthwindSQL.rsOrders
        .MoveNext
        If .EOF Then
            .MoveLast
        End If
    End With
End Sub
```

```
Private Sub cmdPrevious_Click()
    With deNorthwindSQL.rsOrders
        .MovePrevious
        If .BOF Then
            .MoveFirst
        End If
    End With
End Sub
```

Note that you don't have to do anything special to synchronize this navigation with the display in the UserControl. Because they're both attached to the same Command within the same Data Environment, the control and the navigation code automatically work with the same recordset.

Complex Binding with a UserControl

Of course, you may also want to develop a UserControl that uses complex binding—that is, one that binds to an entire row of data at once. This is surprisingly easy once you figure out the trick. To create a complex bound UserControl, you need to follow these steps:

1. Create a new UserControl. Set its DataBindingBehavior property to vbComplexBound.

2. Add at least one intrinsic Visual Basic control that can be bound to the UserControl. You don't have to keep this control, but if you don't add it, the next step won't work.

3. Use the ActiveX Control Interface Wizard from the Add-Ins menu to add DataMember and DataSource properties to your new UserControl.

Note the catch mentioned in Step 2: If you don't have any bindable constituent controls, the ActiveX Control Interface Wizard won't let you add the DataMember and DataSource properties. You don't need to keep the constituent control after you've added the properties, but it has to be there to begin with.

For such a control to be of any use, obviously, you need to have the DataMember and DataSource properties actually do something. Typically, you use them to initialize an internal ADO Recordset object that will then be bound to whatever external data source you use when you instantiate the UserControl. Figure 9.4 shows the frmComplexControl sample form from the DataConsumer sample project, which fleshes out this notion a bit, using the ComplexControl UserControl from the DataConsumerControls sample project.

FIGURE 9.4:

A UserControl with
complex data binding

Some of the code within the ComplexControl UserControl may be of interest. First, there's the code that actually does the work of initializing and managing the internal Recordset object:

```
Private WithEvents mrst As ADODB.Recordset

Private Sub UserControl_Initialize()
    Set mrst = New ADODB.Recordset
End Sub

Public Property Get DataMember() As String
    DataMember = mrst.DataMember
End Property
Public Property Let DataMember( _
 ByVal New_DataMember As String)
    mrst.DataMember = New_DataMember
    PropertyChanged "DataMember"
End Property


Public Property Get DataSource() As DataSource
    Set DataSource = mrst.DataSource
End Property
Public Property Set DataSource( _
 ByVal New_DataSource As DataSource)
    Dim intI As Integer
    Dim intFields As Integer
    Set mrst.DataSource = New_DataSource
    PropertyChanged "DataSource"
    If Text1.Count > 1 Then
        For intI = Text1.Count - 1 To 1 Step -1
            Unload Text1(intI)
        Next intI
    End If
    intFields = mrst.Fields.Count
    If intFields > 0 Then
```

```
        Text1(0).Width = ScaleWidth / intFields
        For intI = 1 To intFields - 1
            Load Text1(intI)
            With Text1(intI)
                .Visible = True
                .Top = 0
                .Width = ScaleWidth / intFields
                .Left = .Width * intI
            End With
        Next intI
    End If
End Property
```

Setting the DataMember and DataSource properties is fairly straightforward, except for the extra work that happens in the Property Set procedure for the DataSource property. The UserControl originally contains only a single TextBox control. When the DataSource is set, the control is able to determine how many fields the target recordset contains and uses this text box as the basis for a control array. This lets the UserControl adapt to any data source.

The UserControl is also designed to proportionately resize all those text boxes so that it can be stretched across a form as appropriate:

```
Private Sub UserControl_Resize()
    Dim intI As Integer
    Dim intBoxes As Integer
    intBoxes = Text1.Count
    For intI = 0 To intBoxes - 1
        With Text1(intI)
            .Width = ScaleWidth / intBoxes
            .Left = .Width * intI
        End With
    Next intI
End Sub
```

And, of course, the UserControl must get data into the text boxes somehow. Since the internal Recordset variable was declared WithEvents, all of its events are available for the code within the UserControl to work with. The logical place to update the user interface is whenever a new record has been completely fetched. Fortunately, the text box array and the recordset's Fields collection have the same indexing, which makes the job simpler:

```
Private Sub mrst_MoveComplete( _
    ByVal adReason As ADODB.EventReasonEnum,  _
```

```
ByVal pError As ADODB.Error, _
adStatus As ADODB.EventStatusEnum, _
ByVal pRecordset As ADODB.Recordset)
    Dim intI As Integer
    On Error Resume Next
    mfLoaded = False
    For intI = 0 To mrst.Fields.Count - 1
        Text1(intI) = mrst.Fields(intI).Value & ""
    Next intI
    mfLoaded = True
End Sub
```

Any changes the user makes through the text boxes have to be written back to the recordset:

```
Private Sub Text1_Change(Index As Integer)
    If mfLoaded Then
        mrst.Fields(Index) = Text1(Index).Text
    End If
End Sub
```

Finally, in this control I've provided wrappers around the Move methods of the bound recordset. This makes it easier to navigate through the recordset when the data source is a Data Environment (or anything else other than a data control):

```
Public Function MoveFirst() As Variant
    If Not mrst Is Nothing Then
        mrst.MoveFirst
    End If
End Function
Public Function MovePrevious() As Variant
    If Not mrst Is Nothing Then
        If Not mrst.BOF Then
            mrst.MovePrevious
        End If
    End If
End Function
Public Function MoveNext() As Variant
    If Not mrst Is Nothing Then
        If Not mrst.EOF Then
            mrst.MoveNext
        End If
    End If
```

```
End Function
Public Function MoveLast() As Variant
    If Not mrst Is Nothing Then
        mrst.MoveLast
    End If
End Function
```

Because the control is complex bound, there's no need to worry about calling the recordset's Update method. Visual Basic will automatically take care of that little bit of bookkeeping whenever there are changes ready to be written.

Given all that work in the control, the code behind frmComplexControl is really rather simple (as it should be, since the purpose of a UserControl is to encapsulate user interface and behavior together):

```
Private Sub cmdFirst_Click()
    ComplexControl1.MoveFirst
End Sub

Private Sub cmdLast_Click()
    ComplexControl1.MoveLast
End Sub

Private Sub cmdNext_Click()
    ComplexControl1.MoveNext
End Sub

Private Sub cmdPrevious_Click()
    ComplexControl1.MovePrevious
End Sub

Private Sub Form_Load()
    With ComplexControl1
        .DataMember = "CustAddress"
        Set .DataSource = deNorthwindSQL
    End With
    deNorthwindSQL.rsCustAddress.MoveFirst
End Sub

Private Sub Form_Resize()
    ComplexControl1.Width = Me.Width
End Sub
```

Using the DataRepeater Control

Visual Basic 6 also includes a new custom control, the DataRepeater control. You can think of the DataRepeater as a helper control. It can't display data by itself, but it can help you build a useful and attractive user interface from other data-bound controls.

Figure 9.5 shows the DataRepeater control in action on frmDataRepeater in the DataConsumer sample project. The DataRepeater itself is the inner rectangle with the scrollbars (everything except the ADO Data control). The text boxes are drawn on the DataRepeater by another custom control.

> **WARNING** In the sample project, this control retrieves data from an Oracle database. If you don't have the Oracle software installed, you'll need to change the properties of the ADO Data control to retrieve data from another source.

FIGURE 9.5:

The DataRepeater control

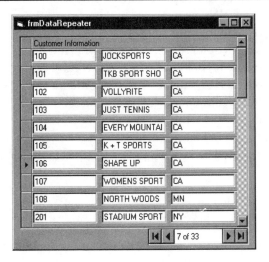

To use the DataRepeater, you must have a compiled custom control that binds to data (a custom control running in the Visual Basic IDE won't work). This sample uses a control called TripleControl, which you'll find in the TripleProject sample. The easiest way to install this control on your computer is to open the TripleProject sample and choose File ➤ Make TripleProject.ocx. TripleControl itself is rather simple: it's just an amalgam of three TextBox controls, exposed by bindable properties named Field1, Field2, and Field3, using the techniques I discussed earlier in the chapter.

TripleControl itself only draws three text boxes. But when it's wrapped by the DataRepeater control, it draws three text boxes as many times as necessary to fill the DataRepeater area. The DataRepeater control supplies the vertical scrollbar, caption, and record selector areas. It also responds to special keystrokes:

- HOME to go to the first record

- END to go to the last record

- PG UP to go back one page of records

- PG DN to go forward one page of records

- Up Arrow to go back one record

- Down Arrow to go forward one record

After you've placed the DataRepeater control on a form, you can set its Repeated-ControlName property to the name of the control that it should use to display data. In the frmDataRepeater sample in the DataConsumer sample project, this is set to TripleProject.TripleControl. You also need to set a data source for the control; here, that's an ADO Data control that connects to the Oracle DEMO database on a server named CASTOR. (You may need to change the properties of this control if your Oracle test server has another name.) Finally, select the RepeaterBindings tab of the Custom property sheet for the DataRepeater control. This tab, shown in Figure 9.6, allows you to choose which bindable properties from the repeated control should be filled from which fields in the data source.

FIGURE 9.6:

Setting bindings in the
DataRepeater control

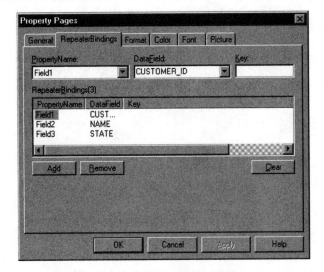

The DataRepeater control is designed to help you display a lot of data on screen
with minimal resource usage. Only the currently selected row of data is actually
drawn on screen using Visual Basic controls such as text boxes. The remaining
rows are simply images constructed by the DataRepeater. This means that only
the current row controls have HWnd properties, for example. But it also means
that you can create very complex interfaces without worrying about resource
usage. Long-time Microsoft Access developers will recognize this strategy as the
same one that's used on Access forms in continuous mode, which the DataRepeater strongly resembles.

NOTE   If you combine a complex bound UserControl resembling the ComplexControl
that was introduced earlier in this chapter with the DataRepeater control, you can
create your own Grid control.

CHAPTER

TEN

Data Shaping

Microsoft supports industry standards when such support suits the company's aims, but it's not afraid to go off in its own direction as well. The SHAPE command is a good example. Although most of what you can do with SQL statements through ADO to standard providers bears at least a close resemblance to ANSI SQL, SHAPE was invented out of whole cloth to support the idea of data shaping. In this chapter, I'll review the basics of data shaping and then show you how this extension to SQL can help you keep track of hierarchies of information.

What Is Data Shaping?

Data shaping is the process of defining a shaped recordset. OK, so, what's a shaped recordset? Well, a shaped recordset is one that can contain more than just data. In particular, the columns of a shaped recordset can contain:

- Data (just like the columns in any other recordset)

- Pointers to another recordset

- Values derived from calculations on the current row of the recordset

- Values derived from calculations over all values in a particular column of the recordset

- Empty, fabricated columns that aren't part of the original data source

As you can see, shaped recordsets are a bit more flexible than regular recordsets. But what is this flexibility good for? That's what I'll be exploring in the rest of this chapter.

NOTE   Empty columns are useful in cases where you need to track some temporary information related to rows while you work with a recordset within an application. I won't be using empty columns in this chapter.

Hierarchical Recordsets

Note in particular that a shaped recordset can contain pointers to other recordsets. By allowing a recordset to contain a pointer to another recordset, a shaped recordset is an ideal way to represent a hierarchy of information. In traditional SQL, you handle a hierarchy by joining tables. This results in redundant information in the resulting recordset. For example, suppose you're interested in information regarding customers and orders. With traditional SQL, you'd create a recordset based on a SQL statement such as

```
SELECT Customers. CompanyName, Orders.OrderDate
FROM Customers INNER JOIN Orders
ON Customers.CustomerID = Orders.CustomerID
```

When you executed this statement, you'd get a recordset that repeated customer names, once for each order the customer has placed.

By contrast, with data shaping you could base a recordset on a SQL statement such as

```
SHAPE {SELECT CustomerID, CompanyName FROM Customers}
APPEND ({SELECT * FROM Orders}
RELATE CustomerID to CustomerID)
```

If you use a shaped recordset to hold the information instead, you'd get a recordset where each customer name occurs only once. This means less data to pass around and, ultimately, better performance.

When you retrieve the value of a field that points to another recordset, you actually get that entire recordset, filtered to include only the related records. This filtered subset of the child recordset is called a chapter. In the example given just above, there are three fields in the recordset created by the SHAPE command: CustomerID, CompanyName, and Chapter1 (the default name of a chapter if no name is supplied using an AS clause). Chapter1 is the recordset of Order information, filtered to include only orders for the first customer at the time that you open the recordset.

Hierarchical recordsets can be nested. That is, a child recordset itself can contain a pointer to yet another child recordset, a grandchild of the original recordset.

For a quick example of using a SHAPE command to retrieve a hierarchical recordset, take a look at frmGrid in the DataShape sample project. This form, shown in Figure 10.1, simply opens a hierarchical recordset and binds it to a Hierarchical FlexGrid control. The code behind this form is simple:

```
Option Explicit

Private mcnn As New ADODB.Connection
```

```
Private mrst As New ADODB.Recordset

Private Sub Form_Load()

    mcnn.Open "Provider=MSDataShape;" & _
     "Data Provider=SQLOLEDB.1;" & _
     "Server=(local);User ID=sa;" & _
     "Initial Catalog=Northwind"

    mrst.Open "SHAPE {" & _
     "SELECT CustomerID, CompanyName " & _
     "FROM Customers} APPEND ({SELECT * " & _
     "FROM Orders} RELATE CustomerID " & _
     "TO CustomerID)", mcnn

    Set hfgMain.DataSource = mrst
End Sub
```

That's all it takes to open a hierarchical recordset and display it in a control that's designed for such things. Now that you've seen the simple part of data shaping, it's time to dig in a bit further.

FIGURE 10.1:

A hierarchical recordset

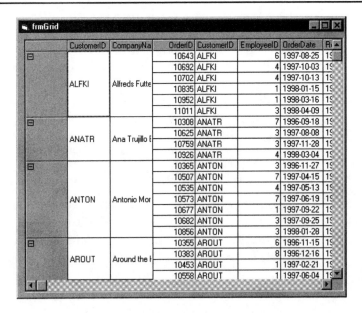

The Data Shaping Service

Data shaping is implemented in a service provider, the Data Shaping Service for OLE DB. A service provider is one that manipulates (but does not supply) data. You need to supply another provider to make the actual connection to the data, and then use the Data Shaping service to create a hierarchical recordset from the data. Connection strings for connections that will use data shaping must specify both the Data Shaping service as the provider and another OLE DB provider as the data provider. For example, a connection string to provide shaped data from a SQL Server database might look like this:

```
Provider=MSDataShape;
Data Provider=SQLOLEDB.1;
Server=(local);
User ID=sa;
Initial Catalog=Northwind
```

You can create a connection string for data shaping out of any existing connection string just by making two changes:

1. Change the Provider keyword in the existing connection string to **Data Provider**.

2. Add **Provider=MSDataShape** to the connection string.

For data shaping to work properly, you must be using client-side cursors. Setting the provider to be the Data Shaping service will automatically set the cursor for any recordset using that connection to be client-side.

Types of Hierarchical Recordsets

The SHAPE statement is able to produce three different types of hierarchical recordsets:

- A relation hierarchy represents a set of parent records and associated child records.

- A parameterized hierarchy also represents parent records and associated child records, but fetches child records on demand.

- A grouping hierarchy represents child records plus a parent recordset composed of aggregate functions.

You'll see each of these types of hierarchical recordsets later in this chapter. In this section, I'll describe their general properties.

Relation Hierarchies

A relation hierarchy represents a set of parent records and associated child records. This recordset is similar to the recordset you can create with a SQL JOIN statement, but it doesn't have the redundancy of a recordset based on a JOIN.

With a relation hierarchy, all the records involved are read into the local cache before the SHAPE statement is processed. This can result in substantial overhead if your recordset is based on a large number of records. However, once the original recordset has been constructed, subsequent fetches are quick because all the data is already cached locally. You can continue to work with records in a relation hierarchy even after closing the connection that the recordset is based on.

Parameterized Hierarchies

A parameterized hierarchy also represents parent records and associated child records, but fetches child records on demand. Just like a relation hierarchy, it contains the same information as a recordset based on a JOIN, but without the redundant rows.

When you open a parameterized hierarchy, all the records in the parent recordset are retrieved. However, child records aren't retrieved until you explicitly open a recordset based on a chapter field. This means that opening a parameterized hierarchy can be much quicker than opening the corresponding relation hierarchy. However, each time you open a child recordset in a parameterized hierarchy, ADO must go back to the data source for more records, so moving through the recordset may be slower than with a relation hierarchy. You must also remain connected to the data source for as long as you want to work with records in a parameterized hierarchy.

Grouping Hierarchies

A grouping hierarchy represents child records plus a parent recordset composed of aggregate functions. This is equivalent to joining a detail SQL statement with an aggregate SQL statement based on the same columns. Because the summary and calculated columns might be based on more than one record, they're automatically non-updateable in a grouping hierarchy.

Like relation hierarchies, all records that a grouping hierarchy are based on are read as soon as you open a recordset on the SHAPE statement.

The SHAPE Statement

As you've seen, hierarchical recordsets are generated by the SHAPE statement. In this section, I'll review the syntax of that statement. First, though, it's good to remember that you don't necessarily have to write SHAPE statements by hand. As you saw in Chapter 6, you can use the Data Environment Designer to generate SHAPE commands visually. You may find that you need to make some modifications to the generated syntax to make it more readable, but, in general, this procedure can save you time.

For example, to generate a SHAPE statement relating Customers, Orders, and Order Details, you could follow these steps:

1. Add a Data Environment to your Visual Basic project.

2. Use the Data Link Properties dialog box to connect this Data Environment to the SQL Server Northwind database.

3. Add a command named Customers, based on the Customers table, to the default connection.

4. Add a child command named Orders, based on the Orders table, to the Customers command. Relate this command to the Customers command using the CustomerID field in both parent and child.

5. Add a child command named OrderDetails, based on the Order Details table, to the Orders command. Relate this command to the Orders command using the OrderID field in both parent and child.

6. Right-click the Customers command and choose Hierarchy Info.

If you follow these particular steps, you'll have created this SHAPE statement:

```
SHAPE
{SELECT * FROM "dbo"."Customers"}  AS Customers
APPEND
```

```
(( SHAPE {SELECT * FROM "dbo"."Orders"}  AS Orders
APPEND
({SELECT * FROM "dbo"."Order Details"}  AS OrderDetails
RELATE 'OrderID' TO 'OrderID') AS OrderDetails)
AS Orders
RELATE 'CustomerID' TO 'CustomerID')
AS Orders
```

This statement includes some qualifiers (such as the dbo to indicate table ownership and the aliasing of SELECTs to command names) that aren't strictly necessary, but they don't hurt.

Syntax of SHAPE

There are actually two different varieties of the SHAPE statement. SHAPE…APPEND is used to create relation and parameterized hierarchies, while SHAPE…COMPUTE is used to create group hierarchies. Either one of these statements can contain aggregate functions or calculated expressions.

SHAPE…APPEND

The general syntax of the SHAPE…APPEND statement is:

```
SHAPE {parent_command} AS parent_alias
APPEND ({child_command} AS child_alias
RELATE parent_column TO child_column…) AS chapter_alias …
```

Here, *parent_command* and *child_command* are usually two SQL statements that return the recordsets that will be built up into the hierarchical recordset. Optionally, you can assign alias names to each of these recordsets, but you're not required to do so. You can also assign an alias to the chapter created from the child recordset; this alias becomes the column name in the main recordset that points to the child recordset.

There are, however, other choices for both parent_command and child_command. They can be:

- The name of a previously shaped recordset

- Another, nested SHAPE statement

- The TABLE keyword, followed by the name of a table from the data source

Because you can nest SHAPE statements, you can create hierarchies of any desired depth.

The curly braces and the parentheses are required parts of the statement.

You can relate the parent and child commands by specifying a pair of fields, or by specifying a group of pairs of fields. For example, this would be a valid RELATE clause:

```
RELATE OrderID TO OrderID, OrderDate TO OrderDetailDate
```

A SHAPE...APPEND statement can also contain multiple APPEND clauses. This has the effect of creating a parent recordset with multiple chapter columns, each of which refers to a subsidiary recordset.

The syntax for a parameterized hierarchy is slightly different in that it includes information on which column to treat as a parameter. It's easiest to show an example of this variation:

```
SHAPE {SELECT CustomerID, CompanyName FROM Customers}
APPEND ({SELECT * FROM Orders WHERE CustomerID = ?}
RELATE CustomerID to PARAMETER 0)
```

Here, the question mark within the definition of the child command indicates the column that should be parameterized at run time, and the PARAMETER 0 in the RELATE clause shows how this parameter relates to the parent command. The effect is that each time the parent command moves to a new row and you request the chapter recordset, the child SQL is issued, with the question mark replaced by the current value of CustomerID from the parent command.

SHAPE...COMPUTE

The general syntax of the SHAPE...COMPUTE statement is:

```
SHAPE {child_command} AS child_alias
COMPUTE child_alias, aggregate_field_list
BY group_field_list
```

The curly braces are required, just as they are in SHAPE...APPEND. The *child_ command* can be one of four things:

- A SQL statement that returns a child recordset

- The name of a previously constructed shaped recordset

- Another SHAPE statement (so these commands can be nested)

- The TABLE keyword followed by the name of a table

In the case of SHAPE...COMPUTE, you must supply an alias for the child command. This alias must be repeated in the column list in the COMPUTE clause and defines the relation between the child recordset and the implied parent recordset.

The aggregate_field_list is optional. If you supply a list here, it must be composed of aggregate functions on the child recordset, and each of these functions defines a column in the generated parent recordset.

The group_field_list is also optional. If you supply a list of columns here, the parent recordset is constructed so that each row has unique values in those columns, and the child recordset is filtered to match. Any columns you list here will become columns in the parent recordset.

If you don't choose to supply a group_field_list, there will be only one row in the parent recordset, and any aggregate it contains will refer to the entire child recordset. If you do supply this list in a BY clause, the parent recordset will contain multiple rows, with the specified grouping.

Aggregate Functions

An aggregate function performs some calculation across all rows of a child (or other descendant) recordset. These aggregate functions all accept fully qualified names for columns. A fully qualified name is simply one that specifies the entire path to a column. For example, if you have a hierarchical recordset in which the top level contains Customers information plus a chapter named Orders, which in turn is a recordset that contains a chapter named OrderDetails, which in turn contains a column named Quantity, the fully qualified name of this column would be

```
Customers.Orders.OrderDetails.Quantity
```

Table 10.1 shows the aggregate functions that are available in the SHAPE syntax.

TABLE 10.1: Aggregate Functions Supported in SHAPE

Function	Description
SUM(column)	Calculates the sum of all values in the specified column.
AVG(column)	Calculates the average of all values in the specified column.
MAX(column)	Retrieves the maximum value from the column.

Continued on next page

TABLE 10.1 CONTINUED: Aggregate Functions Supported in SHAPE

Function	Description
MIN(column)	Retrieves the minimum value from the column.
COUNT(chapter) or COUNT(column)	Counts the number of rows in the chapter or in the column.
STDEV(column)	Calculates the standard deviation of the column.
ANY(column)	Picks a value from the column. It appears that this generally returns the first value, in cases where the column isn't uniform. However, this behavior is not documented and therefore is not guaranteed.

Calculated Expressions

A calculated column can use an arbitrary expression to produce a result, but it can operate only on values in the row of the recordset containing the CALC expression. CALC understands a variety of Visual Basic for Applications (VBA) functions. These are listed in Table 10.2.

TABLE 10.2: VBA Functions Available to CALC

Type of Function	Function
Conversion	Asc, CBool, CByte, CCur, CDate, CDbl, CInt, CLng, CSng, CStr, CVar, CVDate, CVErr, Format, Format$, Hex, Hex$, Oct, Oct$, Val
Date and Time	Date, Date$, DateAdd, DateDiff, DatePart, DateSerial, DateValue, Day, Hour, Minute, Month, Now, Second, Time, Time$, Timer, TimeSerial, TimeValue, WeekDay, Year
Financial	DDB, FV, IPmt, IRR, MIRR, NPer, NPV, Pmt, PPmt, PV, Rate, SLN, SYD
Mathematical	Abs, Atn, Cos, Exp, Fix, Int, Log, Rnd, Sgn, Sin, Sqr, Tan
Miscellaneous	Error, Error$, IIF, IsDate, IsEmpty, IsError, IsNull, IsNumeric, IsObject, QBColor, RGB, TypeName, VarType
String	Chr, ChrB, ChrW, Chr$, ChrB$, InStr$, LCase, LCase$, Left, LeftB, Left$, LeftB$, Len, LTrim, LTrim$, Mid, Mid$, Right, RightB, Right$, RightB$, RTrim, RTrim$, Space, Space$, Str, Str$, StrComp, StrConv, String, String$, Trim, Trim$, UCase, UCase$

Examples of the SHAPE Statement

Let's take a look at some examples of SHAPE statements. You'll find all these examples in frmExample in the DataShape sample project. This form contains a set of command buttons, one for each example. When you click a button, the corresponding example is bound to a Hierarchical FlexGrid control. This lets you quickly see the recordsets returned by each example.

Single-Level Relation Hierarchy

A single-level relation hierarchy relates two recordsets, in this case Customers and Orders:

```
SHAPE {SELECT * FROM Customers}
APPEND ({SELECT * FROM Orders}
RELATE CustomerID TO CustomerID)
```

Multiple-Level Relation Hierarchy

The next step up in complexity is to nest two SHAPE...APPEND commands to create a recordset based on Customers, Orders, and Order Details:

```
SHAPE {SELECT * FROM Customers}
APPEND ((SHAPE {SELECT * FROM Orders}
        APPEND ({SELECT * FROM [Order Details]}
        AS rstOrderDetails
        RELATE OrderID TO OrderID))
RELATE CustomerID TO CustomerID)
```

Parameterized Hierarchy

There's no difference in the recordset retrieved by a parameterized hierarchy and that retrieved by the equivalent relation hierarchy. Here's the parameterized equivalent of the first, single-level example:

```
SHAPE {SELECT * FROM Customers}
APPEND ({SELECT * FROM Orders
WHERE CustomerID = ?}
RELATE CustomerID TO PARAMETER 0)
```

Although this recordset will initially open faster than the equivalent relation hierarchy, you won't see a performance difference between the two on the sample form. That's because the Hierarchical FlexGrid control has to move through all the rows in the recordset to populate itself.

Multiple Relation Hierarchy

By using more than one clause in the APPEND part of the SHAPE statement, you can create a recordset with more than one chapter field, and thus with more than one child recordset:

```
SHAPE {SELECT * FROM Customers}
APPEND({SELECT * FROM Orders WHERE ShippedDate > '1/1/97'}
        RELATE CustomerID TO CustomerID) as rstNewOrders,
       ({SELECT * FROM Orders WHERE ShippedDate <= '1/1/97'}
        RELATE CustomerID TO CustomerID) as rstOldOrders
```

If you scroll through the resulting recordset, you'll see that each parent record is associated with two distinct child recordsets, one each for new and old orders.

Relation Hierarchy with Aggregate

You can also choose to include aggregate columns within a relation hierarchy:

```
SHAPE {SELECT * FROM Customers}
APPEND ({SELECT *  FROM Orders}
         RELATE CustomerID TO CustomerID),
MIN(Chapter1.ShippedDate) AS FirstShip
```

This creates a recordset with Customer and Order information, plus an additional aggregate column that contains the minimum value from any record in the ShippedDate column for each customer.

Grouping Hierarchy

A grouping hierarchy still shows detail and aggregated information, but the parent recordset is created from the child recordset:

```
SHAPE {SELECT Customers.CustomerID AS CustID,
      Customers.CompanyName, Orders.*
      FROM Customers INNER JOIN Orders
      ON Customers.CustomerID = Orders.CustomerID}
      AS rstOrders
COMPUTE rstOrders BY CustID, CompanyName
```

If you run this example, you'll see that the parent fields of CustID and Company-Name are both repeated in the child recordset.

Synchronizing Recordsets

When you're moving through a recordset that contains a chapter field, you can control whether a child recordset based on this field remains synchronized to the parent recordset by setting the parent recordset's StayInSync property appropriately. If you set this property to False, moving the cursor in the parent recordset will have no effect on the child recordset and it remains pointing to the previous chapter. If you set this property to True, the child recordset will be re-fetched whenever you move the cursor in the parent recordset.

For a demonstration of this property, take a look at frmSync in the DataShape sample project. This form simply fetches the same recordset twice, once synchronized and once unsynchronized, and dumps results to a pair of list boxes:

```
Private Sub cmdGo_Click()
    ' Demonstrate the use of StayInSync

    Dim cnn As New ADODB.Connection
    Dim rstParent As New ADODB.Recordset
    Dim rstChild As New ADODB.Recordset

    ' Open a connection
    cnn.Open "Provider=MSDataShape;" & _
      "Data Provider=SQLOLEDB.1;" & _
      "Server=(local);User ID=sa;" & _
      "Initial Catalog=Northwind"

    ' Open a parent recordset, unsynchronized
    rstParent.StayInSync = False
    rstParent.Open "SHAPE {" & _
      "SELECT CustomerID, CompanyName " & _
      "FROM Customers} APPEND ({SELECT " & _
      "CustomerID, OrderDate " & _
      "FROM Orders} RELATE CustomerID " & _
      "TO CustomerID)", cnn

    ' Open the child recordset
    Set rstChild = rstParent.Fields("Chapter1").Value

    ' Step through records and demonstrate results
    With lboNoSync
```

```
        .AddItem "Not synchronized"
        .AddItem " Parent recordset:"
        .AddItem "   " & _
         rstParent.Fields("CustomerID")
        .AddItem " Child recordset"
        .AddItem rstChild.Fields("CustomerID")
        .AddItem "Executing MoveNext"
        rstParent.MoveNext
        .AddItem " Parent recordset:"
        .AddItem "   " & _
         rstParent.Fields("CustomerID")
        .AddItem " Child recordset"
        .AddItem rstChild.Fields("CustomerID")
End With

' Close the recordsets and reopen, synchronized
rstChild.Close
rstParent.Close
rstParent.StayInSync = True
rstParent.Open "SHAPE {" & _
 "SELECT CustomerID, CompanyName " & _
 "FROM Customers} APPEND ({SELECT " & _
 "CustomerID, OrderDate " & _
 "FROM Orders} RELATE CustomerID " & _
 "TO CustomerID)", cnn

' Open the child recordset
Set rstChild = rstParent.Fields("Chapter1").Value

' Step through records and demonstrate results
With lboSync
        .AddItem "Synchronized"
        .AddItem " Parent recordset:"
        .AddItem "   " & _
         rstParent.Fields("CustomerID")
        .AddItem " Child recordset"
        .AddItem rstChild.Fields("CustomerID")
        .AddItem "Executing MoveNext"
        rstParent.MoveNext
        .AddItem " Parent recordset:"
        .AddItem "   " & _
         rstParent.Fields("CustomerID")
```

```
        .AddItem " Child recordset"
        .AddItem rstChild.Fields("CustomerID")
    End With

End Sub
```

Figure 10.2 shows the results of running this procedure.

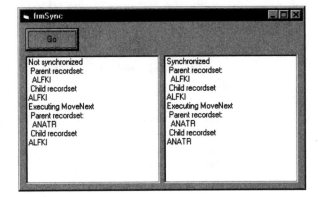

WARNING When you're fetching a child recordset, you must use the Value property of the chapter field in the parent recordset, as shown in the above code sample. If you try to omit this property, you'll get a type mismatch error, even though Value is the default property.

CHAPTER

ELEVEN

Fast Internet Applications with ADO and Visual Basic

- DHTML and ADO

- Remote Data Service

The Internet has become pervasive over the past few years, and it seems as if every development tool in the known universe can now be used to produce Internet applications. Visual Basic is no exception. While there are many Internet-related tools in Visual Basic, in this chapter I'll concentrate on two of them. First, Dynamic HTML (DHTML) provides you with an easy way to move a Visual Basic application from a forms-based interface to a browser-based interface. Second, the Remote Data Service (RDS) allows you to use an ADO data source on another machine, even across the Internet. Because of their dependency on Microsoft software and libraries, both of these techniques are more suited for use on corporate intranets than on the wider Internet, where you can never be sure what browser someone is using.

DHTML and ADO

In this section, you'll learn how to use ADO Code stored in a DHTML application to retrieve and display information in a Web browser. Perhaps the best way to think about this type of application is as a direct replacement for a typical Visual Basic application that uses forms for its user interface. The DHTML application will use Web pages instead of forms, but otherwise it has much the same architecture as a traditional application—that is, it retrieves local data and uses local libraries of code. The major difference is that it will use Internet Explorer instead of stand-alone Visual Basic forms to display its results.

What Is DHTML?

DHTML, as I've already mentioned, stands for Dynamic HTML (or, if you want to be pedantic about it, for Dynamic Hypertext Markup Language). The term is a mouthful, but the idea is quite simple. DHTML takes a standard HTML page and looks at it as a hierarchical collection of objects. These objects can be anything from paragraphs of text to table cells to images to hyperlinks to all the other things that make up an HTML page. Collectively, these objects compose what's called a Document Object Model (DOM). DHTML also endows these objects with properties, methods, and events so that they can be used in development. In fact, by changing the properties of a DOM object, you can change the appearance of a

Web page in a browser without requiring it to fetch a whole new page from the server. DHTML is a client-side technology, implemented entirely on the end user's computer (though, of course, the Web pages can be delivered from a WWW server).

A DHTML application is simply a Visual Basic application that uses the DOM objects instead of standard Visual Basic objects and is designed to be used in an Internet browser. In the next section, you'll learn some of the basics of the Document Object Model. After that, you'll see how to use these objects in a datacentric application.

WARNING   DHTML is, as currently implemented, a browser-specific technology. That is, DHTML applications will only work if the browser you're using is Microsoft Internet Explorer, version 4 or later. Thus, it's most suitable for intranet applications, where corporate standards can dictate the use of a standard browser.

The Document Object Model

The Document Object Model differs in several ways from other object models you may be familiar with. For starters, the parentage of objects is muddy: depending on where it's located on a page, for example, a hyperlink might have any of a number of different objects as a parent. Also, you'll find that some of the objects have rather cryptic names. Figure 11.1, for example, shows a fairly complex HTML page displayed within the TreeView portion of the DHTML Designer. Among other things, this particular page has been parsed to include two FONT objects, one with an NOBR object as a parent, the other with a TD object as a parent.

To make matters even more difficult for the budding DHTML author, pressing F1 within the DHTML Page Designer won't take you to Help for the DOM objects; rather, it brings up help for the designer itself. For help on the DOM, you'll need to manually expand the tree in the MSDN library application that Help launches. First, expand the Platform SDK folder on the Help Contents tab. Within that folder, expand the Internet/Intranet/Extranet Services folder. Within that folder, choose the Dynamic HTML folder. Finally, within that folder you'll find a Document Object Model folder. All the information you need is somewhere below the Document Object Folder, but, alas, none of it is context sensitive. Fortunately it's well organized and cross-referenced.

FIGURE 11.1:

A Web page broken down using the DOM

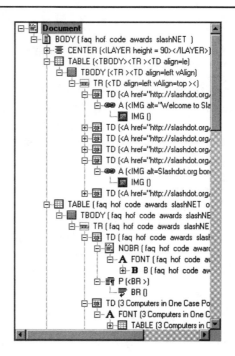

WARNING   When you press F1 from the Visual Basic properties window with a DOM object selected, you'll get a message asking if you want to search for `mshtml.hlp`. Don't bother. This file doesn't exist.

The Document Object Model includes over 125 objects, and learning about these objects in detail would take a whole book. However, you can create useful and interesting DHTML pages using only a fraction of these objects. In this section, I'll cover some general DHTML development concepts and then highlight a few of the objects you'll actually need to create data-enabled DHTML Web pages.

Events and Event Bubbling

All DOM objects support events. Table 11.1 shows the events that are common to all the DOM objects. Table 11.2 shows some additional useful events that apply to specific objects. (As with the other DOM tables in this chapter, these tables are not exhaustive, just illustrative.)

Note that in DOM, event names are lower case, as are property, method, and some object names.

TABLE 11.1: Common DOM Events

Event	Occurs
onmouseover	when the mouse pointer enters an object.
onmouseout	when the mouse pointer leaves an object.
onmousedown	when any mouse button is clicked.
onmouseup	when any mouse button is released.
onmousemove	when movement occurs within an object.
onclick	when the primary mouse button is clicked.
ondblclick	when the primary mouse button is double-clicked.
onkeypress	when any key is pressed and released (repeats if key is held down).
onkeydown	when any key is pressed.
onkeyup	when any key is released.

TABLE 11.2: Some Useful DOM Events

Event	Object	Occurs
onbeforeunload	window	just before a page unloads. Can be cancelled.
onfocus	BUTTON, IMG, TABLE, window	when an object receives the focus.
onhelp	Most objects	when the user presses F1. This event doesn't bubble.
onload	FRAMESET, IMG, window	when an object starts to load.
onresize	window	when an object is resized. This event doesn't bubble.
onunload	window	when a page unloads. Can't be cancelled.

Most events in the Document Object Model bubble, which means that events are handled by parent objects if they're ignored by child objects. This is similar to the way that key events are handled on a Visual Basic form when you set the KeyPreview property to True. For example, if you have an image embedded in a table cell and the mouse passes over that image, the event could be handled by any one of these objects:

- The IMG object itself

- The TD object representing the table cell

- The TR object representing the row in the table

- The TBODY object representing the body of the table

- The TABLE object representing the table itself

- The BODY object representing the entire body of the Web page

Bubbling does *not* stop when one of these objects handles the onmouseover event; the event continues to bubble to higher objects in the chain. When an event occurs, a window.event object is created with context information about that event. For example, window.event.srcElement.id contains the id property of the object that originally fired the event.

If you want to stop bubbling, you can cancel the event in any event handler by setting the window.event.cancelBubble property to True.

Replacing MsgBox

When you start moving your applications to a browser-based interface, you'll discover that you need to come up with new ways to do some things. For example, the humble MsgBox function, though essential in Visual Basic, is rather annoying when you move to a DHTML application. To see why, let's create a simple DHTML application.

To create your first DHTML application, launch Visual Basic and choose DHTML Application from the New Project dialog box. This will create a new project with a single module (containing some utility code) and an instance of the DHTML Page Designer. This designer allows you to create both the user interface and the code of your DHTML page, just as the familiar Form Designer allows you to create both the code and the user interface of a Visual Basic form.

Open the DHTML Page Designer. You'll see that it has a split interface, as shown in Figure 11.2. On the left is a TreeView containing all the elements of the DHTML page as parsed according to the Document Object Model. On the right is a rendering of the page. You'll see in the figure that even a blank page contains two objects, one representing the document as a whole and one representing the body text. You can work with your page either by manipulating objects in the TreeView or by drawing, typing, and using the mouse on the rendered page.

FIGURE 11.2:

DHTML Page Designer

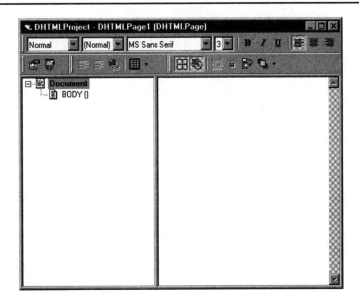

Click in the rendered page and type some text. You'll see it echoed in the BODY object in the TreeView. Type a few paragraphs of text, and the TreeView will display P objects as children of the BODY object. For an initial task, let's add some code to the onmouseover event for the first P object. In order to manipulate any object in code, you need to assign an id property to that object. The id property is an arbitrary, unique string (similar to the Name property of Visual Basic controls). You assign it by selecting the object in the TreeView in the DHTML Page Designer and then typing a value into the Visual Basic properties window for that object. In this example, I've chosen to use idP1 for the first P object.

NOTE   When you assign an id to an object in the DHTML Page Designer, that object is displayed in boldface in the TreeView. Only objects displayed in boldface are accessible to code.

Open the code module for the DHTML page and enter some code in the onmouseover event handler for this object:

```
Private Sub idP1_onmouseover()
    Dim intRet As Integer
    intRet = MsgBox("Click OK or Cancel", _
    vbOKCancel, "Sample MsgBox")
    If intRet = vbOK Then
        idP1.innerText = "You chose OK"
    Else
        idP1.innerText = "You chose Cancel"
    End If
End Sub
```

When you run the project, the Debugging tab of the Project Properties dialog box will be displayed to confirm what action you want to take. You'll want to start the DHTML page that you've been designing, so select Start Component. If you leave the Use Existing Browser check box checked, Visual Basic will look for an existing instance of Internet Explorer and, if it finds one, display the page in that instance. Otherwise, it will launch a new instance.

When the page is open in your browser, run your mouse across the first paragraph. You'll see the message box—but you'll see it in front of the Visual Basic IDE, which will grab the focus from the browser! Worse yet, when you click OK or Cancel, the browser will remain in the background. You can switch back to it and see that the requested change did happen.

WARNING   To stop the application, you must use the Stop toolbar button within the Visual Basic IDE. Just closing the Web browser instance will not stop the application (unlike closing the main form of a conventional Visual Basic application).

If you compile the application, you'll see that the compiled version doesn't have this problem; the message box appears in front of the browser, and the browser doesn't play hide-and-seek. Nevertheless, it's worth converting to a more browser-based way of thinking, for consistency between debugging and running the application as well as for consistency with other Web pages.

Here's the more Web-oriented way to perform the same task:

```
Private Sub idP1_onmouseover()
    Dim intRet As Integer
    intRet = BaseWindow.showModalDialog("MsgBox.htm")
    If intRet = vbOK Then
        idP1.innerText = "You chose OK"
    Else
        idP1.innerText = "You chose Cancel"
    End If
End Sub
```

BaseWindow is a built-in object reference to the current Web browser. Its show-ModalDialog method opens another Web page in a separate browser window and monitors for a return value. The trick here, though, is that you have to create the separate Web page somehow! This one is simple enough that it can just be typed straight into Notepad (or the text editor of your choice) and saved as Msg-Box.htm:

```
<HTML>
<HEAD><TITLE>Sample Dialog</TITLE>
<SCRIPT LANGUAGE="VBScript">
Sub DoOK ()
    window.returnValue = 1
    window.close
End Sub
Sub DoCancel ()
    window.returnValue = 2
    window.close
End Sub
</SCRIPT>
</HEAD>
<BODY>
<P>Click OK or Cancel
<P>
<BUTTON onclick="DoOK">OK</BUTTON> 
<BUTTON onclick="DoCancel">Cancel</BUTTON>
</HTML>
```

So there's a tradeoff here. As you try to make your applications more Web-like, you'll inevitably need to move into doing more straight HTML development, outside the Visual Basic environment. You'll have to decide for yourself what sort of development standards you want to enforce in this area.

DOM Objects

In this section, I'll examine the DOM objects that are most useful for Visual Basic developers. There are 20 objects that are worth knowing about:

- The A object represents the start or destination of a hyperlink (A for Anchor).

- The B object specifies boldface text.

- The BODY object represents the body of the HTML document.

- The DIV object is a container for grouping child objects.

- The document object represents the entire HTML document.

- The H1 through H6 objects render text as heading styles.

- The I object specifies italic text.

- The IMG object represents an embedded image.

- The P object refers to an entire paragraph of text.

- The SPAN object sets off a portion of text as an object.

- The TABLE object represents an entire table.

- The TBODY object represents the body of a table.

- The TD object represents an individual cell in a table.

- The TR object represents a row in a table.

- The window object represents a browser window.

All the samples from this section are contained in the DOMSample project, available on this book's Web site. This sample opens a main page and then uses hyperlinks to navigate to other Dynamic HTML pages within the same project. These hyperlinks work programmatically rather than through the HREF tag. For example, the hyperlink to navigate to the Hyperlinks page uses this code:

```
Private Function Hyperlink2_onclick() As Boolean
    BaseWindow.navigate "DOMSample_dpgHyperlink.html"
End Function
```

WARNING   Note that in order to navigate to a page in the same project, you must separate the project name and the page name with an underscore. This is incorrectly documented in the Visual Basic Help.

Text Manipulation

Figure 11.3 shows some simple text styles and their corresponding interpretations as DOM objects. This is the dpgText page within the DOMSample sample project. A few things to note here:

- When you select an object within the TreeView, the corresponding object on the HTML rendered page is highlighted (if possible).

- Two objects may refer to the same text on the page. For example, the first P object and the first B object both contain the text "An entire bold paragraph."

- Objects in the TreeView are not necessarily displayed in the same order they're shown in the rendered page.

- Some things you might expect to be objects—for example, the centering of the final P object—are actually properties (in this case, the align property of the object).

FIGURE 11.3:

Sample text page and its DOM representation

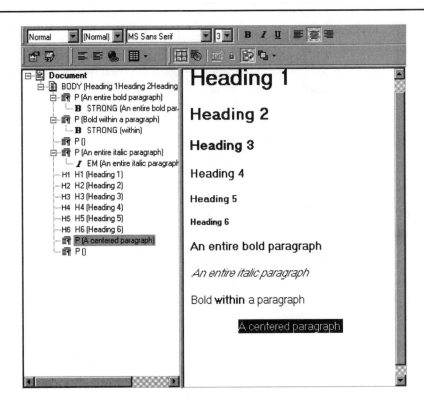

When you're manipulating text, you're most likely to want to work with properties of the P object. Table 11.3 lists the properties that you'll probably find most useful in this regard.

TABLE 11.3: Some Properties of the P Object

Property	Explanation
innerHTML	The entire contents of the paragraph, including any formatting tags (such as the <B></B> tags that specify boldface)
innerText	The typed text in the paragraph, not including any formatting tags
outerHTML	The entire paragraph, including the paragraph tags themselves
parentElement	The parent of this object in the parsed DOM hierarchy
style	A collection of style attributes for this object
title	ToolTip to use when the mouse is hovered over the paragraph

To change the text of a paragraph, you'll probably want to set its innerText property, thereby preserving the formatting. To change the appearance of a paragraph, you can modify the object returned by the style property of the paragraph. This object has many of the properties you'd expect, including:

- backgroundColor
- backgroundImage
- color
- font
- visibility

For example, you may want to have a paragraph change color when the mouse pointer passes over it. You can do this with a pair of Event procedures:

```
Private mstrSaveColor As String

Private Sub idColorChange_onmouseout()
    idColorChange.Style.Color = mstrSaveColor
End Sub

Private Sub idColorChange_onmouseover()
```

```
    mstrSaveColor = idColorChange.Style.Color
    idColorChange.Style.Color = "BLUEVIOLET"
End Sub
```

Color values are strings, and these strings can be either standard color names or hex values. To see the values that you can use, search the DOM help for "Color Table."

Document Organization

There are a number of objects that make it easier for you to work with documents and pieces of documents. These include the A, BODY, DIV, document, SPAN, and window objects.

A objects represent hyperlinks within your document. You don't have to do anything special to make the hyperlinks work; that's built into the HTML. You can edit the href property to change the destination of a hyperlink on the fly if you'd like. However, if you want to add your own actions to the default action for a hyperlink, you need to do a bit of programming. Here's some code from the dpgHyperlink sample page in the DOMSample project:

```
Private Function idClickMe_onclick() As Boolean
    idPara2.innerText = "About to jump to Microsoft"
    idClickMe_onclick = True
End Function
```

That is, if you intercept the default action for the hyperlink, you need to explicitly tell Internet Explorer to go ahead and do that default action when you're done. If you don't set the return value of the procedure to True, then your code will run, but the hyperlink won't function as a hyperlink.

DIV and SPAN provide two ways to group objects within your application. You can highlight as much text as you'd like in the DHTML Page Designer, then click the Wrap Selection In <DIV>...</DIV> toolbar button to create a DIV object. This has the effect of giving you a single object that you can manipulate to change the style, for example, of multiple paragraphs. On the other hand, you can select any part of a paragraph and click the Wrap Selection In <SPAN>...</SPAN> toolbar button to give you an object smaller than a paragraph (perhaps a few words that you want to highlight when the mouse pointer passes over them). Of course, for an even wider selection, you can manipulate the properties of the BODY object, which represents all the text on screen. The dpgHyperlink sample page in the

DOMSample project includes examples of manipulating the style of each of these three objects:

```
Private mstrSaveColor As String

Private Sub idBodyChangeColor_onmouseout()
    idBody.Style.Color = mstrSaveColor
End Sub

Private Sub idBodyChangeColor_onmouseover()
    mstrSaveColor = idBody.Style.Color
    idBody.Style.Color = "LIME"
End Sub

Private Sub idDivChangeColor_onmouseout()
    idDiv1.Style.Color = mstrSaveColor
End Sub

Private Sub idDivChangeColor_onmouseover()
    mstrSaveColor = idDiv1.Style.Color
    idDiv1.Style.Color = "LIME"
End Sub

Private Sub idSpanChangeColor_onmouseout()
    idSpan1.Style.Color = mstrSaveColor
End Sub

Private Sub idSpanChangeColor_onmouseover()
    mstrSaveColor = idSpan1.Style.Color
    idSpan1.Style.Color = "LIME"
End Sub
```

Visual Basic provides an object named Document, which is a built-in instance of the DOM document object. In other words, you don't have to assign an id to this object to use it. This object represents the entire document open in the browser window. More important is the BaseWindow object, a built-in instance of the window object, representing the browser window itself. This object makes available a number of useful methods:

Alert   Displays an alert dialog box with an OK button.

Close   Closes the browser window.

MoveTo   Moves the window.

Navigate   Loads a new page.

ResizeTo   Resizes the window.

ShowModalDialog   Opens a browser dialog box.

Here's some sample code for the four methods we haven't already seen. Note that with the moveTo and resizeTo methods, the measurements are given in pixels.

```
Private Function idAlert_onclick() As Boolean
    BaseWindow.alert "This is an alert"
End Function

Private Function idClose_onclick() As Boolean
    BaseWindow.Close
End Function

Private Function idMoveTo_onclick() As Boolean
    BaseWindow.moveTo 100, 100
End Function

Private Function idResizeTo_onclick() As Boolean
    BaseWindow.resizeTo 100, 100
End Function
```

Tables

On database-connected pages, you'll probably make heavy use of HTML tables. Fortunately, although the table object model is fairly complex, referring to individual cells (likely what you'll want to do) is pretty simple.

When you create a table, you'll get:

- A TABLE object representing the entire table

- A TBODY object representing the body of the table

- A TR object representing each row in the table

- A TD object representing each cell in the table

If you just want to modify data, all you need to do is assign ids to the TD objects and you're off. The dpgTable sample page in the DOMSample project illustrates the process of setting values in a table's cells:

```
Private Function TextField1_onchange() As Boolean
    idCell1.innerText = TextField1.Value
```

```
        idCell2.innerText = StrReverse(TextField1.Value)
        idCell3.innerText = Len(TextField1.Value)
        idCell4.innerText = TextField1.Value & "!"
End Function
```

NOTE   In an HTML text field, the onchange event occurs only when the user commits the text—for example, by tabbing out of the control.

A Simple DHTML Application

Let's walk through the steps necessary to create a simple DHTML application that uses ADO to fetch records from a local database. In this particular case, we'll use the sales information in the SQL Server version of the Northwind database. Figure 11.4 shows the finished page open in Internet Explorer. This page is saved as dpgHitList in the DHTMLDemo sample project.

FIGURE 11.4:

The Product Hit List sample page

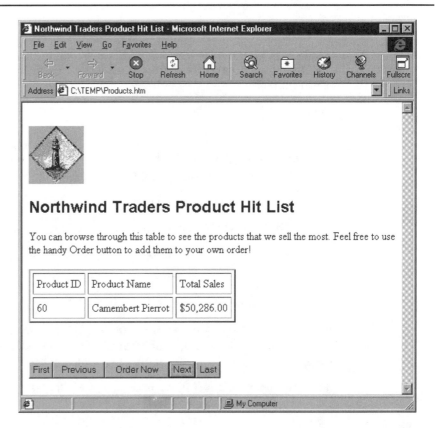

To create this sample, you need to start by designing the Web page. While you can do this entirely within Visual Basic, the DHTML Page Designer is so pathetic as to be pretty much useless for page design, unless you already know HTML quite well (in which case you probably have your own preferred tool already). Even if the only software you have available is Visual Basic 6, you still have a better editor than the DHTML Page Designer available, because Internet Explorer 4 includes FrontPage Express. You might have to use the Add/Remove Software Control Panel applet to install this component of Internet Explorer if you did a minimal install the first time through. While not "industrial strength," this editor is probably good enough for anything that most Visual Basic developers will try to do.

So, the first step is to create a static Web page, without interactive controls, using the Web page editor of your choice. Figure 11.5 shows this first step. You'll see that there are no command buttons on the page and no data in the table. You'll add those elements later from within Visual Basic.

FIGURE 11.5:

Designing the Web page

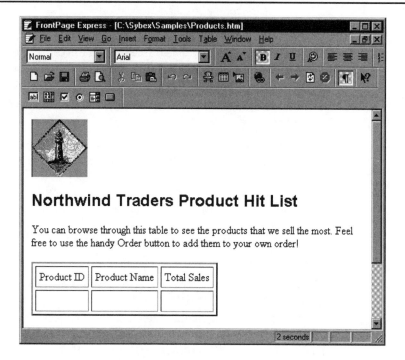

When you're satisfied with your page, create a new Visual Basic project and choose DHTML Application from the New Project dialog box. Visual Basic will create an application with one module (with a bit of utility code already in it) and one DHTML Page Designer. You now need to load the page you've already created into the designer. Click the DHTML Page Designer Properties toolbar button within the designer and you'll get a choice of ways to save the HTML. You can either include the HTML directly in the Visual Basic file or save it as an external page. This dialog box also lets you choose an existing HTML file to open—which is what you want to do in this case—so click the Save HTML In An External File option and open the file that you've already created.

NOTE
The DHTML Page Designer also includes a Launch Editor toolbar button, so you can load the page back into a better editor any time you want to do so. By default, this button loads the page into Notepad. To choose another editor, select Tools ➤ Options from the Visual Basic menu and set an External HTML Editor on the Advanced tab of the resulting dialog box. You'll need to shut down and restart Visual Basic for the change to take effect.

Next, you'll need to add a source of data to your project. In the DHTMLDemo sample project, the dpgHitList page uses a Data Environment to grab its data. This Data Environment is connected to the SQL Server version of the Northwind database and contains a command, ProductSales, based directly on a SQL statement:

```
SELECT Products.ProductID, Products.ProductName,
SUM([Order Details].UnitPrice * [Order Details].Quantity)
AS LinePrice
FROM Products INNER JOIN [Order Details] ON
Products.ProductID = [Order Details].ProductID
GROUP BY Products.ProductID, Products.ProductName
ORDER BY SUM([Order Details].UnitPrice *
[Order Details].Quantity) DESC
```

You also need to modify the HTML to allow you to change some of its elements. While the DHTML Page Designer automatically parses the loaded page down to the smallest level of the Document Object Model, it won't allow you to work with any object in code unless that object has had an ID assigned. By default, nothing has an ID assigned, so you'll need to take care of this. In the designer, expand the tree until you get to the table cells that will hold the data, and assign id properties to each of these TD objects. In the dpgHitList sample page, I've used idProductID, idProductName, and idTotalSales for these IDs. It's easy to identify objects with IDs in the TreeView in the DHTML Page Designer; their names are displayed in boldface text.

You can add buttons to the page in the designer the same way you add buttons to a form. When you open the Visual Basic Toolbox, you'll find that it opens to an HTML tab containing only controls suitable for HTML forms. The controls you'll find here include:

Button   Roughly the same as a Visual Basic command button

SubmitButton   A special button for submitting results from forms

ResetButton   A special button for resetting a form

TextField   Roughly the same as a Visual Basic text box

TextArea   Roughly the same as a multiline text box

PasswordField   A text box designed to not display what the user types

Option   Roughly the same as an option button

Checkbox   Roughly the same as the Visual Basic check box

Select   Can be used for a list box or a combo box

Image   Roughly the same as the Visual Basic image control

Hyperlink   For inserting hyperlinks

HorizontalRule   For dividing a page visually

FileUpload   A specialized control for sending files to the server

HiddenField   An invisible text box

InputImage   A graphical input area

List   A list box control

On the dpgHitList sample page in the DHTMLDemo project, I've added five buttons and assigned each of them an id value so that they're programmable. These are the record navigation buttons plus the Order Now button (the latter is present just as decoration).

The final step to this simple application is to add code behind the page. First, there's the code to ensure that data is loaded into the table cells that are originally blank. When the page's onload event occurs, the code executes the Command object that we created in the Data Environment. This ensures that it's through fetching data before any more code is executed. Next, the code uses a shared procedure to actually fill in the table:

```
Private Sub DHTMLPage_Load()
    deNorthwindSQL.ProductSales
    LoadData
End Sub

Private Sub LoadData()
    If deNorthwindSQL.rsProductSales.BOF _
    Or deNorthwindSQL.rsProductSales.EOF Then
        idProductID.innerHTML = ""
        idProductName.innerHTML = ""
        idTotalSales.innerHTML = ""
    Else
        idProductID.innerHTML = _
         deNorthwindSQL.rsProductSales("ProductID")
        idProductName.innerHTML = _
         deNorthwindSQL.rsProductSales("ProductName")
        idTotalSales.innerHTML = _
         Format(deNorthwindSQL.rsProductSales( _
         "LinePrice"), "$#,##00")
    End If
End Sub
```

The navigation buttons move the record pointer in the recordset created by the Command object. Then they reload the data using the same shared procedure:

```
Private Function cmdFirst_onclick() As Boolean
    deNorthwindSQL.rsProductSales.MoveFirst
    LoadData
End Function

Private Function cmdLast_onclick() As Boolean
    deNorthwindSQL.rsProductSales.MoveLast
    LoadData
End Function

Private Function cmdNext_onclick() As Boolean
    If Not deNorthwindSQL.rsProductSales.EOF Then
        deNorthwindSQL.rsProductSales.MoveNext
        If deNorthwindSQL.rsProductSales.EOF Then
```

```
            deNorthwindSQL.rsProductSales.MoveLast
        End If
        LoadData
    End If
End Function


Private Function cmdPrevious_onclick() As Boolean
    If Not deNorthwindSQL.rsProductSales.BOF Then
        deNorthwindSQL.rsProductSales.MovePrevious
        If deNorthwindSQL.rsProductSales.BOF Then
            deNorthwindSQL.rsProductSales.MoveFirst
        End If
        LoadData
    End If
End Function
```

Finally, the unimplemented Order Now button raises an alert:

```
Private Function cmdOrderNow_onclick() As Boolean
    BaseWindow.alert _
      "Sorry, ordering system is not running!"
End Function
```

Using ADO with DHTML

In this section, I'll cover two more examples of using ADO with DHTML pages, to give you some ideas about how you can hook up your applications to this new user interface. First, I'll look at a DHTML version of the frmCars sample application from the Data Environment sample project (this sample was used in Chapter 6). The second application demonstrates using the BindingCollection object to create a bound DHTML page.

Managing Data in Code

Figure 11.6 shows the Car Tracker sample application running as a browser application. You can view the source for this by opening the dpgCars DHTML Page Designer within the DHTMLDemo project.

FIGURE 11.6:

ADO Data on a
DHTML page

The code behind this Web page is based on the code that was used on the form-based version of the same sample. The Web page uses HTML fields instead of Visual Basic intrinsic controls, but the id values for those fields are set to the same names that the VB controls used, which makes it easier to move the code. Here's the code from behind the page:

NOTE   This sample uses the Cars database that was first discussed in Chapter 6. You can create this database by running the `cars.sql` script if you haven't done so already.

```
Option Explicit

Private fAddNew As Boolean
```

```
Private Function cmdAddNew_onclick() As Boolean
    txtID.disabled = True
    txtYear.disabled = False
    txtMake.disabled = False
    txtModel.disabled = False
    txtID.Value = "<Identity>"
    txtYear.Value = ""
    txtMake.Value = ""
    txtModel.Value = ""
    txtMake.focus
    fAddNew = True
    cmdUpdate.disabled = False
    cmdAddNew.disabled = True
    cmdDelete.disabled = True
End Function

Private Function cmdDelete_onclick() As Boolean
    Dim intRet As Integer
    intRet = MsgBox("Are you sure?", vbYesNo)
    If intRet = vbYes Then
        deCars.DeleteCar txtID.Value
    End If
    deCars.rstblCars.Requery
    LoadData
End Function

Private Function cmdFirst_onclick() As Boolean
    deCars.rstblCars.MoveFirst
    LoadData
End Function

Private Function cmdLast_onclick() As Boolean
    deCars.rstblCars.MoveLast
    LoadData
End Function

Private Function cmdNext_onclick() As Boolean
    If Not deCars.rstblCars.EOF Then
        deCars.rstblCars.MoveNext
        If deCars.rstblCars.EOF Then
            deCars.rstblCars.MoveLast
        End If
```

```
            LoadData
        End If
End Function


Private Function cmdPrevious_onclick() As Boolean
    If Not deCars.rstblCars.BOF Then
        deCars.rstblCars.MovePrevious
        If deCars.rstblCars.BOF Then
            deCars.rstblCars.MoveFirst
        End If
        LoadData
    End If
End Function


Private Function cmdUpdate_onclick() As Boolean
    If fAddNew Then
        deCars.InsertCar txtYear.Value, _
         txtMake.Value, txtModel.Value
        fAddNew = False
        txtID.Value = ""
        txtYear.Value = ""
        txtMake.Value = ""
        txtModel.Value = ""
    Else
        deCars.UpdateCar txtID.Value, txtYear.Value, _
         txtMake.Value, txtModel.Value
    End If
    deCars.rstblCars.Requery
    cmdUpdate.disabled = True
    cmdAddNew.disabled = False
    If deCars.rstblCars.RecordCount > 0 Then
        cmdDelete.disabled = False
    End If
End Function


Private Sub DHTMLPage_Load()
    deCars.tblCars
    If deCars.rstblCars.RecordCount = 0 Then
        txtID.disabled = True
        txtYear.disabled = True
        txtMake.disabled = True
        txtModel.disabled = True
```

```
                cmdDelete.disabled = True
        Else
                cmdDelete.disabled = False
        End If
        cmdUpdate.disabled = True
        LoadData
End Sub

Private Sub LoadData()
    If deCars.rstblCars.BOF Or deCars.rstblCars.EOF Then
        txtID.Value = ""
        txtMake.Value = ""
        txtModel.Value = ""
        txtYear.Value = ""
    Else
        txtID.Value = deCars.rstblCars("ID")
        txtMake.Value = deCars.rstblCars("Make")
        txtModel.Value = deCars.rstblCars("Model")
        txtYear.Value = deCars.rstblCars("Year")
    End If
End Sub

Private Sub DHTMLPage_Unload()
    deCars.rstblCars.Close
End Sub

Private Function txtModel_onchange() As Boolean
    If Not fAddNew Then
        cmdUpdate.disabled = False
        cmdDelete.disabled = True
        cmdAddNew.disabled = True
    End If
    txtModel_onchange = True
End Function

Private Function txtYear_onchange() As Boolean
    If Not fAddNew Then
        cmdUpdate.disabled = False
        cmdDelete.disabled = True
        cmdAddNew.disabled = True
    End If
    txtYear_onchange = True
```

```
End Function

Private Function txtMake_onkeypress() As Boolean
    If Not fAddNew Then
        cmdUpdate.disabled = False
        cmdDelete.disabled = True
        cmdAddNew.disabled = True
    End If
    txtMake_onkeypress = True
End Function
```

If you review the code from the forms-based version of the same project, you'll see that there were few changes required. Here's a summary of what had to be done to move this data entry application from a form to a DHTML page:

- The Hierarchical FlexGrid control used to display the original table on the form has been removed from the DHTML page. Although you can use many ActiveX controls directly on DHTML pages, the Hierarchical FlexGrid isn't one of them. If you try to add such a control to a DHTML page, you'll get an error from Visual Basic.

- Visual Basic controls have an Enabled property; DOM input fields have a disabled property. So every occurrence of Enabled in the original code had to be changed to disabled, and the Boolean value reversed as well.

- Whenever the code works with the value in a control, the Value property has to be specified explicitly so that the code gets just the user's text to work with.

- The SetFocus method for Visual Basic controls is replaced by the focus method for input fields.

- The DHTMLPage_Load event includes an explicit call to the Command object used to retrieve the data, to make certain that the command is executed before the page attempts to load any data.

- The onchange events need to include a line that sets the return value to True, so that the default action (displaying the typed character) is performed after the code behind the page runs.

As you can see, it's a relatively straightforward exercise to translate an existing application from using a form to using a DHTML page. Indeed, it's possible to imagine a Visual Basic wizard that would perform most of the work, similar to the job that the ActiveX Document Migration Wizard does now. There's a niche product just waiting for some enterprising developer to get to work on!

Using Bound Fields in DHTML

Back in Chapter 6, you learned about the BindingCollection object that allows you to do run-time binding between data sources and data consumers. Input controls on DHTML pages can also work as data consumers in this fashion, allowing you to design bound DHTML pages. For example, the dpgOracle page in the DHTMLDemo sample project uses this technique to display (and edit) data from an Oracle database. Figure 11.7 shows this application in action. As with the other applications in this chapter, it's not a marvel of good Web page design—but it does serve to get data displayed in a Web browser.

FIGURE 11.7:

Bound controls on a DHTML page

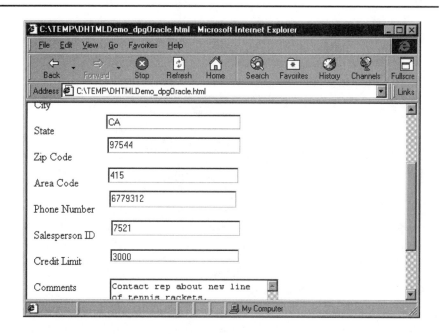

This application uses a Data Environment named deOracle to connect to the DEMO database on a server named CASTOR (if your test Oracle server has a different name, just edit the properties of the Connection object in the Data Environment accordingly). This Data Environment includes a single Command object named Customers, based on a relatively simple SQL statement:

```
SELECT CUSTOMER.* FROM CUSTOMER
```

In order to make the displayed data editable, the Command is set to use client-side cursors. If you use server-side cursors with an Oracle database via the Microsoft-supplied Oracle OLE DB Provider, all your data will be read only no matter what cursor type you choose. The client-side provider adds some special magic that lets Oracle data be updated. The sample is also set to use optimistic locking and cache 100 records locally (good default settings for shared data access in many cases).

The DHTML page consists of a series of text strings (the equivalent of regular label controls) and input fields. Each input field has been given an id starting with txt, just as if it was a TextBox control. Besides the record navigation code (which is the same as for the other DHTML pages we've seen), there's only a small amount of code behind this page:

```
Dim mcolBind As BindingCollection

Private Sub BaseWindow_onload()
    Set mcolBind = New BindingCollection
    With mcolBind
        Set .DataSource = deOracle
        .DataMember = "Customers"
        .Add txtCustomer_ID, "Value", "CUSTOMER_ID"
        .Add txtName, "Value", "NAME"
        .Add txtAddress, "Value", "ADDRESS"
        .Add txtCity, "Value", "CITY"
        .Add txtState, "Value", "STATE"
        .Add txtZip_Code, "Value", "ZIP_CODE"
        .Add txtArea_Code, "Value", "AREA_CODE"
        .Add txtPhone_Number, "Value", "PHONE_NUMBER"
        .Add txtSalesperson_ID, "Value", "SALESPERSON_ID"
        .Add txtCredit_Limit, "Value", "CREDIT_LIMIT"
        .Add txtComments, "Value", "COMMENTS"
    End With
End Sub
```

In order to support the BindingCollection object, the project has a reference to the Microsoft Data Binding Collection library. You'll note that the code is in the BaseWindow_onload event, rather than the DHTMLPage_onload event that I've used in previous examples. That's because the page's event occurs as soon as any part of the page is loaded, which will be before all the input fields are present. The window's load event occurs when the page is entirely loaded.

The code works like any other binding code. It creates a BindingCollection object and uses its Add method to specify the controls to bind, the property to use in binding (the DOM Value property, in this case), and the field from the DataMember to bind. That's it! Once this code is in place, you can treat the DHTML page like a bound form, moving through records and having changes automatically committed when you move to another record.

You can also use the binding collection technique to bind input fields on a DHTML page to an ADO Data control. The ADO Data control is one of the controls that you can embed directly on an HTML page. The dpgDataControl page in the DHTMLDemo project demonstrates this technique. This particular page uses run-time binding with the ADO Data control to retrieve a couple of fields from the SQL Server version of the Northwind sample database:

```
Dim mcolBind As BindingCollection

Private Sub BaseWindow_onload()
    Set mcolBind = New BindingCollection
    With mcolBind
        Set .DataSource = Adodc1
        .Add txtCustomerID, "Value", "CustomerID"
        .Add txtCompanyName, "Value", "CompanyName"
    End If
End Sub
```

Unfortunately, there are a couple of annoyances to using the ADO Data control in this fashion. First, the connection string builder doesn't work when you drop the control on a DHTML page design surface. Rather than try to type an OLE DB connection string by hand from memory, you may want to drop an ADO Data control on a scratch form, use the builder from there, and then copy the final string to the instance of the control on the DHTML page. Second, the ADO Data control is not marked safe for scripting. This means that if you have Internet Explorer security set to Medium (the default) or High, you'll get a warning when you try to initialize a page with this control, and have to tell Internet Explorer that the page is safe to load before it will go fetch your data.

Remote Data Service

While DHTML is an interesting and flashy technology, it's primarily suited for intranets. All the action takes place on the client computer, and the data source needs to be available by the traditional ADO means (local data or a server that you can connect to by an OLE DB connection). Remote Data Service, or RDS (formerly Advanced Data Connector, ADC), is designed for a simple purpose: to allow OLE DB and ADO to retrieve information from a server on the "other side" of a Web server. Thus, RDS is a mixed client and server technology. Some of the RDS components run on the client, while others must be installed on a Web server that also hosts the database you're retrieving information from.

In this section, you'll learn the basics of RDS and see how to use it in a variety of ways from Visual Basic.

> **NOTE**
>
> The samples for this section are in the RDSDemo sample project. They were tested using a server running Windows NT Enterprise Edition with Service Pack 4, Internet Information Server 4 (from the Windows NT Option Pack), and SQL Server 7 installed. The server name for the samples is MUSHROOM. You'll need to change this to match your own server name, of course.

Examining RDS

The basic idea of RDS is to enable the use of Hypertext Transfer Protocol (HTTP), one of the major transmission protocols of the Internet, between the client application and a middleware layer. In this case, the middleware layer consists of Microsoft Internet Information Server (IIS). IIS in turn uses server-side RDS components to query the database and return results to the client. Since HTTP is a *stateless* protocol (that is, one HTTP message knows nothing about the messages that have come before), RDS is most suited to use with a *disconnected recordset*: one that does not maintain a persistent connection to the server. Typically, an RDS client program will retrieve results into a local recordset, disconnect that recordset from the server, and then later reconnect the recordset to send back updates (if necessary). Figure 11.8 shows the basic RDS process.

FIGURE 11.8:

Simple RDS components

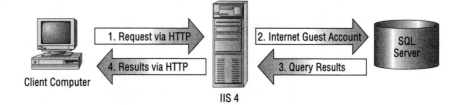

Because of the number of separate components involved and their distribution across multiple computers, RDS can be something of a minefield to set up (the inadequate documentation and lack of samples using Visual Basic doesn't help much, either). The biggest configuration headache is probably security. You could embed a username and password in your client application, but that's often not an acceptable way to proceed, particularly if the application is going to be using a Web page over the Internet (instead of just an intranet). More likely, you'll want to handle security completely on the server. Assuming you're using the SQL Server OLE DB provider, here are some things to keep in mind:

- The SQL Server software and the IIS software must be installed and running on the same computer. The database, of course, can be elsewhere on your network.

- You need to enable anonymous access on the Web server. To check this, open the Internet Service Manager and select Properties for the Default Web Site. Choose the Directory Security tab and click the Edit button in the Anonymous Access and Authentication Control section. Select the Allow Anonymous Access check box and click the Edit button for the Account used. Select the Internet guest account, which will be an account starting with IUSR (for example, for the Web server MUSHROOM this account is IUSR_MUSHROOM) and check the Enable Automatic Password Synchronization check box. This ensures that Windows NT will recognize the account as a valid domain account.

- You also need to make sure the Web account has the permission to log on locally, so that it can get to your SQL Server databases. Open the Windows NT User Manager and select Policies ➤ User Rights. Select Log On Locally from the combo box and make sure your Internet guest account appears in the list.

- You also need to tell SQL Server that this account should be allowed to retrieve data. In SQL Enterprise Manager, expand the Security folder for the database you want to connect to and click on the Logins node. Right-click on this node and choose New Login. Type in the domain and name of the Internet Guest account (for example, for a server named MUSHROOM in a domain named CANYON, enter CANYON\MUSHROOM), click the option button for Windows NT Authentication, choose your domain, and select the Grant Access option button. Select the default database that you're going to retrieve data from. Then select the Database Access tab and check all databases that you want to access over the Internet.

- Finally, you need to specify when you send the original RDS request that the server should use Windows NT Integrated Security rather than SQL Server security. This ensures that all the work you've done to set up the operating system account as a SQL Server user is worthwhile. To do this, include `Integrated Security=SSPI` in your OLE DB connection string.

Once everything is set up, the easiest way to check your work is to actually retrieve and change some data from the server. I'll show you four ways to do this, in order of increasing complexity:

- Using a disconnected recordset

- Using the RDS.DataControl object

- Using the RDS.DataSpace object

- Using a custom business object

Using a Disconnected Recordset

The frmMSRemote form in the RDSDemo sample project demonstrates the most basic way to use RDS:

1. Fetch a recordset using the MSRemote OLE DB Provider.

2. Disconnect the recordset from its data source.

3. Reconnect the recordset if changes are to be made.

The MSRemote OLE DB provider doesn't connect directly to a data source itself. Instead, it takes the Internet name of another computer and a connection string that's valid on that computer. MSRemote looks for IIS on the other computer, sends it the connection string, and lets IIS make the connection using OLE DB on its own computer. Thus, for this sample the connection string is

```
Provider=MS Remote; ➡
Remote Server=http://mushroom; ➡
Remote Provider=SQLOLEDB; ➡
DATA SOURCE=MUSHROOM; ➡
DATABASE=Northwind; ➡
Integrated Security=SSPI
```

Here the Remote Server option is the only thing that the MSRemote provider looks at. It takes the rest of the OLE DB connection string and passes it off to the IIS server running at that address. You'll see that the remaining part of the string is a standard connection string for the SQL Server OLE DB Provider. Note the use of the Integrated Security option as discussed in the previous section.

Here's the entire code used for fetching the data:

```
Private mrstCustomers As New ADOR.Recordset
Private Sub Form_Load()
    Dim cn As New ADODB.Connection
    ' Connect to the server
    cn.Open "Provider=MS Remote;" & _
     "Remote Server=http://mushroom;" & _
     "Remote Provider=SQLOLEDB;" & _
     "DATA SOURCE=MUSHROOM;DATABASE=Northwind" & _
     ";Integrated Security=SSPI"
    ' Set the recordset options
    Set mrstCustomers.ActiveConnection = cn
    mrstCustomers.Source = _
     "SELECT * FROM Customers"
    mrstCustomers.CursorLocation = adUseClient
    mrstCustomers.CursorType = adOpenStatic
    mrstCustomers.LockType = adLockBatchOptimistic
    ' Open the recordset
    mrstCustomers.Open
    ' Set the marshalling option
    mrstCustomers.MarshalOptions = _
     adMarshalModifiedOnly
    ' Disconnect the recordset
    Set mrstCustomers.ActiveConnection = Nothing
    cn.Close
    Set cn = Nothing
```

```
        ' Load the data to the UI
        LoadData
        mfLoaded = True
    End Sub

    Private Sub LoadData()
        ' Move the current recordset row to the form
        mfLoaded = False
        With mrstCustomers
            txtCustomerID = .Fields("CustomerID") & ""
            txtCompanyName = .Fields("CompanyName") & ""
            txtContactName = .Fields("ContactName") & ""
            txtContactTitle = .Fields("ContactTitle") & ""
            txtAddress = .Fields("Address") & ""
            txtCity = .Fields("City") & ""
            txtRegion = .Fields("Region") & ""
            txtPostalCode = .Fields("PostalCode") & ""
            txtCountry = .Fields("Country") & ""
            txtPhone = .Fields("Phone") & ""
            txtFax = .Fields("Fax") & ""
            ' And update the record counter
            txtRecord = .AbsolutePosition & " of " & _
              .RecordCount
        End With
        mfLoaded = True
    End Sub
```

There are a few points of interest here. First, you'll notice that the Recordset object is declared as ADOR.Recordset instead of ADODB.Recordset. ADOR is the ProgID for the Microsoft ActiveX Data Objects Recordset Library. This library matches the regular ADO library precisely for the Recordset object, but it contains no other objects. In a client program that doesn't need other objects, this can save you a bit of overhead. (Of course, here it's only used for demonstration, since the connection object comes from the regular ADO library.)

Next, you can see the steps necessary to create a disconnected recordset:

1. Open a connection to the data source (in this case, using the MS Remote OLE DB provider).

2. Set the ActiveConnection property of the recordset to use this connection.

3. Set other properties of the recordset to control what type of cursor you'll get. Note that with a disconnected recordset, even if you call for a dynamic or keyset cursor, you'll receive a static cursor, since there's no way for a disconnected recordset to receive updates from other users. You must choose client-side cursors, since you're not going to remain connected to the server.

4. Be sure to set the lock type to adLockBatchOptimistic. If you neglect this step, even though the disconnected recordset will cache multiple changes locally, it will only save a single change (at most) to the server and you won't get any error messages about the other changes being lost. If you don't specify a lock type, you won't be able to make any changes to the recordset at all.

5. Open the recordset.

6. Set the MarshalOptions property to adMarshalModifiedOnly. This tells ADO to send only changed records to the server when you reconnect, rather than every record, and will vastly speed up operations.

7. Set the ActiveConnection property to Nothing and close the connection (this is what makes it a disconnected recordset). Although you may think this would invalidate the recordset, in fact what it does is keep it in client-side memory.

Once you've got such a recordset, you can work with it just as you can with any other recordset. For example, there are no surprises in the record navigation code, nor in the code that saves changes from the user interface back to the recordset:

```
Private Sub cmdFirst_Click()
    mrstCustomers.MoveFirst
    LoadData
End Sub

Private Sub cmdLast_Click()
    mrstCustomers.MoveLast
    LoadData
End Sub

Private Sub cmdNext_Click()
    If Not mrstCustomers.EOF Then
        mrstCustomers.MoveNext
        If mrstCustomers.EOF Then
            mrstCustomers.MoveLast
```

```
            End If
        End If
        LoadData
    End Sub


    Private Sub cmdPrevious_Click()
        If Not mrstCustomers.BOF Then
            mrstCustomers.MovePrevious
            If mrstCustomers.BOF Then
                mrstCustomers.MoveFirst
            End If
        End If
        LoadData
    End Sub
    Private Sub txtAddress_Change()
        ' Write changes to the recordset
        If mfLoaded Then
            mrstCustomers.Fields("Address") = _
             txtAddress.Text & ""
            mfDirty = True
            cmdSaveChanges.Enabled = True
        End If
    End Sub
    ' Code for other textbox change events is similar
```

To save changes back to the server, you simply open another connection and assign the recordset's ActiveConnection property back to that connection:

```
    Private Sub cmdSaveChanges_Click()
        Dim cn As New ADODB.Connection
        mfLoaded = False
        ' Reconnect to the server
        cn.Open "Provider=MS Remote;" & _
         "Remote Server=http://mushroom;" & _
         "Remote Provider=SQLOLEDB;" & _
         "DATA SOURCE=MUSHROOM;DATABASE=Northwind" & _
         ";Integrated Security=SSPI"
        Set mrstCustomers.ActiveConnection = cn
        mrstCustomers.UpdateBatch
        mfDirty = False
        cmdSaveChanges.Enabled = False
        ' Need to update the client recordset
        ' before we disconnect again
```

```
            mrstCustomers.Resync
            LoadData
            Set mrstCustomers.ActiveConnection = Nothing
            cn.Close
            Set cn = Nothing
            mfLoaded = True
    End Sub
```

The UpdateBatch method takes all the locally cached changes and returns them to the server. If any of the changes fail (for example, because someone else edited the record), then all changes are discarded. If you're working in a busy database, you may wish to reconnect and save changes any time a record is edited.

Finally, the frmMSRemote form in the RDSDemo sample application implements a warning on the form's QueryUnload event, since it's possible for the user to attempt to close the form with multiple data changes pending:

```
    Private Sub Form_QueryUnload(Cancel As Integer, _
      UnloadMode As Integer)
        Dim intRet As Integer
        If mfDirty Then
            intRet = MsgBox( _
              "Would you like to save your changes?", _
              vbYesNo, "frmMSRemote")
            If intRet = vbYes Then
                cmdSaveChanges_Click
            End If
        End If
        mfDirty = False
        mrstCustomers.Close
    End Sub
```

Using the RDS.DataControl Object

To continue with the other techniques in this section, you need to be sure that the Microsoft Remote Data Services library is loaded (under Project ➤ References, of course). This library provides two objects of interest. You'll learn about the Data-Space object in the next section of this chapter. For now, it's time to look at the RDS.DataControl object, which provides a bindable, remotable source of data. You can see this object in action on the frmRemoteDataControl form in the RDS-Demo sample project.

Creating and binding a recordset via this control is very similar to other binding techniques you've seen elsewhere in this book:

```
' Bindable source for the recordset
Private mdc As RDS.DataControl
' Bindings for this source
Private mBindCol As BindingCollection
Private Sub Form_Load()
    ' Initialize the data control
    Set mdc = New RDS.DataControl
    With mdc
        .Connect = "Provider=SQLOLEDB;" & _
         "DATA SOURCE=MUSHROOM;DATABASE=Northwind" & _
         ";Integrated Security=SSPI"
        .SQL = "SELECT * FROM Customers"
        .Server = "http://mushroom"
        .ExecuteOptions = adcExecAsync
        .Refresh
        Do While .ReadyState = adcReadyStateLoaded
            DoEvents
        Loop
    End With
    ' And bind it to the UI
    Set mBindCol = New BindingCollection
    With mBindCol
        Set .DataSource = mdc
        .Add txtCustomerID, "Text", "CustomerID"
        .Add txtCompanyName, "Text", "CompanyName"
        .Add txtContactName, "Text", "ContactName"
        .Add txtContactTitle, "Text", "ContactTitle"
        .Add txtAddress, "Text", "Address"
        .Add txtCity, "Text", "City"
        .Add txtRegion, "Text", "Region"
        .Add txtPostalCode, "Text", "PostalCode"
        .Add txtCountry, "Text", "Country"
        .Add txtPhone, "Text", "Phone"
        .Add txtFax, "Text", "Fax"
    End With
    txtRecord = mdc.Recordset.AbsolutePosition & _
      " of " & mdc.Recordset.RecordCount
    mfLoaded = True
End Sub
```

As you can see, you need to set a few properties of this "control" (actually an object in memory, not something you can place directly on a form) before using it:

- The Connect property holds an OLE DB connect string that's valid on the server you'll be connecting to.

- The SQL property holds the SQL statement to execute.

- The Server property holds the Internet address of the IIS server that will handle creating the recordset.

- The ExecuteOptions property can be set (as it is here) for asynchronous operation, so that the user could proceed with another operation if the data took a long time to fetch.

Once you've called the DataControl's Refresh method, you're all set. You just create a new BindingCollection object and use it to bind form fields to recordset fields, and you've automatically got a bound, updateable, disconnected recordset. The recordset is disconnected automatically because it's been fetched via the stateless HTTP protocol.

Record navigation is done by calling the standard methods of the DataControl's exposed Recordset object:

```
Private Sub cmdFirst_Click()
    mfLoaded = False
    mdc.Recordset.MoveFirst
    txtRecord = mdc.Recordset.AbsolutePosition & _
     " of " & mdc.Recordset.RecordCount
    mfLoaded = True
End Sub

Private Sub cmdLast_Click()
    mfLoaded = False
    mdc.Recordset.MoveLast
    txtRecord = mdc.Recordset.AbsolutePosition & _
     " of " & mdc.Recordset.RecordCount
    mfLoaded = True
End Sub

Private Sub cmdNext_Click()
    mfLoaded = False
    If Not mdc.Recordset.EOF Then
        mdc.Recordset.MoveNext
```

```
        If mdc.Recordset.EOF Then
            mdc.Recordset.MoveLast
        End If
    End If
    txtRecord = mdc.Recordset.AbsolutePosition & _
     " of " & mdc.Recordset.RecordCount
    mfLoaded = True
End Sub

Private Sub cmdPrevious_Click()
    mfLoaded = False
    If Not mdc.Recordset.BOF Then
        mdc.Recordset.MovePrevious
        If mdc.Recordset.BOF Then
            mdc.Recordset.MoveFirst
        End If
    End If
    txtRecord = mdc.Recordset.AbsolutePosition & _
     " of " & mdc.Recordset.RecordCount
    mfLoaded = True
End Sub
```

Because this recordset is disconnected, you must explicitly save any changes back to the server before destroying the recordset. The DataControl object wraps the entire reconnect-and-save operation in a single method. Once again, the form includes code to help prevent the user from inadvertently losing changes by closing it:

```
Private Sub cmdSaveChanges_Click()
    mdc.SubmitChanges
    mfDirty = False
End Sub
Private Sub Form_QueryUnload(Cancel As Integer, _
  UnloadMode As Integer)
    Dim intRet As Integer
    If mfDirty Then
        intRet = MsgBox( _
         "Would you like to save your changes?", _
         vbYesNo, "frmMSRemote")
        If intRet = vbYes Then
            cmdSaveChanges_Click
        End If
    End If
    mfDirty = False
End Sub
```

Using the RDS.DataSpace Object

Besides the DataControl, the RDS library also provides a DataSpace object. You can think of the DataSpace as letting you get a bit more involved with the internal operation of the DataControl; you'll still need a DataControl object if you want to bind your results to visual controls.

The frmDataSpace form in the RDSDemo project demonstrates the use of the RDS.DataSpace object. Almost all the code in this sample is exactly the same as the code in the previous section. The only major difference is in the code that retrieves the data in the first place:

```
Private mds As New RDS.DataSpace
' Server-side data factory object
Private mdf As Object
Private mrstCustomers As ADOR.Recordset
' Bindable source for the recordset
Private mdc As RDS.DataControl
' Bindings for this source
Private mBindCol As BindingCollection
' Flag that data is loaded
Private Sub Form_Load()
    ' Create a DataFactory object on the server
    Set mdf = mds.CreateObject("RDSServer.DataFactory", _
     "http://mushroom")
    ' Use the DataFactory to grab a recordset
    Set mrstCustomers = mdf.query("Provider=SQLOLEDB;" & _
        "DATA SOURCE=MUSHROOM;DATABASE=Northwind" & _
        ";Integrated Security=SSPI", "SELECT * FROM Customers")
    ' Initialize the data control
    Set mdc = New RDS.DataControl
    Set mdc.SourceRecordset = mrstCustomers
    ' And bind it to the UI
    Set mBindCol = New BindingCollection
    With mBindCol
        Set .DataSource = mdc
        .Add txtCustomerID, "Text", "CustomerID"
        .Add txtCompanyName, "Text", "CompanyName"
        .Add txtContactName, "Text", "ContactName"
        .Add txtContactTitle, "Text", "ContactTitle"
        .Add txtAddress, "Text", "Address"
        .Add txtCity, "Text", "City"
```

```
            .Add txtRegion, "Text", "Region"
            .Add txtPostalCode, "Text", "PostalCode"
            .Add txtCountry, "Text", "Country"
            .Add txtPhone, "Text", "Phone"
            .Add txtFax, "Text", "Fax"
        End With
        txtRecord = mdc.Recordset.AbsolutePosition & _
          " of " & mdc.Recordset.RecordCount
        mfLoaded = True
    End Sub
```

This code starts by using the DataSpace object to create an object of class RDSServer.DataFactory on the specified server (`http://mushroom` in this case). The RDSServer library is installed when you install IIS 4, and it provides the generic business object that is used implicitly by the DataControl and explicitly by the DataSpace to retrieve data.

The DataFactory object in turn (here late-bound, since the RDSServer library isn't installed on the client) is used to create a recordset, which is then bound to the DataControl object simply by setting the SourceRecordset property. After that, the rest of the operations of this form use the DataControl, just as the previous example did.

Invoking Business Objects on the Server

Why go to all the trouble of using the DataSpace object explicitly when the Data-Control takes care of all those details for you? Well, take another look at this line of code:

```
Set mdf = mds.CreateObject("RDSServer.DataFactory", _
    "http://mushroom")
```

Look familiar? The syntax of DataSpace.CreateObject is similar to that of the intrinsic Visual Basic CreateObject function, with the addition of an argument to specify the server. And there's where the real power of RDS comes in: you're not limited to creating objects of the RDSServer.DataFactory class. You can create your own server-side business objects and use them to retrieve data into disconnected recordsets via HTTP using the rest of the RDS services.

A few points about using custom business objects:

- If you attempt to create an object on a server that doesn't exist or can't be reached, you'll get an error on the DataSpace.CreateObject method. This will be error –2147012867, Internet Client Error: Cannot Connect to Server.

- If you attempt to create an unknown or unusable object, the DataSpace.CreateObject method will still happily proceed without error. But the first time you attempt to use a method of the object, you'll get error –2147024891, Unexpected Error.

- All objects created in this way are late-bound. Since you're connecting to the object over the Internet, the usual slight performance degradation to late-binding doesn't really matter. On the plus side, this means that you don't need the TypeLib for the custom object to be installed on the client.

- Because the remoting is done over the stateless HTTP protocol, there's no way to have persistent properties in a business object that's used by RDS. Each time you call a method from the object, it's recreated on the server.

In order for a custom business object to be usable from RDS, you have to tell IIS that the object is safe to launch. This requires creating a key in the Registry (there's a reg file in the sample code that shows you how to do this):

```
HKEY_LOCAL_MACHINE
 \SYSTEM
  \CurrentControlSet
  \Services
  \W3SVC
   \Parameters
   \ADCLaunch
    \MyServer.MyObject
```

Obviously, you replace MyServer.MyObject with the actual ProgID and ClsID of your custom business object.

For an example of this technique, look at frmCustomObject in the RDSDemo sample project. In order for this sample to work, you'll need to build the RDS-ServerDemo project on the computer that's running IIS and SQL Server (or build it on another computer and use the Visual Basic Package and Deploy Wizard to install it). You'll also need to run the RDSServerDemo.reg file to create the launch permissions key in the Registry.

NOTE   Microsoft has created a tool, ClsIdView, to make registering RDS servers easier. It also helps locate any other problems with data access libraries on your server. You can download this tool from http://support.microsoft.com/download/support/mslfiles/Clsidvw.exe.

WARNING   If you're debugging a business object, you'll find that IIS does not release the DLL once it's loaded. In order to make changes and recompile, you'll need to use the Services applet in Control Panel to stop and restart the World Wide Web publishing service.

The frmCustomObject sample form starts by creating an object of the appropriate custom class and then calls its GetCountries method to retrieve a list of countries. Next, it lets the user select a country and retrieves the records from that country:

```
Private Sub Form_Load()
    ' Create a DataFactory object on the server
    Set mdf = mds.CreateObject("RDSServerDemo.DataFactory", _
    "http://mushroom")
    Set mrstCountries = mdf.GetCountries
    Do Until mrstCountries.EOF
        lboCountry.AddItem mrstCountries.Fields("Country")
        mrstCountries.MoveNext
    Loop
End Sub
Private Sub lboCountry_Click()
    Dim ctl As Control
    ' Use the DataFactory to grab a recordset
    Set mrstCustomers = mdf.GetCustomers(lboCountry.Text)
    ' Initialize the data control
    Set mdc = New RDS.DataControl
    Set mdc.SourceRecordset = mrstCustomers
    ' And bind it to the UI
    Set mBindCol = New BindingCollection
    With mBindCol
        Set .DataSource = mdc
        .Add txtCustomerID, "Text", "CustomerID"
        .Add txtCompanyName, "Text", "CompanyName"
        .Add txtContactName, "Text", "ContactName"
        .Add txtContactTitle, "Text", "ContactTitle"
        .Add txtAddress, "Text", "Address"
        .Add txtCity, "Text", "City"
        .Add txtRegion, "Text", "Region"
        .Add txtPostalCode, "Text", "PostalCode"
        .Add txtCountry, "Text", "Country"
```

```
            .Add txtPhone, "Text", "Phone"
            .Add txtFax, "Text", "Fax"
        End With
        txtRecord = mdc.Recordset.AbsolutePosition & _
          " of " & mdc.Recordset.RecordCount
        mfLoaded = True
        For Each ctl In Me.Controls
            ctl.Enabled = True
        Next ctl
        txtCustomerID.Enabled = False
        cmdSaveChanges.Enabled = False
    End Sub
```

As you can see, once you've created a data factory object of any class, you can call its methods just like you call any other object method in Visual Basic. When there are changes to return, the client program just sends the entire changed recordset back to the server. This is necessary, of course, because the business object is stateless.

```
    Private Sub cmdSaveChanges_Click()
        mdf.SubmitChanges mrstCustomers
        mfDirty = False
    End Sub
```

The business object itself is implemented in an ActiveX DLL with a single class. That class exposes four methods. First, there's one that's not used at all in the sample code:

```
    Const conVersion = "10"

    Public Function Version() As String
        ' Calling this method provides an easy way to
        ' test proper business object registration
        Version = conVersion
    End Function
```

Providing a simple method like this in your custom business classes allows you to check quickly whether you've got the connection to the class set up and everything registered properly. You can use the DataSpace object's CreateObject method to create the class, then call its Version method. If you get the hard-coded string back, all is well. If not, something's not right. (Perhaps you forgot to give the object launch permissions?)

The GetCountries method returns a list of all the values of the Country field in the Customers table in the Northwind database on the local server:

```
Public Function GetCountries() As ADODB.Recordset
    ' Return all countries in the table
    Dim cn As New ADODB.Connection
    Dim rst As New ADODB.Recordset

    cn.CursorLocation = adUseClient
    cn.Open "Provider=SQLOLEDB;" & _
     "Data Source=(local);" & _
     "Initial Catalog=Northwind;" & _
     "Integrated Security=SSPI"

    rst.Open _
     "SELECT Country From Customers GROUP BY Country", _
     cn, adOpenKeyset, adLockBatchOptimistic

    Set GetCountries = rst
    Set rst.ActiveConnection = Nothing
End Function
```

Although the client program assigns the result of this function to an ADOR recordset, the function itself uses an ADODB recordset. It has to have the entire ADO library loaded so it can use the Connection object. Fortunately, there's no problem in assigning the two types of recordsets back and forth.

You'll see that the function itself does the entire work of opening and connecting to the database. Obviously, you could use code here to specify a database user with higher privileges than you want to give to the Internet guest account.

Note also that although the recordset is disconnected within the function, the connection is left open. This is necessary because if you closed the connection, the recordset would close too! Everything gets cleaned up neatly at the end of the function.

When the client program calls GetCustomers with the name of a country, the server executes a query to retrieve just those customers:

```
Public Function GetCustomers(strCountry As String) _
  As ADODB.Recordset
    ' Return all customers in the specified country
    Dim cn As New ADODB.Connection
```

```
      Dim rst As New ADODB.Recordset

      cn.CursorLocation = adUseClient
      cn.Open "Provider=SQLOLEDB;" & _
        "Data Source=(local);" & _
        "Initial Catalog=Northwind;" & _
        "Integrated Security=SSPI"

      rst.Open "SELECT * From Customers WHERE Country = '" & _
        strCountry & "'", cn, adOpenKeyset, _
        adLockBatchOptimistic

      Set GetCustomers = rst
      Set rst.ActiveConnection = Nothing
End Function
```

Finally, the code used to submit changes is also simple:

```
Public Function SubmitChanges( _
  rstCustomers As ADODB.Recordset)

      Dim cn As New ADODB.Connection
      Dim rst As New ADODB.Recordset

      cn.CursorLocation = adUseClient
      cn.Open "Provider=SQLOLEDB;" & _
        "Data Source=(local);" & _
        "Initial Catalog=Northwind;" & _
        "Integrated Security=SSPI"

      rst.Open rstCustomers, cn
      rst.UpdateBatch
      rst.Close
      Set rst = Nothing
      cn.Close
      Set cn = Nothing
End Function
```

Opening a recordset using an existing recordset as the source and a specified connection has the effect of reconnecting the disconnected recordset that was shipped in from the client. Because the client is using changed records marshalling, this recordset will contain only the updated records, rather than all the records that were originally sent out. If you needed to do some sort of custom conflict resolution between multiple users, this function would be the place for the code.

This example just scratches the surface of what you can do with a custom business object instantiated via RDS. As the name suggests, such objects are a good place to implement business rules for distributed applications. For example, if you used such an object to return a list of customers, you could check credit ratings when edited customers were returned and take action based on the ratings. Such rules would be enforced no matter which client created the objects.

CHAPTER

TWELVE

Using ADO MD to Summarize Data

- Basics of Multidimensional Data

- Understanding Multidimensional Data

- Introduction to Microsoft OLAP Server

- ADO MD Objects

- Additional ADO MD Techniques

In Chapter 2, you learned that ADO is designed to be extensible—that is, you can load multiple libraries, each of which adds some objects designed to work with the core ADO objects. This chapter covers one of those libraries, the Microsoft ActiveX Data Objects (Multidimensional), or ADO MD, library.

This library provides objects that are designed to help you work with both the schema and data provided by multidimensional data sources. In this chapter, I'll dig into the basics of multidimensional data, especially as provided by the new Microsoft OLAP Server, and then show how you can use the ADO MD objects to work with this data.

Basics of Multidimensional Data

In this section, I'll explore the basics of multidimensional data. First, I'll take a quick look at the basic concept and explain what distinguishes multidimensional data from the relational data you're probably more familiar with. Then I'll introduce Microsoft OLAP Server (formerly code-named "Plato") and show you how it helps slice and dice your data. Finally, I'll review the basic objects in the ADO MD object model. If you're anxious to work with ADO MD in Visual Basic code and are already familiar with multidimensional data, you might want to skip ahead to the next section.

Understanding Multidimensional Data

So what's this "multidimensional" thing all about, anyhow? It's about summarizing masses of data in a way that makes sense to human beings. Given, say, 500,000 individual sales receipts, how do you find patterns in them? Normally, the answer is that you summarize the data by looking for similarities and counting noses. Each way of summarizing the data amounts to a dimension.

Grouping queries give you a means to summarize along a single dimension. For example, you might use a GROUP BY clause in a query to determine what proportion of the sales for the last year were from stores in the US, as opposed to stores in Canada or Mexico. In this case, "location" would be the dimension of interest and the field to group by.

If you're familiar with Microsoft Access, you know about crosstab queries, which let you summarize data along two dimensions at once. For example, you could use a crosstab to answer the question "What were the sales in stores in the US, Canada, and Mexico during 1997 and 1998?" The crosstab query takes two dimensions (location and time, in this case) and populates a grid with some summary measure for all combinations of those dimensions.

What multidimensional data does is extend this concept to more than two dimensions. For example, you might define dimensions of Yearly Income, Marital Status, and Education Level, and ask what sales came from low-income families where the buyer was married and had a high school degree—as opposed to all other combinations of those three factors. Figure 12.1 shows an application (the Cube Browser that ships with Microsoft OLAP Server) displaying the results of just such a multidimensional query.

FIGURE 12.1:

Multidimensional data

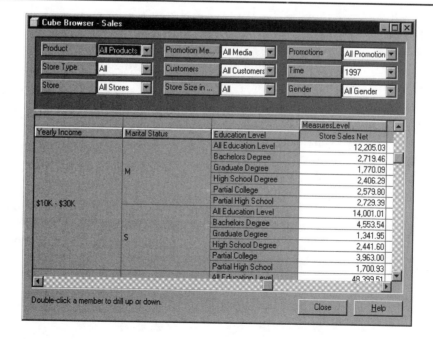

Introduction to Microsoft OLAP Server

Although there are many sources of multidimensional data available, the examples in this chapter work with Microsoft OLAP Server. This server ships with SQL Server 7, although you need to run a separate installation program to get it up and running on your system. The sample project for this chapter is configured to assume that you've got Microsoft OLAP Server running on the same computer as both SQL Server 7 and Visual Basic. As always, you may need to modify the connection strings in the samples if your configuration is different.

> **WARNING**   In the samples, the server name is BEAVER. Although the Microsoft SQL Server OLE DB provider recognizes "(local)" as a valid name for the SQL Server running on the local machine, the Microsoft OLAP Server OLE DB provider does not.

To get started, I'll review the basic terminology and concepts used by Microsoft OLAP Server. I'll also briefly discuss the Microsoft OLAP Manager, which is a Microsoft Management Console (MMC) application that provides access to data from Microsoft OLAP Server.

> **NOTE**   ADO MD is based on the OLE DB for OLAP specification, which Microsoft is developing as a somewhat open standard. For information on other companies supporting this standard, see `http://www.microsoft.com/data/oledb/olap/indsupp.htm`.

OLAP itself stands for Online Analytical Processing—as distinct from OLTP, Online Transaction Processing. If you think about a standard data entry application that takes in orders from all your branch offices and stores them in relational tables, that's an OLTP application. Now think about trying to do complex grouping and multidimensional queries within the confines of that OLTP application. Obviously, there'd be a performance problem there. The data in an OLTP application is stored in a way that speeds data entry and has minimal disk requirements. But this format (relational tables) is not optimal for summarizing the data and hunting for patterns in it.

That's where OLAP comes in. The basic idea is to trade off increased storage space now for increased speed of querying later. In addition, Microsoft OLAP

Server can work with Microsoft SQL Server to collect and summarize data from multiple heterogeneous databases as a single entity subject to multidimensional analysis.

Cubes, Dimensions, and Measures

The basic unit of storage and analysis in Microsoft OLAP Services is the cube. Cubes contain dimensions and measures. Dimensions come from dimension tables, while measures come from fact tables.

A dimension table contains relational data that you'd like to summarize by. For example, you might have a clients table, which you could group by Country, State, and City, or an inventory table, where you might want to group detail information by Year, Month, Week, and Day of sale.

A single cube can have multiple dimensions, each based on one or more dimension tables. A dimension represents a category for analyzing business data: geographical region or time in the examples above. Typically, a dimension has a natural hierarchy so that lower results can be "rolled up" into higher results: cities aggregated into states, or state totals into country totals. Each type of summary that can be retrieved from a single dimension is called a level, so you speak of a city level or a state level in a geographic dimension.

A fact table contains the basic information that you wish to summarize. This might be order detail information, payroll records, stock prices, or anything else that's amenable to summing and averaging. Any table that has supplied a field to a Sum or Avg function in a totals query is a good candidate for a fact table.

A cube must contain at least one measure, based on a column in a fact table (or a calculated expression), that you'd like to analyze. Cubes can also contain multiple measures. For example, a cube containing stock price information might use high, low, and close as measures. This cube could let you look at, say, the average closing price for three stocks over five years.

Of course, fact tables and dimension tables must be related—hardly surprising, given that you use the dimension tables to group information from the fact table. There are two basic OLAP schemas for relating these tables. In a star schema, every dimension table is related directly to the fact table. In a snowflake schema, some dimension tables are related indirectly to the fact table. For example, if your cube includes tblOrderDetails as a fact table, with tblCustomers and tblOrders as dimension tables, and tblCustomers is related to tblOrders, which in turn is related to tblOrderDetails, then you're dealing with a snowflake schema.

MOLAP, ROLAP, and HOLAP

Microsoft OLAP Services offers three different ways to make the trade-off between size and speed: Multidimensional OLAP (MOLAP), Relational OLAP (ROLAP), and Hybrid OLAP (HOLAP). Although this trade-off has no bearing on the logical ADO MD model of the data (it's strictly a matter of physical storage), you'll probably run across these terms—so it pays to understand them.

MOLAP copies all the data and all the aggregates to the OLAP server, where they are stored in an optimized multidimensional format. MOLAP gives the best query performance of the three types, because everything is right there when it's queried. On the other hand, it also takes up the most space and requires the most time to prepare.

ROLAP storage leaves the original data in the relational tables where it's already stored. ROLAP uses a separate set of relational tables to store and retrieve the aggregate data that the server uses to calculate cubes. ROLAP is the best bet for large data sets that are infrequently queried, since it minimizes up-front processing time and storage requirements.

HOLAP, as you might guess, is a hybrid of these two approaches. The original data remains in relational tables, but aggregations are stored on the server in the optimized multidimensional format. HOLAP is intermediate between ROLAP and MOLAP in speed and storage requirements. You might also have HOLAP storage in which some of the aggregations are left in ROLAP form.

Microsoft OLAP Manager

Installing Microsoft OLAP Server also installs Microsoft OLAP Manager. Just like SQL Enterprise Manager (and the Windows NT 5 administrative tools), this application runs within the confines of the Microsoft Management Console, a plug-in-oriented application that uses a TreeView to represent and manage hierarchical objects. Figure 12.2 shows Microsoft OLAP Manager at work. In this case, I've drilled down to the Sales cube in the FoodMart sample database that ships as part of Microsoft OLAP Server.

FIGURE 12.2:

Microsoft OLAP Manager

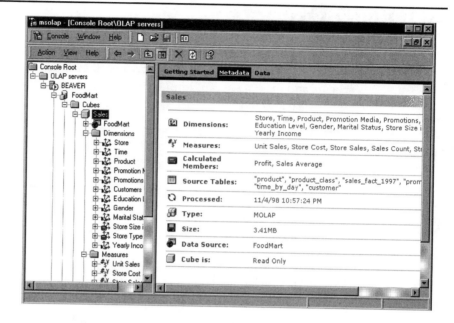

Explaining the use of the Microsoft OLAP Manager is beyond the scope of this book. Fortunately, the designers did an excellent job of making it nearly intuitive to use. When you first launch the Manager, it displays a hyperlinked "Getting Started" page that will walk you through a basic tutorial. And, although it includes an editor for complex operations, you'll find that the built-in wizards will do almost any task for you. If you right-click the Cubes folder beneath a database name and choose New Cube ➤ Wizard, it will walk you through the process of using a series of wizards to build, store, and process your data:

- Cube Wizard

- Dimension Wizard

- Storage Design Wizard

You can also right-click a cube and choose "Browse Data" to see the information stored in the cube. This will open the Cube Browser application that you saw in Figure 12.1.

ADO MD Objects

Although ADO MD is an extension to regular ADO, it actually defines more objects than ADO itself does! That's because it includes objects to model both the schema and the data of multidimensional data sources. Figure 12.3 shows the ADO MD object model.

FIGURE 12.3:

ADO MD object model

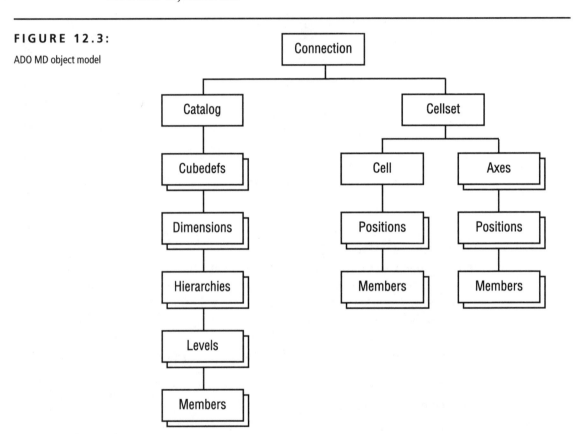

In this section, I'll examine each of these objects briefly, describe its relation to what you can see in the Microsoft OLAP Manager (the sample multidimensional provider I'm using), and show you its use in Visual Basic code. This isn't meant to be an exhaustive reference. If you want to see all the methods and properties of the ADO MD objects, refer to the Microsoft ADO MD Programmer's Reference, part of the Platform SDK.

Schema Objects

The schema objects in the ADO MD object model are used for retrieving design information about the particular multidimensional data source you're retrieving data from. You can't get to any of the actual data from these objects. You also can't create any new objects by manipulating the ADO MD schema objects. These objects are limited strictly to retrieving information on existing objects.

Catalog

The Catalog object represents schema information for a single multidimensional database. This object isn't very interesting, but it's necessary as the way to get to all the other schema objects. You can experiment with the Catalog object by clicking the Catalog button on the frmObjects form in the ADOMDSamples sample project. This runs the following code:

```
Private Sub cmdCatalog_Click()

    Dim cnn As New ADODB.Connection
    Dim cat As New ADOMD.Catalog
    Dim prp As ADODB.Property

    Screen.MousePointer = vbHourglass
    cnn.Open "Provider=MSOLAP.1; " & _
      "Integrated Security=SSPI;Data Source=BEAVER;" & _
      "Initial Catalog=FoodMart;"
    Set cat.ActiveConnection = cnn
    With lboProperties
        .Clear
        .AddItem "Name: " & cat.Name
        .AddItem "ActiveConnection: " & _
        cat.ActiveConnection
    End With
    Screen.MousePointer = vbDefault

End Sub
```

This code retrieves the two properties of the Catalog object and displays them in a list box on the form. (Unlike the other ADO MD objects, the Catalog object does not have a Properties collection to iterate.)

Note the similarity of the MSOLAP OLE DB provider connection string to the string used by the SQL Server OLE DB provider. Here the Data Source parameter names the OLAP server to use and the Initial Catalog parameter names the database to investigate.

You'll see also that this code sets the mouse pointer to the hourglass while the connection is being made. Retrieving schema information from the Microsoft OLAP Server via ADO MD is quite slow.

If you like, you can connect to an OLAP catalog without explicitly using an ADO Connection object:

```
cat.ActiveConnecton = "Provider=MSOLAP.1; " & _
    "Integrated Security=SSPI;Data Source=BEAVER;" & _
    "Initial Catalog=FoodMart;"
```

CubeDef

The CubeDef object represents a single cube from a multidimensional data source. The Catalog object contains a collection of CubeDef objects that you can iterate using For Next or For Each syntax. When you retrieve an individual Cube-Def, you can inspect its properties, as in this sample code from the frmObjects form in the ADOMDSamples project:

```
Private Sub cmdCubeDef_Click()

    Dim cat As New ADOMD.Catalog
    Dim cdf As ADOMD.CubeDef
    Dim prp As ADODB.Property

    Screen.MousePointer = vbHourglass
    cat.ActiveConnection = "Provider=MSOLAP.1; " & _
      "Integrated Security=SSPI;Data Source=BEAVER;" & _
      "Initial Catalog=FoodMart;"
    Set cdf = cat.CubeDefs(0)
    With lboProperties
        .Clear
        .AddItem "Name: " & cdf.Name
        .AddItem "Description: " & cdf.Description
        For Each prp In cdf.Properties
            .AddItem prp.Name & ": " & prp.Value
        Next prp
    End With
```

```
        Screen.MousePointer = vbDefault

End Sub
```

Table 12.1 lists some of the properties of the CubeDef object. The properties in the table are all provider-supplied properties; that is, they might or might not be present, depending on the OLE DB provider used to initialize the cube. This table lists properties from the MSOLAP provider. As you can see in the source code above, there are also some properties (Name and Description) that are intrinsic to the object and are not included in the Properties collection.

TABLE 12.1: CubeDef Properties from the MSOLAP Provider

Property	Description
CATALOG_NAME	Name of the parent Catalog object. Note that this substitutes for a more standard Parent property.
LAST_SCHEMA_UPDATE	Date and time of the last design change to this cube.
LAST_DATA_UPDATE	Date and time of the last data change to this cube.
CUBE_NAME	Name of the cube.
DESCRIPTION	Readable description of the cube.

The CubeDef object provides two intrinsic properties regardless of the provider used: Name and Description. These will not necessarily match the provider-supplied properties. For instance, with the MSOLAP provider, `CubeDef.Properties-("DESCRIPTION")` may return Null while `CubeDef.Description` returns an empty string.

The CubeDef object has no methods.

Dimension

The Dimension object represents a dimension within a cube. A dimension is a single way of summarizing data—for example, by geographic location. The Dimension button on the frmObjects form in the ADOMDSamples project calls code that instantiates a Dimension object and then retrieves its properties:

```
Private Sub cmdDimension_Click()

    Dim cat As New ADOMD.Catalog
```

```
Dim dmn As ADOMD.Dimension
Dim prp As ADODB.Property

Screen.MousePointer = vbHourglass
cat.ActiveConnection = "Provider=MSOLAP.1; " & _
  "Integrated Security=SSPI;Data Source=BEAVER;" & _
  "Initial Catalog=FoodMart;"
Set dmn = cat.CubeDefs(0).Dimensions(0)
With lboProperties
    .Clear
    .AddItem "Name: " & dmn.Name
    .AddItem "UniqueName: " & dmn.UniqueName
    .AddItem "Description: " & dmn.Description
    For Each prp In dmn.Properties
        .AddItem prp.Name & ": " & prp.Value
    Next prp
End With
Screen.MousePointer = vbDefault

End Sub
```

As with the other ADO MD objects, the Dimension object has both intrinsic properties (supplied by ADO MD itself) and provider-supplied properties (supplied, in this case, by the MSOLAP provider). Table 12.2 shows some of the properties for a Dimension object. The Type column in this table contains "I" for intrinsic properties and "P" for provider-supplied properties. Note that the intrinsic properties do *not* show up when you iterate through the Properties collection; you must retrieve them specifically by name.

TABLE 12.2: Selected Properties of the Dimension Object

Property	Type	Description
Name	I	Name of the dimension.
Description	I	Description of this dimension (can be empty).
UniqueName	I	Unambiguous name for the dimension. Since you can have, for example, a Dimension and a Level with the same name, this property provides a way to disambiguate the two in code.
CATALOG_NAME	P	Name of the owning Catalog object.

Continued on next page

TABLE 12.2 CONTINUED: Selected Properties of the Dimension Object

Property	Type	Description
CUBE_NAME	P	Name of the parent CubeDef object.
DIMENSION_CAPTION	P	Value to be used to identify this dimension to human beings.
DIMENSION_ORDINAL	P	Number of this dimension among all the dimensions in the cube. Note that this will not necessarily be its place in the Dimensions collection.
DIMENSION_CARDINALITY	P	Number of unique values at the most detailed level of drilldown in this dimension.

Hierarchy

The Hierarchy object represents a way in which a dimension can be summarized or "rolled up." Each Dimension object has a collection of Hierarchy objects (the Hierarchies collection), one of which is identified as being the highest level of rollup. You can retrieve the properties of a Hierarchy object with code similar to this code from behind the Hierarchy button on the frmObjects form in the ADOMDSamples project:

```
Private Sub cmdHierarchy_Click()

    Dim cat As New ADOMD.Catalog
    Dim hrc As ADOMD.Hierarchy
    Dim prp As ADODB.Property

    Screen.MousePointer = vbHourglass
    cat.ActiveConnection = "Provider=MSOLAP.1; " & _
      "Integrated Security=SSPI;Data Source=BEAVER;" & _
      "Initial Catalog=FoodMart;"
    Set hrc = cat.CubeDefs(0).Dimensions(0).Hierarchies(0)
    With lboProperties
        .Clear
        .AddItem "Name: " & hrc.Name
        .AddItem "UniqueName: " & hrc.UniqueName
        .AddItem "Description: " & hrc.Description
        For Each prp In hrc.Properties
            .AddItem prp.Name & ": " & prp.Value
        Next prp
```

```
    End With
    Screen.MousePointer = vbDefault

End Sub
```

Table 12.3 lists some of the properties of a Hierarchy object supplied by the MSOLAP provider. Once again, the properties are identified as to whether they are intrinsic or provider supplied.

TABLE 12.3: Selected Properties of the Hierarchy Object

Property	Type	Description
Name	I	Name of the hierarchy.
Description	I	Description of this hierarchy (can be empty).
UniqueName	I	Unambiguous name for the hierarchy.
CATALOG_NAME	P	Name of the owning Catalog object.
CUBE_NAME	P	Name of the parent CubeDef object.
HIERARCHY_CARDINALITY	P	Number of unique values in the bottom level of the hierarchy.
ALL_MEMBER	P	Name of the Hierarchy Member that includes the entire hierarchy in rolled-up fashion.

Level

The Level object represents a single part of a hierarchy—for example, the city information in a geographic level. By this time, the code for retrieving the properties of a Level object should come as no surprise. Note that ADO MD lends itself to long strings of nested hierarchical objects, unlike regular ADO.

```
    Private Sub cmdLevel_Click()

        Dim cat As New ADOMD.Catalog
        Dim lvl As ADOMD.Level
        Dim prp As ADODB.Property

        Screen.MousePointer = vbHourglass
        cat.ActiveConnection = "Provider=MSOLAP.1; " & _
          "Integrated Security=SSPI;Data Source=BEAVER;" & _
```

```
     "Initial Catalog=FoodMart;"
Set lvl = cat.CubeDefs(0).Dimensions(0). _
 Hierarchies(0).Levels(1)
With lboProperties
    .Clear
    .AddItem "Caption: " & lvl.Caption
    .AddItem "Depth: " & lvl.Depth
    .AddItem "Name: " & lvl.Name
    .AddItem "UniqueName: " & lvl.UniqueName
    .AddItem "Description: " & lvl.Description
    For Each prp In lvl.Properties
        .AddItem prp.Name & ": " & prp.Value
    Next prp
End With
Screen.MousePointer = vbDefault

End Sub
```

Levels have more of the intrinsic type of properties than the other schema objects above them in the object model. Table 12.4 shows some of the properties of the Level object (when MSOLAP is used as the provider).

TABLE 12.4: Selected Properties of the Level Object

Property	Type	Description
Name	I	Name of the level.
Description	I	Description of the level (can be empty).
UniqueName	I	Unambiguous name for the level.
Caption	I	Label to use for this level.
Depth	I	Number of levels between this level and the top of the hierarchy.
CATALOG_NAME	P	Name of the owning Catalog object.
CUBE_NAME	P	Name of the parent CubeDef object.
LEVEL_CARDINALITY	P	Number of unique values in this level.

Member

The Member object represents the basic unit of information that's summarized in a particular data cube. To make matters somewhat confusing, there's only one Member object in the type library, but it's used in several different ways. Here it's a child of the Level object; in a few pages you'll meet it again as a child of the Position object.

You can think of a Member as the building block of a cube. Members in a Level are the different values that that particular level can take on. To retrieve the information on a member, just retrieve it from the Level's Members collection, as in this code from the Member button of the frmObjects sample in the ADOMDSamples project:

```
Private Sub cmdMember_Click()

    Dim cat As New ADOMD.Catalog
    Dim mbr As ADOMD.Member
    Dim prp As ADODB.Property

    Screen.MousePointer = vbHourglass
    cat.ActiveConnection = "Provider=MSOLAP.1; " & _
      "Integrated Security=SSPI;Data Source=BEAVER;" & _
      "Initial Catalog=FoodMart;"
    Set mbr = cat.CubeDefs(0).Dimensions(0). _
      Hierarchies(0).Levels(1).Members(0)
    With lboProperties
        .Clear
        .AddItem "Caption: " & mbr.Caption
        .AddItem "ChildCount: " & mbr.ChildCount
        .AddItem "Description: " & mbr.Description
        .AddItem "LevelDepth: " & mbr.LevelDepth
        .AddItem "LevelName: " & mbr.LevelName
        .AddItem "Name: " & mbr.Name
        .AddItem "Type: " & mbr.Type
        .AddItem "UniqueName: " & mbr.UniqueName
        For Each prp In mbr.Properties
            .AddItem mbr.Name & ": " & prp.Value
        Next prp
    End With
    Screen.MousePointer = vbDefault

End Sub
```

The MSOLAP provider doesn't add any provider-specific properties to a Member object in a Level. Table 12.5 lists the intrinsic properties for such a Member object.

TABLE 12.5: Properties of a Member in a Level

Property	Type	Description
Caption	I	Label to use for the member.
ChildCount	I	Number of child members of this member.
Description	I	Description of the member.
LevelDepth	I	Number of levels between the parent Level of this member and the top of the hierarchy.
LevelName	I	Parent Level of this member.
Name	I	Name of the member.
Type	I	Type of this member. Possible values are adMemberRegular (for an instance of a business entity), adMemberMeasure (for a summarized value), adMemberFormula (for a calculated member), adMemberAll (for the "All" member of a Hierarchy), and adMemberUnknown.
UniqueName	I	Unambiguous name for the member.

Members in Levels are recursive. That is, a Member returns a ChildCount property, and if that count is greater than zero, it has a Children collection of Member objects of its own. This is the information that's used in progressive drilldown and filtering of a Dimension. The children of a Member of a Level are those Members of the next Level in the Hierarchy whose parent in the original data is the parent Member. If you think this is confusing, you're right. Figure 12.4 may make this a bit clearer. Note that all the children of the members in the level "Store Country" are themselves members in the level "Store State."

FIGURE 12.4:

A portion of the object hierarchy of the Sales cube

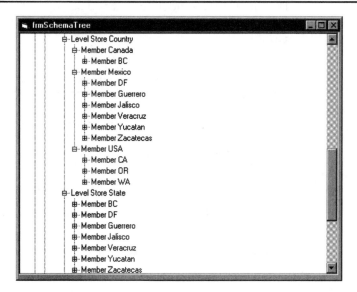

NOTE   Figure 12.4 is drawn from the frmSchemaTree sample form in the ADOMDSamples project. Just about all the code behind this form, which allows you to see graphically the relation between the ADO MD schema objects, is TreeView bookkeeping code that won't be reviewed here.

Data Objects

In addition to the schema objects, ADO MD defines a selection of objects that you can use to return the data from a Cube. Just as a relational database gives rise to recordsets, a multidimensional database gives rise to cellsets. ADO MD defines a set of objects that you can use to create and explore these cellsets. Figure 12.5 displays some of the data from the sample Sales cube on a Hierarchical FlexGrid on a Visual Basic form (this is frmCellset from the ADOMDSamples project).

Data from a multi-dimensional cellset

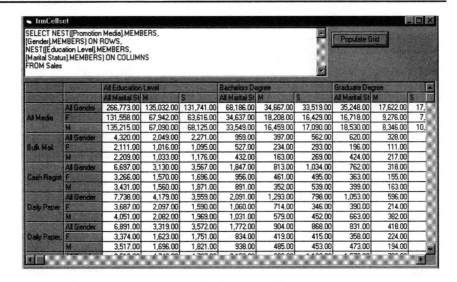

Because the data in a cube consists of summary information, it's never editable. So you don't have to worry about the complexities you sometimes face when editing recordsets. Cellsets (and their constituent objects) are always read-only.

Cellset

The Cellset object represents the results of a single multidimensional query. It's analogous to a Recordset object in regular ADO. A cellset has a source, just as a recordset does. However, where the source of a recordset is a SQL statement, the source of a cellset is a Multidimensional expression (MDX) statement. MDX is a set of extensions to SQL designed to capture the selection, drilldown, and filtering qualities of multidimensional data manipulation. The basic idea is that an MDX statement specifies a series of axes and a cube to select them from. For instance, the MDX statement that led to the information in Figure 12.5 is:

```
SELECT
NEST([Promotion Media].MEMBERS,
[Gender].MEMBERS) ON ROWS,
NEST([Education Level].MEMBERS,
[Marital Status].MEMBERS) ON COLUMNS
FROM Sales
```

This statement specifies a cellset where rows are aggregated first on the Promotion Media dimension and then on the Gender dimension, Columns are aggregated first on the Education Level dimension and then on the Marital Status dimension, and all the data is drawn from the cube named Sales.

The frmCellset form in the ADOMDSamples project first opens a cellset and then modifies a Hierarchical FlexGrid to display the contents of the cellset. You can't bind a cellset directly to any other control, since a cellset isn't a recordset (but see the discussion of opening a recordset from a cellset later in this chapter). Instead, data is copied piece by piece from the cellset to the Hierarchical FlexGrid control.

Once you've created a valid MDX statement, opening a cellset is simple:

```
Dim cat As New ADOMD.Catalog
Dim cst As New ADOMD.Cellset

txtSource.Text = "SELECT NEST([Promotion Media].MEMBERS, " & _
  vbCrLf & "[Gender].MEMBERS) ON ROWS, " & _
  vbCrLf & "NEST([Education Level].MEMBERS, " & _
  vbCrLf & "[Marital Status].MEMBERS) ON COLUMNS" & _
  vbCrLf & "FROM Sales"
' Get the data into the cellset
cat.ActiveConnection = "Provider=MSOLAP.1; " & _
  "Integrated Security=SSPI;Data Source=BEAVER;" & _
  "Initial Catalog=FoodMart;"
cst.Source = txtSource.Text
Set cst.ActiveConnection = cat.ActiveConnection
cst.Open
```

Although the Cellset does not have a default collection, it's most easily thought of as a collection of Cells—and, in fact, the Item method of the Cellset returns a Cell object. A cellset can have more than two axes. The Item method takes as many arguments as the number of axes contained in the cellset. So, in the case of the sample shown here, you need to provide two arguments (row and column) to retrieve a cell from a cellset.

NOTE For the formal syntax of MDX statements, refer to the ADO MD documentation in the MDAC SDK.

Cell

The Cell object represents one piece of information from a single multidimensional query. It's analogous to a Field object in regular ADO. However, there's a major difference due to the fact that cellsets can have multiple axes and have no concept of "current record." In a recordset, you first navigate to the record of interest by (for example) a series of calls to MoveNext, and then retrieve the Field of interest. In a cellset, you navigate directly to the cell of interest by specifying its position along all the axes in the cellset.

In the frmCellset form of the ADOMDSamples project, a two-dimensional loop transfers cell values directly from the cellset to the Hierarchical FlexGrid control:

```
' Now iterate through the cellset and transfer it
' to the grid
For intCol = 0 To cst.Axes(0).Positions.Count - 1
    For intRow = 0 To cst.Axes(1).Positions.Count - 1
        With fgResults
            .Col = intCol + .FixedCols
            .Row = intRow + .FixedRows
            .Text = cst(intCol, intRow).FormattedValue
        End With
    Next intRow
Next intCol
```

This code relies on the cellset having only two axes and retrieves cells by calling the (default) Item method of the cellset object. If there were three axes, the line setting properties would perhaps read:

```
.Text = cst(intPage, intCol, intRow).FormattedValue
```

The Cell object has three properties of interest:

- Value holds the value of the summary for the cell in question.

- FormattedValue holds the value with server-side formatting.

- Ordinal holds a number uniquely identifying the cell within the cellset.

Providers may also add properties of their own to the Cell object.

Axis

The Axis object represents one of the dimensions that you've actually chosen in constructing a Cellset. For example, consider the sample MDX statement we used a few pages ago:

```
SELECT
NEST([Promotion Media].MEMBERS,
[Gender].MEMBERS) ON ROWS,
NEST([Education Level].MEMBERS,
[Marital Status].MEMBERS) ON COLUMNS
FROM Sales
```

This statement gives rise to two Axis objects (the collection is named Axes), one to represent the rows and one to represent the columns. Axis(0) includes the column information (Education Level and Marital Status) while Axis(1) holds the row information (Promotion Media and Gender). In the frmCellset sample, the Dimension-Count property of the Axis object is used to determine how many non-scrollable rows the grid will contain:

```
.FixedCols = cst.Axes(1).DimensionCount
For intCol = 0 To .FixedCols - 1
    .MergeCol(intCol) = True
Next intCol
.FixedRows = cst.Axes(0).DimensionCount
For intRow = 0 To .FixedRows - 1
    .MergeRow(intRow) = True
Next intRow
```

Name and DimensionCount are the only two intrinsic properties of the Axis object. However, the Axis object is also the parent of the Positions collection, which is an important part of properly labeling your multidimensional data.

Position and Member

The Position object provides information about one of the values along an Axis. You'll seldom do anything directly with the Position object. However, Position objects each have a Members collection that contains information on which exact values make up that point on the Axis. For example, in an axis consisting of Promotion Media and Gender, one of the Position objects would contain two Member objects, Bulk Mail and All Gender, representing the values of the particular dimensions making up that position.

In the frmCellset sample in the ADOMDSamples project, these Members (which should not be confused with the Member objects found when iterating through the schema, as discussed earlier) are used to fill in the information in the fixed cells of the Hierarchical FlexGrid:

```
With fgResults
    For intRow = 0 To cst.Axes(1).Positions.Count - 1
        For intCol = 0 To .FixedCols - 1
            .Row = intRow + .FixedRows
            .Col = intCol
            .Text = cst.Axes(1).Positions(intRow). _
            Members(intCol).Caption
        Next intCol
    Next intRow
    For intCol = 0 To cst.Axes(0).Positions.Count - 1
        For intRow = 0 To .FixedRows - 1
            .Row = intRow
            .Col = intCol + .FixedCols
            .Text = cst.Axes(0).Positions(intCol). _
            Members(intRow).Caption
        Next intRow
    Next intCol
End With
```

Additional ADO MD Techniques

ADO MD, of course, is not a completely independent object model. It's integrated with the ADO object model. There are two ways in which you can use ADO and ADO MD together. First, it's possible to get schema information from a multidimensional data source into a recordset rather than examining it hierarchically. Second, you can "flatten" a cellset into a recordset and use it like any other read-only ADO recordset.

WARNING The integration, alas, isn't perfect. While you can create a Data Environment or a Data Link based on the MSOLAP OLE DB provider, you won't find any useful information in either one. Data Environments and Data Links are unable to retrieve MSOLAP information.

Using OpenSchema to List Objects

You saw earlier in a chapter how to use the ADO MD object model to drill down into schema information. But you'll recall from Chapter 3 that the ADO Connection object includes an OpenSchema method to retrieve generalized schema information. ADO MD extends the OpenSchema method by providing six additional constants:

- adSchemaCubes

- adSchemaDimensions

- adSchemaHierarchies

- adSchemaLevels

- adSchemaMeasures

- adSchemeMembers

Figure 12.6 shows the frmSchema form from the ADOMDSamples project. In this particular case, it's displaying the contents of a recordset containing all the Dimensions to be found on a particular server.

FIGURE 12.6:

Recordset with Dimension information

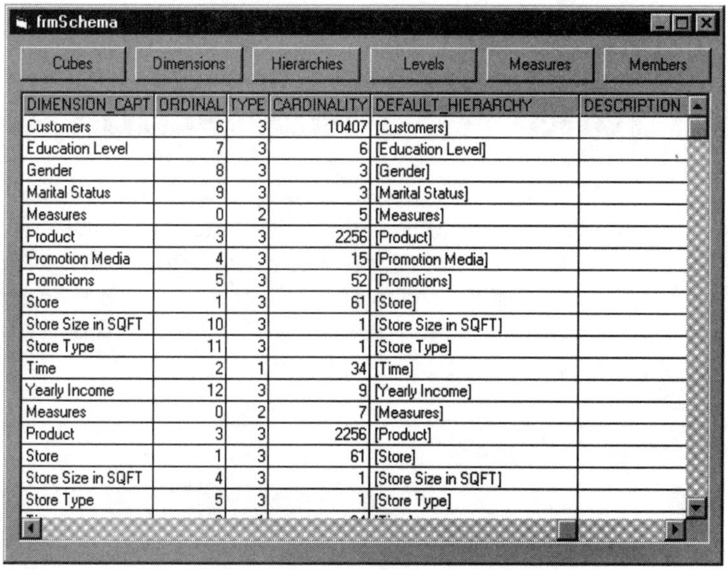

DIMENSION_CAPT	ORDINAL	TYPE	CARDINALITY	DEFAULT_HIERARCHY	DESCRIPTION
Customers	6	3	10407	[Customers]	
Education Level	7	3	6	[Education Level]	
Gender	8	3	3	[Gender]	
Marital Status	9	3	3	[Marital Status]	
Measures	0	2	5	[Measures]	
Product	3	3	2256	[Product]	
Promotion Media	4	3	15	[Promotion Media]	
Promotions	5	3	52	[Promotions]	
Store	1	3	61	[Store]	
Store Size in SQFT	10	3	1	[Store Size in SQFT]	
Store Type	11	3	1	[Store Type]	
Time	2	1	34	[Time]	
Yearly Income	12	3	9	[Yearly Income]	
Measures	0	2	7	[Measures]	
Product	3	3	2256	[Product]	
Store	1	3	61	[Store]	
Store Size in SQFT	4	3	1	[Store Size in SQFT]	
Store Type	5	3	1	[Store Type]	

The code that generated this particular recordset is:

```
Private Sub cmdDimensions_Click()

    Dim cnn As New ADODB.Connection
    Dim rst As ADODB.Recordset

    Screen.MousePointer = vbHourglass
    fgResults.Clear
    cnn.Open "Provider=MSOLAP.1; " & _
     "Integrated Security=SSPI;Data Source=BEAVER;" & _
     "Initial Catalog=FoodMart;"
    Set rst = cnn.OpenSchema(adSchemaDimensions)
    Set fgResults.DataSource = rst
    fgResults.Refresh
    Screen.MousePointer = vbDefault

End Sub
```

As you can see, the only multidimensional elements to this code snippet are the connection string used (via the MSOLAP provider) and the adSchemaDimensions constant that tells the OpenSchema method how to populate its recordset.

The OpenSchema method is most useful when you want to get an overall view of the contents of an entire server, since it lists all the objects regardless of which cube they belong to. If you're trying to determine information about a particular cube, you're probably better off drilling down through the ADO MD object hierarchy.

WARNING   Because the OpenSchema recordsets contain information on all the cubes on a server, they can grow quite large. In particular, opening a recordset of all Member information on a server with many cubes is likely to be a very slow operation.

Opening a Recordset from a Cellset

If you like, you can "flatten" a cellset into a recordset. You do so by creating a Recordset object, but using a multidimensional connection string and an MDX statement as the source rather than using a SQL statement. You can see an example of this technique in frmRecordset in the ADOMDSamples project, shown in Figure 12.7.

FIGURE 12.7:

Recordset based on multi-dimensional data

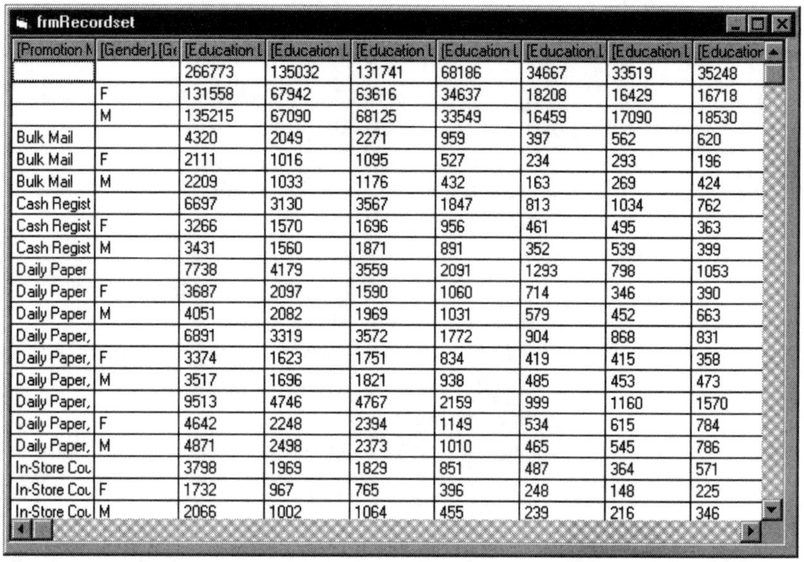

[Promotion M	[Gender],[Ge	[Education L	[Education L	[Education L	[Education L	[Education L	[Education L	[Education ▲
		266773	135032	131741	68186	34667	33519	35248
	F	131558	67942	63616	34637	18208	16429	16718
	M	135215	67090	68125	33549	16459	17090	18530
Bulk Mail		4320	2049	2271	959	397	562	620
Bulk Mail	F	2111	1016	1095	527	234	293	196
Bulk Mail	M	2209	1033	1176	432	163	269	424
Cash Regist		6697	3130	3567	1847	813	1034	762
Cash Regist	F	3266	1570	1696	956	461	495	363
Cash Regist	M	3431	1560	1871	891	352	539	399
Daily Paper		7738	4179	3559	2091	1293	798	1053
Daily Paper	F	3687	2097	1590	1060	714	346	390
Daily Paper	M	4051	2082	1969	1031	579	452	663
Daily Paper,		6891	3319	3572	1772	904	868	831
Daily Paper,	F	3374	1623	1751	834	419	415	358
Daily Paper,	M	3517	1696	1821	938	485	453	473
Daily Paper,		9513	4746	4767	2159	999	1160	1570
Daily Paper,	F	4642	2248	2394	1149	534	615	784
Daily Paper,	M	4871	2498	2373	1010	465	545	786
In-Store Cou		3798	1969	1829	851	487	364	571
In-Store Cou	F	1732	967	765	396	248	148	225
In-Store Cou	M	2066	1002	1064	455	239	216	346

The code that generated this recordset is simple and doesn't explicitly use any ADO MD objects. Instead, it takes direct advantage of the MSOLAP provider to return the recordset of interest:

```
Private Sub Form_Load()

    Dim cnn As New ADODB.Connection
    Dim rst As New ADODB.Recordset

    Screen.MousePointer = vbHourglass
    fgResults.Clear
    cnn.Open "Provider=MSOLAP.1; " & _
     "Integrated Security=SSPI;Data Source=BEAVER;" & _
     "Initial Catalog=FoodMart;"
    rst.Source = "SELECT NEST([Promotion Media].MEMBERS, " & _
     vbCrLf & "[Gender].MEMBERS) ON ROWS, " & _
     vbCrLf & "NEST([Education Level].MEMBERS, " & _
     vbCrLf & "[Marital Status].MEMBERS) ON COLUMNS" & _
     vbCrLf & "FROM Sales"
    rst.ActiveConnection = cnn
    rst.Open
    Set fgResults.DataSource = rst
```

```
fgResults.Refresh
Screen.MousePointer = vbDefault

End Sub
```

The provider follows three rules in creating the recordset:

1. There is one row in the recordset for each combination of members on the row axis of the implied cellset.

2. There is one field in the recordset for each combination of members on the column axis of the implied cellset.

3. The values returned at the intersection of these records and fields are derived from the unformatted Value property of the cells in the implied cellset.

The major advantage to returning a recordset instead of a cellset is that the recordset can be used in any context where a regular ADO recordset is valid. For example, it can be bound to a grid control (as in this example) or even passed back over HTTP via RDS (see Chapter 11). On the other hand, the formatting of the recordset is uninspiring, and the concatenated field names can be difficult to work with. If you're developing an interface that allows people to work with multidimensional data interactively, you're almost certainly better off using cellsets rather than recordsets.

Creating Data Sources with Visual Basic

■ Overview of Creating Data Sources

■ Creating an ActiveX Data Source Control

■ Creating an OLE DB Provider

Throughout this book, I've been using Visual Basic at the downstream end of ADO connections: as the consumer of data supplied by some external data source. But what about the other end of the connection? Well, as it happens, you can create data sources in Visual Basic as well. In this chapter, I'll examine several ways to create your own data source using Visual Basic, and show how your own VB programs can play a role as data providers as well as data consumers. When you've seen this side of the equation, you'll finally know how to use VB for an end-to-end OLE DB and ADO solution.

Overview of Creating Data Sources

Visual Basic 6 provides you with two different ways to create data sources:

- You can build an ActiveX control that acts as a bindable data source within Visual Basic.

- You can build a class that acts as an OLE DB Provider, using the OLE DB Simple Provider (OSP) Toolkit.

In this chapter, you'll see both of these approaches used. Depending on your needs and constraints, they're both useful ways to handle the problem of making a data source available.

Choosing a Plan of Attack

Given these two alternatives (native ActiveX control or OLE DB Simple Provider), how should you choose which way to build your data source in Visual Basic? Here are a few points you should consider:

- Will the data source be used on bound forms in Visual Basic? This suggests that a native ActiveX control is the best choice.

- Do you need to get at this data source from other OLE DB data consumers, not written in Visual Basic? Then you'll need to use OSP.

- Do you have the time, patience, and disk space to install the Microsoft Data Access Components (MDAC) SDK? You'll need it to use OSP.

- Will the client computers have the current MDAC installed? They'll need it for OSP. Then again, you're likely to need this no matter what approach you use for data access.

- Would you like a familiar user interface for the developers who use your control? An ActiveX control is probably the way to go here.

Creating an ActiveX Data Source Control

In this section, I'll show you how to create a simple ActiveX data control. This control is contained in the RegDataControl.vbp sample project. There's code to test it in the DataControlTest.vbp sample project. You can open both the control and the supporting code to test it by opening the DataControl.vbg sample project group.

This particular control is designed to retrieve information from the Windows Registry. Figure 13.1 shows this control in action (this is the frmSimpleTest form in the DataControlTest sample project). The control is providing, in this case, an interface to the key names contained under the HKEY_CURRENT_USER\Software key in the Windows Registry on my test computer.

FIGURE 13.1:

Using the RegData control

The RegData control exposes a number of properties that allow the developer to control the information it retrieves from the Registry:

- The Action property tells the control whether it should retrieve a list of keys or a list of values.

- The RootKey property tells the control which Registry Hive it should retrieve data from.

- The Path property tells the control where in the specified Root Key it should start retrieving data.

- The Recordset property exposes the control's data at run time.

The choice of the Registry as the location to retrieve data from is purely arbitrary. You can, of course, create a data control to return practically any information from any source that you can place in a recordset. Some possibilities include:

- A recordset of folders or files (or both!) on a specific hard drive

- A recordset containing the names of external applications that your program can launch

- A recordset listing network machine names

- A recordset of recommended Web sites

Because you're using ADO, there's no need for the original information to be in recordset or traditional RDBMS form. With ADO, you can create a recordset, append fields to it, and populate those fields from an array easily. This lets you use the Visual Basic data binding interfaces with information from any source whatsoever.

> **NOTE**
> The RegData control uses code in basRegistry to retrieve information from the Registry. Because this code is peripheral to the main point of this chapter, I won't review it in detail. Listing 13.1 shows the code from basRegistry. If you'd like to know more about using VBA to retrieve information from the Registry, see *Visual Basic Language Developer's Handbook* by Ken Getz and Mike Gilbert (ISBN 0-7821-2162-4, available from Sybex in early 2000).

LISTING 13.1

```
Option Explicit

Type FILETIME
        dwLowDateTime As Long
        dwHighDateTime As Long
End Type

Type SECURITY_ATTRIBUTES
        nLength As Long
        lpSecurityDescriptor As Long
        bInheritHandle As Boolean
End Type
```

```
Private Declare Function RegOpenKeyEx _
  Lib "advapi32.dll" Alias "RegOpenKeyExA" _
  (ByVal hKey As Long, ByVal lpSubKey As String, _
  ByVal ulOptions As Long, ByVal samDesired As Long, _
  phkResult As Long) As Long
Private Declare Function RegCloseKey _
  Lib "advapi32" _
  (ByVal hKey As Long) As Long
Private Declare Function RegEnumKeyEx _
  Lib "advapi32.dll" Alias "RegEnumKeyExA" _
  (ByVal hKey As Long, ByVal dwIndex As Long, _
  ByVal lpName As String, lpcbName As Long, _
  lpReserved As Long, ByVal lpClass As String, _
  lpcbClass As Long, lpftLastWriteTime As FILETIME) As Long
Private Declare Function RegEnumValue _
  Lib "advapi32.dll" Alias "RegEnumValueA" _
  (ByVal hKey As Long, ByVal dwIndex As Long, _
  ByVal lpValueName As String, lpcbValueName As Long, _
  lpReserved As Long, lpType As Long, _
  lpData As Any, lpcbData As Any) As Long
Const conSuccess = 0
Const conKeyQueryValue = &H1
Const conKeySetValue = &H2
Const conKeyCreateSubKey = &H4
Const conKeyEnumerateSubKeys = &H8
Const conKeyNotify = &H10
Const conKeyCreateLink = &H20
Const conReadControl = &H20000

Const conKeyRead = conKeyQueryValue + conKeyEnumerateSubKeys + _
  conKeyNotify + conReadControl
Const conKeyWrite = conKeySetValue + conKeyCreateSubKey + _
conReadControl
Const conKeyExecute = conKeyRead
Const conKeyAllAccess = conKeyQueryValue + conKeySetValue + _
  conKeyCreateSubKey + conKeyEnumerateSubKeys + _
  conKeyNotify + conKeyCreateLink + conReadControl

Function ListSubkeys(hKeyRoot As Long, strSubkey As String) As Variant
    Dim hSubkey As Long
    Dim cEnum As Long
    Dim hKey As Long
```

```vb
Dim lngResult As Long
Dim strNameBuff As String
Dim cbNameBuff As Long
Dim strClassBuff As String
Dim cbClassBuff As Long
Dim typFileTime As FILETIME
Dim astrKeys() As String
Dim intI As Integer

intI = 1

' Open the key passed in
lngResult = RegOpenKeyEx(hKeyRoot, strSubkey, _
 0&, conKeyAllAccess, hSubkey)

' Make sure the call succeeded
If lngResult = conSuccess Then

    ' Loop through all subkeys
    Do
        ' Set up buffers
        strNameBuff = Space$(255)
        cbNameBuff = Len(strNameBuff)
        strClassBuff = Space$(255)
        cbClassBuff = Len(strClassBuff)

        ' Call RegEnumKeyEx
        lngResult = RegEnumKeyEx(hSubkey, cEnum, _
         strNameBuff, cbNameBuff, ByVal 0&, _
         strClassBuff, cbClassBuff, typFileTime)

        ' If successful, add to the array
        If lngResult = conSuccess Then
            ReDim Preserve astrKeys(1 To intI)
            astrKeys(intI) = Left(strNameBuff, cbNameBuff)
            intI = intI + 1
        End If

        ' Increment subkey index
        cEnum = cEnum + 1
    Loop Until lngResult <> 0
```

```
            ' Close the subkey
            lngResult = RegCloseKey(hSubkey)
        End If
        ' Return the array
        ListSubkeys = astrKeys()
End Function


Function ListValues(hKeyRoot As Long, strSubkey As String) As Variant
    Dim hSubkey As Long
    Dim cEnum As Long
    Dim lngResult As Long
    Dim strNameBuff As String
    Dim cbNameBuff As Long
    Dim lngType As Long
    Dim abytData(1 To 2048) As Byte
    Dim cbData As Long
    Dim astrValues() As String
    Dim intI As Integer

    intI = 1

    ' Open the key passed in
    lngResult = RegOpenKeyEx(hKeyRoot, strSubkey, _
     0&, conKeyAllAccess, hSubkey)

    ' Make sure the call succeeded
    If lngResult = conSuccess Then

        ' Loop through all values
        Do
            ' Set up buffers
            strNameBuff = Space$(255)
            cbNameBuff = Len(strNameBuff)
            Erase abytData
            cbData = UBound(abytData)

            ' Call RegEnumValue
            lngResult = RegEnumValue(hSubkey, cEnum, _
             strNameBuff, cbNameBuff, ByVal 0&, _
             lngType, abytData(1), cbData)

            ' If successful, add to the array
```

```
    If lngResult = conSuccess Then
        ReDim Preserve astrValues(1 To intI)
        astrValues(intI) = Left(strNameBuff, cbNameBuff)
        intI = intI + 1
    End If

        ' Increment value index
        cEnum = cEnum + 1
    Loop Until lngResult <> 0

    ' Close the key
    lngResult = RegCloseKey(hSubkey)
  End If
  ListValues = astrValues()
End Function
```

Creating the User Interface

As you saw in Figure 13.1, the RegData control uses an interface very much like that of the regular ADO Data control: four buttons for first, previous, next, and last record, and a text area. This is also the interface that's used by the regular data control, and by the data control area on Microsoft Access forms. As such, it's very likely to be familiar to developers who will be using your custom data controls. Unless you have a very good reason to design a different user interface, you should stick to this one.

Figure 13.2 shows the user interface of the RegData UserControl in the designer. It contains these elements:

- A single PictureBox control, whose job is to provide the sunken border around the rest of the constituent controls.

- A single Label control, with its background set to transparent so that the PictureBox background shows through. The Caption property of this Label control provides the text area of the UserControl.

- Four CommandButton controls.

FIGURE 13.2:

Designing the RegData
control

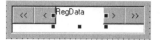

To make this control act in the expected manner, there's code in its Resize event
that serves to arrange the constituent controls neatly. Remember, because this is a
UserControl, this code executes when the RegData control is resized at design time.

```
Private Sub UserControl_Resize()
    ' Make things look neat
    ' Size the PictureBox to fill the UserControl
    Picture1.Move 0, 0, Width, Height
    ' Put the First button all the way left
    cmdFirst.Move 0, 0, cmdFirst.Width, Height - 60
    ' Stack the Previous button beside it
    cmdPrevious.Move cmdFirst.Left + cmdFirst.Width, 0, _
     cmdPrevious.Width, Height - 60
    ' Put the Last button all the way right
    cmdLast.Move (Width - cmdLast.Width) - 60, 0, _
     cmdLast.Width, Height - 60
    ' Stack the Next button beside it
    cmdNext.Move cmdLast.Left - cmdNext.Width, 0, _
     cmdNext.Width, Height - 60
    ' Size the label as high as its text
    lblCaption.Height = TextHeight("A")
    ' And stick it between the buttons
    lblCaption.Move cmdPrevious.Left + cmdPrevious.Width, _
     ((Height - 60) / 2) - (lblCaption.Height / 2), _
     cmdNext.Left - (cmdPrevious.Left + cmdPrevious.Width)
End Sub
```

Handling Properties

As with any UserControl, much of the code in the RegData control is concerned
with handling properties. This code has to perform several tasks. First, to make
things simpler in the property sheet of an instance of the control, it helps to define
enumerated values for properties that have only a fixed set of values:

```
' Enums to make setting things in the
' property sheet simpler
```

```
' Allowed RootKey settings
Public Enum rdRootKeyType
    rdHKEY_CLASSES_ROOT = &H80000000
    rdHKEY_CURRENT_USER = &H80000001
    rdHKEY_LOCAL_MACHINE = &H80000002
    rdHKEY_USERS = &H80000003
End Enum

' Allowed ActionType settings
Public Enum rdActionType
    rdActionKeys = 0
    rdActionValues = 1
End Enum
```

> **NOTE** It's good practice to preface any enumerated values with an abbreviation for your control so that they don't conflict with public members of other controls.

Also on a global level, the control has private variables to hold its properties, and default values that will be used when the control is first created:

```
' Default values for properties
' These are used when an instance of the
' control is first created
Const conDefaultRootKey = rdHKEY_CURRENT_USER
Const conDefaultPath = ""
Const conDefaultAction = rdActionKeys

' Private variables that hold the exposed
' custom properties for this control
Private menuRootKey As rdRootKeyType
Private mstrPath As String
Private menuAction As rdActionType

' Recordset that holds this control's data
Private WithEvents mrs As ADODB.Recordset
```

Every property needs a Property Let procedure, a Property Get procedure, or both:

```
' Recordset property
' Note that this property is read-only
' The recordset can only be populated by
```

```vb
' the control's own code
Public Property Get Recordset() As ADODB.Recordset
    Set Recordset = mrs
End Property


' Caption property
Public Property Let Caption(ByVal NewCaption As String)
    lblCaption.Caption = NewCaption
    PropertyChanged "Caption"
End Property
Public Property Get Caption() As String
    Caption = lblCaption.Caption
End Property


' Rootkey property
Public Property Let RootKey(ByVal NewRootKey As rdRootKeyType)
    menuRootKey = NewRootKey
    PropertyChanged "RootKey"
End Property
Public Property Get RootKey() As rdRootKeyType
    RootKey = menuRootKey
End Property


' Path property
Public Property Let Path(ByVal NewPath As String)
    ' Registry key paths use backslashes, and we
    ' don't want to see leading or trailing ones. Do
    ' what we can to fix up user mistakes here.
    NewPath = Replace(NewPath, "/", "\")
    If Left(NewPath, 1) = "\" Then
        NewPath = Mid(NewPath, 2)
    End If
    If Right(NewPath, 1) = "\" Then
        NewPath = Left(NewPath, Len(NewPath) - 1)
    End If
    mstrPath = NewPath
    PropertyChanged "Path"
End Property
Public Property Get Path() As String
    Path = mstrPath
End Property
```

```
' Action Property
Public Property Let Action(ByVal NewAction As rdActionType)
    menuAction = NewAction
    PropertyChanged "Action"
End Property
Public Property Get Action() As rdActionType
    Action = menuAction
End Property
```

WARNING   You can't use public variables for the properties of a UserControl, because of the need to call the PropertyChanged method when each property is set.

You also need code in the UserControl to initialize the properties, save their values when an instance of the UserControl is persisted, and retrieve their values when a saved UserControl is recreated:

```
Private Sub UserControl_InitProperties()
    ' Initialize control to defaults
    menuRootKey = conDefaultRootKey
    mstrPath = conDefaultPath
    menuAction = conDefaultAction
    lblCaption.Caption = Ambient.DisplayName
    Set UserControl.Font = Ambient.Font
End Sub

Private Sub UserControl_ReadProperties(PropBag As PropertyBag)
    ' Read any persiste properties for the control
    lblCaption.Caption = PropBag.ReadProperty("Caption", _
     Ambient.DisplayName)
    menuRootKey = PropBag.ReadProperty("RootKey", _
     conDefaultRootKey)
    mstrPath = PropBag.ReadProperty("Path", _
     conDefaultPath)
    menuAction = PropBag.ReadProperty("Action", _
     conDefaultAction)
End Sub

Private Sub UserControl_WriteProperties(PropBag As PropertyBag)
    ' Persist properties when the control is saved
    PropBag.WriteProperty "Caption", lblCaption.Caption, _
     Ambient.DisplayName
```

```
        PropBag.WriteProperty "RootKey", menuRootKey, _
          conDefaultRootKey
        PropBag.WriteProperty "Path", mstrPath, _
          conDefaultPath
        PropBag.WriteProperty "Action", menuAction, _
          conDefaultAction
    End Sub
```

Handling Data

Of course, a control that will be a data source must have code concerned with data. The first thing you need to do is to set the DataSourceBehavior property of the UserControl to vbDataSource. This is what puts the "glue" into place that will let this control play in the data-binding game.

When a consumer of data from this control wants to retrieve data, it calls the GetDataMember sub:

```
Private Sub UserControl_GetDataMember( _
  DataMember As String, Data As Object)
      ' Required for controls that are a datasource
      ' We only support a default DataMember
    GetRecordset
    Set Data = mrs
End Sub
```

GetDataMember has to perform two functions. First, it needs to somehow, from somewhere, get the data that your control is going to provide. Then it needs to set a recordset representing that data into the Data argument that's passed back to the consumer.

In the case of RegData, the data comes from the Registry, under control of the properties of the control, using the GetRecordset procedure:

```
Private Sub GetRecordset()
      ' Get the data that this control is the source for
    Dim varData As Variant
    Dim intI As Integer

    On Error GoTo HandleErr

      ' Create a new recordset with a single field
    Set mrs = New ADODB.Recordset
```

```
mrs.CursorLocation = adUseClient
mrs.Fields.Append "Data", adVarChar, 40, _
 adFldIsNullable

' Open the recordset with no data so we can add
' rows to it
mrs.Open , , adOpenStatic, adLockBatchOptimistic

If menuAction = rdActionKeys Then
    ' Get an array of all subkeys
    varData = ListSubkeys(menuRootKey, mstrPath)
    For intI = LBound(varData) To UBound(varData)
        ' And add them to the recordset
        mrs.AddNew "Data", varData(intI)
    Next intI
Else    ' rdActionValues
    ' Get an array of all values
    varData = ListValues(menuRootKey, mstrPath)
    ' And add them to the recordset
    For intI = LBound(varData) To UBound(varData)
        mrs.AddNew "Data", varData(intI)
    Next intI
End If

' Commit all the rows
mrs.UpdateBatch adAffectAll
' Position the pointer
mrs.MoveFirst

ExitHere:
    Exit Sub

HandleErr:
    Set mrs = Nothing
    Resume ExitHere
End Sub
```

GetRecordset finds the data using these steps:

1. Initialize the module-level recordset variable and tell it to use a client-side cursor. Remember, you must use a client-side cursor in order to create a disconnected recordset (one that does not have an ADO Connection object, either explicit or implicit, open at all times).

2. Append a single field to the recordset, named Data, so there will be somewhere to put the data. (This gives rise to a single entry, "Data," in the DataField property of any control that's bound to this UserControl.)

3. Open the recordset using a batch optimistic cursor, so that data can be added to it.

4. Depending on the properties of the control, call either ListSubkeys or ListValues to retrieve the data. Each of those procedures returns an array.

5. Iterate through the array, adding each value as a row to the recordset.

6. Commit the recordset using the UpdateBatch method to make its data available.

7. Set the recordset current record pointer to the first record.

In case of any error, GetRecordset returns an empty recordset. This makes sense in this particular case: If the developer sets conflicting or nonsensical properties for an instance of the RegData control, it simply retrieves no data.

Finally, there are some utility procedures involved with the data. Clicking any of the buttons on the UserControl causes the internal recordset to navigate in the expected direction. The control also exposes a Refresh method, which lets clients tell it when new properties have been set and new data must be retrieved:

```
' Refresh method
Public Sub Refresh()
    GetRecordset
End Sub


' Internal functions that move through
' the recordset when the buttons are clicked
Private Sub cmdFirst_Click()
    If Not mrs Is Nothing Then
        mrs.MoveFirst
    End If
End Sub

Private Sub cmdLast_Click()
    If Not mrs Is Nothing Then
        mrs.MoveLast
    End If
End Sub
```

```
Private Sub cmdNext_Click()
    If Not mrs Is Nothing Then
        If Not mrs.EOF Then
            mrs.MoveNext
        End If
        If mrs.EOF Then
            mrs.MoveLast
        End If
    End If
End Sub

Private Sub cmdPrevious_Click()
    If Not mrs Is Nothing Then
        If Not mrs.BOF Then
            mrs.MovePrevious
        End If
        If mrs.BOF Then
            mrs.MoveFirst
        End If
    End If
End Sub
```

NOTE   Exposing a Refresh method is a design decision. As an alternative, the Property Let procedures for the control could call GetRecordset to automatically refresh the data when new values are set.

A More Complex Example

The DataControlTest sample project also contains a form named frmRegData-ControlTest that demonstrates a more complex example of using the RegData User-Control. On this form, shown in Figure 13.3, the RegData UserControl is invisible at run time.

FIGURE 13.3:

Data from the RegData
UserControl on a grid

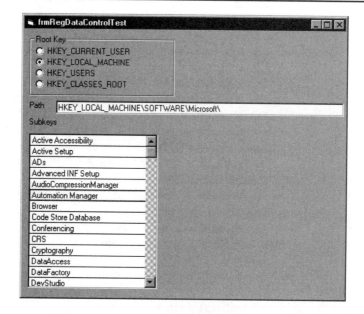

The frmRegDataControlTest sample form interacts with the RegData control at
run time. As the user manipulates the form's user interface, the code sets new values for the control's properties and refreshes its data. For example, when the user
double-clicks a displayed subkey, the control "drills down" one more level in the
Registry and gets the subkeys (or values, if there are no subkeys) for that level:

```
Private Sub fgData_DblClick()
    ' Drill down one level when a subkey is
    ' double-clicked
    RegData1.Path = RegData1.Path & "\" & fgData.Text
    RegData1.Refresh
    If ((RegData1.Recordset Is Nothing) And _
     (RegData1.Action = rdActionKeys)) Then
        ' If we can't retrieve any subkeys, try to
        ' retrieve values
        RegData1.Action = rdActionValues
        RegData1.Refresh
    End If
    Set fgData.DataSource = RegData1.Recordset
    If RegData1.Recordset Is Nothing Then
        fgData.Clear
```

```
            End If
            BuildPath
    End Sub
    Private Sub BuildPath()
            ' Fix up the display
            If optHKCU Then
                txtPath = "HKEY_CURRENT_USER\" & RegData1.Path
            ElseIf optHKLM Then
                txtPath = "HKEY_LOCAL_MACHINE\" & RegData1.Path
            ElseIf optHKCR Then
                txtPath = "HKEY_CLASSES_ROOT\" & RegData1.Path
            ElseIf optHKU Then
                txtPath = "HKEY_USERS\" & RegData1.Path
            End If
            If RegData1.Action = rdActionKeys Then
                lblGrid.Caption = "Subkeys"
            Else
                lblGrid.Caption = "Values"
            End If
            If RegData1.Path <> "" Then
                txtPath = txtPath & "\"
            End If
    End Sub
```

ActiveX Data Source controls (like the RegData control) are as flexible as any other data control. For example, you can also use them completely invisibly by using the BindingCollection object to bind them to any other data consumer. But their main drawback is that you can't use them outside of an ActiveX control container such as a Visual Basic form. If you want to expose data to other OLE DB consumers, you'll need to use the OLE DB Simple Provider toolkit.

Creating an OLE DB Provider

Creating a UserControl that has the vbDataSource value for its DataSource-Behavior property is a good solution for creating data sources that you want to use exclusively within Visual Basic. But what if you want to create an actual OLE DB provider that's available to any OLE DB consumer? That's where the OLEDB-SimpleProvider interface comes in.

OLEDBSimpleProvider is a version of the OLE DB interface that contains the basic, most necessary members used by any data consumer. In order to implement this interface, you'll need the OLE DB Simple Provider Toolkit. This toolkit is part of the Microsoft Data Access Components (MDAC) SDK. This SDK is automatically shipped to Microsoft Developer Network (MSDN) members as a part of their annual subscription. However, it's also available for free on the Web (as long as you don't mind a 37-megabyte download) from the Microsoft Universal Data Access site (`http://www.microsoft.com/data`).

WARNING   The Visual Basic Help mentions a constant vbOLEDBProvider. This constant doesn't actually exist; it was part of a beta version of Visual Basic 6 that was removed from the product but not from the Help. To create an OLE DB Provider with Visual Basic, you *must* use the OSP Toolkit.

When you're installing the MDAC SDK, you can choose which components to install. The only thing you really need for this section is the OLE DB Simple Provider Toolkit. Although that toolkit takes up less than 100KB of disk space, you'll still need about 120MB free to complete the installation.

Implementing OLE DB Simple Provider

I could walk you through building all the code for a simple provider from scratch, but there's an easier way. When you install the OLE DB Simple Provider Toolkit, it places a sample Visual Basic project in the `osp\vb` subfolder of the install location that you choose. Rather than writing all the code for a simple provider, it's much easier to make a copy of this code and modify it for your own purposes.

I'll demonstrate this strategy in the creation of the Language Resource Provider sample application. This OLE DB Provider will be used to provide a localized interface for a product. It lets the consumer set a language as the DataMember and then returns a recordset consisting of resource IDs and localized strings in that language. For purposes of this book, the acceptable DataMember values will be "English" and "Pig Latin." However, as you'll see in the code, it would be easy to extend the component to accept other values for this property.

The provider begins as a new ActiveX DLL project (the final project is available on this book's Web site as the OSPSample project). This project contains two multiuse classes, LRDataSource and LROSP. The first of these classes has its

DataSourceBehavior set to vbDataSource. This will be the class that you can bind other Visual Basic applications to. The project also needs references to three libraries:

- The Microsoft OLE DB Simple Provider 1.5 Library contains the OLEDB-SimpleProvider interface definition.

- The Microsoft OLE DB Error Library has error codes for OLE DB operations.

- The Microsoft Data Source Interfaces enable the Visual Basic data source behavior for the project.

Setting the reference to the OLE DB Error Library is trickier than it needs to be. It's possible for a single DLL to contain multiple type libraries, and in fact the OLE DB Error Library is the second type library in the `oledb32.dll` file. Unfortunately, Visual Basic provides no means for you to set a reference to the second type library in a DLL through the user interface. Believe it or not, you'll need to close your project and edit the vbp file in a text editor to do this! You can copy the applicable line from the `SampleOSP_VB.vbp` file that ships with the OLE DB Simple Provider Toolkit or from this book's sample app `OSPSample.vbp` file. Here's the start of this file:

```
Type=OleDll
Reference=*\G{00020430-0000-0000-C000-
000000000046}#2.0#0#..\..\WINNT\System32\stdole2.tlb#OLE Automation
Reference=*\G{E0E270C2-C0BE-11D0-8FE4-
00A0C90A6341}#1.5#409#..\..\WINNT\System32\SIMPDATA.TLB#Microsoft OLE
DB Simple Provider 1.5 Library
Reference=*\G{C8B522D5-5CF3-11CE-ADE5-00AA0044773D}#1.0#0#..\..\Program
Files\Common Files\System\ole db\Oledb32.dll\2#Microsoft OLE DB Error
Library
Reference=*\G{7C0FFAB0-CD84-11D0-949A-
00A0C91110ED}#1.0#0#..\..\WINNT\System32\msdatsrc.tlb#Microsoft Data
Source Interfaces
Class=MyDataSource; MyDataSource.cls
Class=MyOSPObject; MyOSPObject.cls
Startup="(None)"
```

The boldfaced line above is the one that you'll need to copy to your own Visual Basic project file in order to set this reference. Once you've done this, you can open up the Project ➤ References dialog box to confirm that you can use the library.

The next step is to fill in the boilerplate code for the two classes by copying it directly from the code in the SampleOSP_VB project. I copied the entire contents of `MyDataSource.cls` to `LRDataSource.cls` and the entire contents of `MyOSP-Object.cls` to `LROSP.cls`.

> **WARNING** The sample project from the OLE DB Simple Provider Toolkit doesn't use `Option Explicit`. You should insert this statement at the top of each class in your project. Doing so, unfortunately, will expose several errors in the sample code, which uses variables without declaring them, as well as one place where the Boolean constant False is mistyped as "Flase." It's hard to think of a better demonstration of the worth of Option Explicit!

The next step is to modify the copied code to work with the data you want to provide. The modifications to `LRDataSource.cls` are minimal. This class exists only to pass on the DataMember to the other class, and to return the data that it provides. All I've done in this case is change the name of the property used within the other class to hold the DataMember value, and change the name of the class variable that gets instantiated. Here's the full code for the LRDataSource class:

```
Option Explicit

Private Sub Class_GetDataMember(DataMember As String, _
  Data As Object)

    If DataMember = "" Then Err.Raise (E_FAIL)

    Dim LR As New LROSP
    LR.Language = DataMember
    LR.LoadData

    Set Data = LR

End Sub
```

The modifications to LROSP are somewhat more extensive. First, the property **Language** needs to be created. Since no special processing has to happen when this property is set, it can be implemented as a simple public variable, replacing the existing FilePath variable:

```
Public Language As String
```

Next, the LoadData procedure needs to be modified. This is the procedure that fetches the data you want your provider to provide. It loads it into an array named MyOSPArray for the rest of the code within the class to use. The sample project supplied with the OLE DB Simple Provider Toolkit uses FilePath to specify a text file, and then loads the array with semicolon-separated data from that file. The code in the LROSP class in the OSPSample project uses the Language property to identify a language and creates an array based on the chosen language:

```
Public Sub LoadData()
    Dim intI As Integer

    On Error GoTo ErrorTrap

    ReDim MyOSPArray(0 To 10, 1 To 2)
    RowCount = 10
    ColCount = 2

    MyOSPArray(0, 1) = "ResourceID"
    MyOSPArray(0, 2) = "Data"

    For intI = 1 To 10
        MyOSPArray(intI, 1) = CStr(1000 + intI)
    Next intI
    Select Case Language
        Case "English"
            MyOSPArray(1, 2) = "OK"
            MyOSPArray(2, 2) = "Cancel"
            MyOSPArray(3, 2) = "Next"
            MyOSPArray(4, 2) = "Previous"
            MyOSPArray(5, 2) = "Refresh"
            MyOSPArray(6, 2) = "First"
            MyOSPArray(7, 2) = "Last"
            MyOSPArray(8, 2) = "Update"
            MyOSPArray(9, 2) = "Delete"
            MyOSPArray(10, 2) = "New"
        Case "Pig Latin"
            MyOSPArray(1, 2) = "OKway"
            MyOSPArray(2, 2) = "Ancelcay"
            MyOSPArray(3, 2) = "Extnay"
            MyOSPArray(4, 2) = "Eviouspray"
            MyOSPArray(5, 2) = "Efreshray"
            MyOSPArray(6, 2) = "Irstfay"
```

```
            MyOSPArray(7, 2) = "Astlay"
            MyOSPArray(8, 2) = "Updateway"
            MyOSPArray(9, 2) = "Eleteday"
            MyOSPArray(10, 2) = "Ewnay"
        Case Else
            Err.Raise (E_FAIL)
    End Select
    Exit Sub
ErrorTrap:
    Err.Raise (E_FAIL)
    Resume
End Sub
```

NOTE

Note that the array has as many columns as the recordset has fields, and as many rows as the number of records plus one. The zeroth row is reserved for field names that you want to present to the data consumer.

The template code from the Toolkit project also contains a SaveData sub. This sub is called from the Class_Terminate event to persist changes back to the original disk file. In the case of the LROSP class, there's no way to persist changes, since the values are hard-coded into the class. But since you might want to modify this code in the future (for example, to save changes to a disk file or the Registry), I've left in an empty SaveData procedure:

```
Public Sub SaveData()
    On Error GoTo ErrorTrap
    Exit Sub
ErrorTrap:
    Err.Raise (E_FAIL)
End Sub
```

The remaining code in the sample Toolkit project is written on the assumption that the data is internally stored in the array; it manipulates the array rather than the original data source. What this means is that I didn't have to make any further modifications to use the code to provide my language resource data.

The next step is to compile the DLL. Although this registers the DLL's classes on your system, it's not enough to make the DLL be recognized as an OLE DB provider. In order to do this, you need to make a copy of the SampleOSP_VB.reg file from the OLE DB Simple Provider Toolkit. For the OSPSample project, this copy is named LR.reg. Open the copy and change the descriptive strings and class names to match your project. Here's what's in LR.reg:

```
REGEDIT4

[HKEY_CLASSES_ROOT\OSPSample]
@="Language Resource Provider"

[HKEY_CLASSES_ROOT\OSPSample\CLSID]
@="{CA2B8981-FE2D-11D2-BE1D-006008E092A3}"
"OLEDB_SERVICES"=dword:00000000

[HKEY_CLASSES_ROOT\CLSID\{CA2B8981-FE2D-11D2-BE1D-006008E092A3}]
@="OSPSample"

[HKEY_CLASSES_ROOT\CLSID\{CA2B8981-FE2D-11D2-BE1D-006008E092A3}\
➥InprocServer32]
@="c:\\Program Files\\Common Files\\System\\OLE DB\\MSDAOSP.DLL"
"ThreadingModel"="Both"

[HKEY_CLASSES_ROOT\CLSID\{CA2B8981-FE2D-11D2-BE1D-006008E092A3}\ProgID]
@="OSPSample"

[HKEY_CLASSES_ROOT\CLSID\{CA2B8981-FE2D-11D2-BE1D-006008E092A3}\
➥VersionIndependentProgID]
@="OSPSample"

[HKEY_CLASSES_ROOT\CLSID\{CA2B8981-FE2D-11D2-BE1D-006008E092A3}\
➥OLE DB Provider]
@="Language Resource Provider"

[HKEY_CLASSES_ROOT\CLSID\{CA2B8981-FE2D-11D2-BE1D-006008E092A3}\
➥OSP Data Object]
@="OSPSample.LRDataSource"
```

Note that there's a GUID (Globally Unique Identifier) assigned to the OLE DB provider. In this case, it's CA2B8981-FE2D-11D2-BE1D-006008E092A3, but you can't just reuse some other provider's GUID. You need to generate a GUID just for your provider. The simplest way to do this is to use the tool GuidGen.exe, which is included on the Visual Basic CD-ROM.

GuidGen (shown in Figure 13.4) is a simple utility. When you need a new unique identifier, run it, select the appropriate format (here, the format used by the Registry), and copy the resulting GUID to the clipboard. Then you can paste it into your code or, as here, Registry file.

FIGURE 13.4:

GuidGen

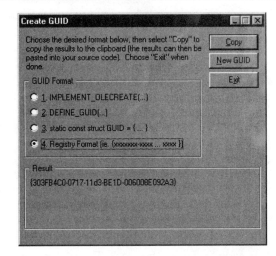

After you've created the Registry file for your provider, run this file on the system where your provider will be used. This will merge the special keys into the Registry to tell the system that your provider really is an OLE DB provider.

Using the OLE DB Simple Provider

Once you've created your provider, compiled it, and registered it on your system, you're ready to use it to retrieve data. How do you use it? The answer is that it's a bona fide OLE DB provider that you can use in any context where an OLE DB provider is expected.

Figure 13.5 shows the frmTest form from the OSPTest sample project. This project uses the Language Resource Provider that I created to allow you to switch its user interface between the two supported languages.

FIGURE 13.5:

Testing the Language
Resource Provider

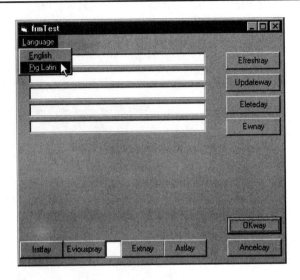

The OSPTest sample project doesn't need any references to any special libraries. Instead, it does its work just by calling the Language Resource Provider. Here's the code that does the work. There's one procedure to set the UI to English, and another to set it to Pig Latin. The only other code is used to pick a default UI language when the form is loaded:

```
Option Explicit

Private Sub Form_Load()
    ' Initialize to English UI
    mnuLanguageEnglish_Click
    End Sub

Private Sub mnuLanguageEnglish_Click()
    ' Change the UI language to English
    Dim cnn As New ADODB.Connection
    Dim rst As New ADODB.Recordset
    Dim ctl As Control

    ' Open a recordset from our Provider
    cnn.Provider = "OSPSample"
    cnn.Open
    rst.Open "English", cnn
```

```
    ' Loop through all the controls, looking for Tags
    For Each ctl In Me.Controls
        If Len(ctl.Tag & "") > 0 Then
            ' Look for a matching row in the recordset
            rst.Find "ResourceID = " & ctl.Tag
            ' If one is found, use it for the caption
            If Not rst.EOF Then
                ctl.Caption = rst.Fields("Data")
            End If
        End If
    Next ctl

End Sub

Private Sub mnuLanguagePigLatin_Click()
    ' Change the UI language to Pig Latin
    Dim cnn As New ADODB.Connection
    Dim rst As New ADODB.Recordset
    Dim ctl As Control

    ' Open a recordset from our Provider
    cnn.Provider = "OSPSample"
    cnn.Open
    rst.Open "Pig Latin", cnn

    ' Loop through all the controls, looking for Tags
    For Each ctl In Me.Controls
        If Len(ctl.Tag & "") > 0 Then
            ' Look for a matching row in the recordset
            rst.Find "ResourceID = " & ctl.Tag
            ' If one is found, use it for the caption
            If Not rst.EOF Then
                ctl.Caption = rst.Fields("Data")
            End If
        End If
    Next ctl

End Sub
```

As you can see, the code to use data from the Language Resource Provider is quite simple—and the same as the code to use data from any other OLE DB provider! The language procedures follow these steps:

1. Open a connection using the Language Resource Provider (with the project name that we chose to compile the provider under).

2. Open a recordset using either "English" or "Pig Latin" as the DataMember in the Source property.

3. For each control on the form that has a value in its Tag property, use the ADO Find method to look for a row in the recordset that has that value in its ResourceID field.

4. Set the caption of the control to the value in the Data field on the same row of the recordset.

Note that all the ADO code, including the use of the Open and Find methods, is identical to code for any other OLE DB provider.

If you compile this sample on your computer, you'll find that the Language Resource Provider works in other contexts that expect an OLE DB provider. For example, Figure 13.6 shows that this provider appears in the list of providers available to any Data Link file.

FIGURE 13.6:

Choosing the Language Resource Provider for a data link file

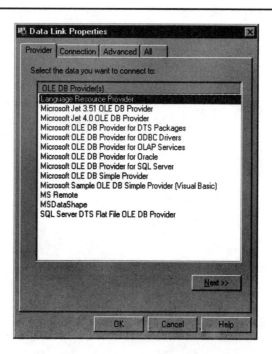

APPENDIX

A

A SQL Language Primer

■ The SELECT Statement

■ Data Modification Statements

■ Other SQL Statements

SQL stands for Structured Query Language. While you can certainly use ADO with Visual Basic without knowing SQL—thanks to the capabilities of advanced rapid design components such as the Data Environment and Data Reports—you'll be limited in how far you can go. In order to really tap the power of ADO in retrieving information from diverse data stores, you need to understand the syntax and use of SQL.

The good news is that there's a standard dialect of SQL, promulgated by the American National Standards Institute, usually known as ANSI SQL (or SQL-92, since the 1992 standard is the one most often referred to). The bad news is that while products usually base their SQL on ANSI SQL, vendors tend to diverge from the standard in more or less significant ways. However, for the simple SQL statements you'll need to retrieve, update, insert, and delete data, you can (for the most part) safely assume that "plain vanilla" standard SQL will work.

In this appendix, you'll learn enough SQL to get started. For further details on advanced SQL, you'll want to refer to the vendor documentation. In particular, you may find these references useful:

- For the Jet Engine, *Microsoft Jet Database Engine Programmer's Guide* (Microsoft Press, 1997).

- For Microsoft SQL Server, *Transact-SQL Reference*, part of the SQL Server Books Online.

- For Oracle, *Oracle8 SQL Reference*, part of the Oracle 8 HTML documentation.

If you're going to be seriously working with a particular vendor's database through ADO, you'll find one of these books to be very useful.

The SELECT Statement

The SELECT statement is probably the single most important statement in the SQL language. It's used to retrieve data into a resultset. This data might be contained in one or many columns, contained in a single table, or spread across many tables. It might be sorted or filtered. It might even be aggregated. The SELECT statement is made up of a number of clauses, each introduced by a SQL keyword.

Here's an example, based on the SQL Server Northwind sample database, that incorporates all the clauses you'll learn in this section:

```
SELECT Customers.CustomerID, Customers.Country,
 Count(Orders.OrderID) AS OrderCount
FROM Customers INNER JOIN Orders
 ON Customers.CustomerID = Orders.CustomerID
WHERE Customers.Country = 'USA'
 GROUP BY Customers.CustomerID, Customers.Country
 HAVING Count(Orders.OrderID) = 10
 ORDER BY Customers.CustomerID
```

This SQL statement returns a resultset of information that includes columns for the CustomerID and Country fields from the Customers table and the count of the OrderID field in the Orders table. The two tables are joined so that rows having the same CustomerID value in both tables are matched to one another. The results are drawn only from rows belonging to customers in the USA. The number of orders for each customer is counted, and only customers with exactly 10 orders are included in the resultset. These customers are sorted in CustomerID order.

Let's look at each of these clauses in more detail.

The SELECT Clause

Here's a simplified syntax diagram for the SELECT clause. This syntax (along with the rest of the examples in this chapter) is based on SELECT as it's supported by SQL Server 7, but all or most of it should work in any full-featured database program:

```
SELECT [ ALL | DISTINCT ]
[ TOP n [PERCENT] ]
{ *
    | { table_name | view_name | table_alias }.*
    | { column_name | expression }
    [ [AS] column_alias ]
    | column_alias = expression
} [,...n]
```

WARNING This syntax diagram doesn't contain every element understood by every database program I've used in this book. I've simplified the syntax diagrams to include only the most common items.

In these syntax diagrams, I'll use these standard conventions:

- SQL keywords are in all upper case.

- Placeholders for database objects are in italics.

- Square brackets surround optional items.

- Vertical bars separate choices. So, for example, SELECT [ALL | DISTINCT] indicates that a SELECT clause can contain either the ALL or the DISTINCT keyword, but not both.

- Braces surround required items.

- The [, . . . n] indicates that the preceding item can be repeated one or more times, separated by commas.

As you can see, even the SELECT clause itself is complex. I'll dissect it a piece at a time, with examples from the Customers table in the SQL Server Northwind database. You can't have a SELECT statement without a FROM clause, so there will be a simple FROM clause in these examples even though I won't explain the full syntax of FROM until the next section.

The simplest SELECT uses the * symbol to return all columns from all records in a table:

```
SELECT * FROM Customers
```

You can also specify all columns from a particular table or view:

```
SELECT Customers.* FROM Customers
```

In this case, since there's only one table in the FROM clause, you'll still get the same results that you would with a simple SELECT * statement. However, as you'll see in the next section, you can include multiple tables in the FROM clause, and using the *table_name.** syntax allows you to see only the columns from a specific table. You'll also see in the next section how to create a table alias in the FROM clause.

For even more selectivity, you can specify individual columns to display:

```
SELECT Customers.CustomerID, Customers.ContactName
FROM Customers
```

As you've seen, you can specify column names with the syntax *table_name .column_name*. If either name has an illegal character in it, you can use square brackets to surround the name. For example, if the field and table names had spaces, this would be a valid SELECT statement:

```
SELECT [Customers Table].[Customer ID]
FROM [Customers Table]
```

If field names are unambiguous (unique across all tables in the FROM clause), you don't need to specify the table names:

```
SELECT Country FROM Customers
```

You can also assign an alias to any column. This will have the result of giving a name that you specify to the resulting column in any recordset based on this SQL statement. In this statement, the ContactName column would be returned with the alias Contact:

```
SELECT Customers.CustomerID,
 Customers.ContactName AS Contact
FROM Customers
```

You can also use expressions to create calculated columns. For example, you might want to display only a part of the customer ID:

```
SELECT Left(Customers.CustomerID, 2) AS ID,
 Customers.ContactName AS Contact
FROM Customers
```

This statement creates a calculated column named ID by applying the Left() function to the Customers.CustomerID column. You'll need to refer to the documentation for your individual database program to determine which functions are supported in expressions.

If you prefer, you can use the *column_alias=expression* syntax to rewrite this example:

```
SELECT ID = Left(Customers.CustomerID, 2),
 Customers.ContactName AS Contact
FROM Customers
```

The ALL and DISTINCT keywords control how the resultset will handle duplicate rows. Using ALL (the default) includes duplicate rows in the resultset. Using DISTINCT limits the resultset by removing all duplicate rows. For example, this query will return many duplicate rows when run against the Northwind sample database:

```
SELECT ALL Country FROM Customers
```

This query will not return any duplicate rows, even though many customers have the same country:

```
SELECT DISTINCT Country FROM Customers
```

Finally, you can use TOP *n* and TOP *n* PERCENT to limit the number of rows that will be returned. This query will return only the first five rows it retrieves:

```
SELECT TOP 5 CompanyName FROM Customers
```

And this query will return roughly one-quarter of the rows from the table:

```
SELECT TOP 25 PERCENT CompanyName FROM Customers
```

The FROM Clause

The FROM clause is used to specify the set of source tables that the query will use for data. Here's a syntax diagram for the FROM clause:

```
[ FROM {<table_source>} [,...n] ]

<table_source> ::=
table_name [ [AS] table_alias ]
| view_name [ [AS] table_alias ]
| <joined_table>

<joined_table> ::=
<table_source> <join_type> <table_source> ON <search_condition>
| <table_source> CROSS JOIN <table_source>
| <joined_table>

<join_type> ::=
[ INNER | { { LEFT | RIGHT | FULL } [OUTER] } ]
JOIN
```

You've already seen how the simplest of FROM clauses lets you specify a table to retrieve data from:

```
SELECT * FROM Customers
```

You can also use a table alias to rename a table for purposes of a query (in this case, C is the alias for the Customers table):

```
SELECT C.CustomerID FROM Customers AS C
```

Note that this can allow you to shorten the SELECT clause, at the cost of readability.

What about two tables? That's where the concept of joined tables comes in. To explore joins, we'll use two tables, Table1 and Table2. Figure A.1 shows these two tables, each of which has two fields, and the data that they contain.

FIGURE A.1:

Sample tables for testing join types

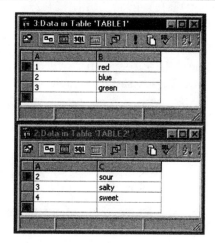

For starters, what happens if you just try the simplest way to retrieve the data from both tables in a single query with the simplest possible syntax:

```
SELECT * FROM Table1, Table2
```

The answer is that you'll get a resultset that looks like this:

A	B	A	C
1	red	2	sour
2	blue	2	sour
3	green	2	sour
1	red	3	salty
2	blue	3	salty
3	green	3	salty
1	red	4	sweet
2	blue	4	sweet
3	green	4	sweet

(9 row(s) affected)

This is probably not what you were expecting to see. The technical term for this type of join is *Cartesian product*. In a Cartesian product, every row from each table in the FROM clause is joined together with every row in every other table in the FROM clause. While this can be useful on occasion, usually what you want is to locate rows that match on some key field. To do that, you create an inner join:

```
SELECT *
FROM Table1 INNER JOIN Table2
  ON Table1.A = Table2.A
```

The INNER JOIN keyword specifies that you only want to see matching rows, and the ON clause specifies which fields should be matched. With the sample data you already saw, the result of this query now has the expected rows:

A	B	A	C
2	blue	2	sour
3	green	3	salty

```
(2 row(s) affected)
```

Outer joins allow you to somewhat relax the restriction on matching rows. The purpose of an outer join is to include all rows from one table while choosing only matching rows from the other table. As an example, here's one type of outer join:

```
SELECT *
FROM Table1 LEFT OUTER JOIN Table2
  ON Table1.A = Table2.A
```

This resultset includes all rows from the table on the left of the join, and matching rows from the table on the right of the join:

A	B	A	C
1	red	NULL	NULL
2	blue	2	sour
3	green	3	salty

```
(3 row(s) affected)
```

Since there is no matching data in Table2 for the first row in Table1, SQL Server returns NULL as the value for the fields in Table2 matching that row. As you'd expect, there's also a RIGHT OUTER JOIN.

```
SELECT *
FROM Table1 RIGHT OUTER JOIN Table2
  ON Table1.A = Table2.A
```

This returns all rows from the table on the right side of the join, and matching rows from the table on the left side of the join:

A	B	A	C
2	blue	2	sour
3	green	3	salty
NULL	NULL	4	sweet

```
(3 row(s) affected)
```

Combining the two types of outer join gives you a FULL OUTER JOIN:

```
SELECT *
FROM Table1 FULL OUTER JOIN Table2
  ON Table1.A = Table2.A
```

This returns all data from either table, matching rows where possible:

A	B	A	C
2	blue	2	sour
3	green	3	salty
NULL	NULL	4	sweet
1	red	NULL	NULL

```
(4 row(s) affected)
```

You can also use the CROSS JOIN keyword to explicitly specify the Cartesian product:

```
SELECT *
FROM Table1 CROSS JOIN Table2
```

In this case, of course, you don't include a joining condition, since you want all combinations of rows from the two tables.

The joining condition need not be strict equality. For example, this is a valid query:

```
SELECT *
FROM Table1 INNER JOIN Table2
  ON Table1.A < Table2.A
```

In this case, the resultset matches every row in Table1 with every row in Table2, and then keeps only those rows where the join condition evaluates to True:

```
A         B         A         C
_____    _____    _____    _____
1         red       2         sour
1         red       3         salty
1         red       4         sweet
2         blue      3         salty
2         blue      4         sweet
3         green     4         sweet

(6 row(s) affected)
```

If there are more than two tables in the query, you can nest join clauses. For example, this is legal SQL for retrieving records from a set of five joined tables:

```
SELECT Customers.CompanyName, Employees.LastName
FROM Customers INNER JOIN
Orders ON
Customers.CustomerID = Orders.CustomerID INNER JOIN
[Order Details] ON
Orders.OrderID = [Order Details].OrderID INNER JOIN
Products ON
[Order Details].ProductID = Products.ProductID INNER JOIN
Employees ON
Orders.EmployeeID = Employees.EmployeeID
```

This query retrieves the names of employees who have taken orders from each customer. In a case like this, the joining conditions are evaluated left to right. If you'd like to make the order of evaluation more clear, or force evaluation in a different order, you can use parentheses within the FROM clause. For example, you could also get the same resultset with this SQL statement:

```
SELECT Customers.CompanyName, Employees.LastName
FROM ((((Customers INNER JOIN
Orders ON
Customers.CustomerID = Orders.CustomerID) INNER JOIN
[Order Details] ON
Orders.OrderID = [Order Details].OrderID) INNER JOIN
Products ON
[Order Details].ProductID = Products.ProductID) INNER JOIN
Employees ON
Orders.EmployeeID = Employees.EmployeeID)
```

The WHERE Clause

The WHERE clause of a SELECT query allows you to filter the rows that will be returned by the query. Here's the general syntax for this clause:

```
WHERE <search_condition>
```

Not very complex, is it? The key lies in constructing search conditions. In this section, I'll show you a few examples to give you an idea of what you can do with a WHERE clause.

A search condition is an expression that can be evaluated to True or False for each row that might be included in the resultset. For a simple example, here's how to pick out a specific value in a text column:

```
SELECT * FROM Customers
WHERE ContactTitle = 'Owner'
```

Or you can ask for rows that match one of a set of values by using the IN keyword:

```
SELECT * FROM Customers
WHERE ContactTitle IN ('Owner', 'Sales Manager')
```

You can also use the Boolean <> or NOT operators to exclude rows with a specific value:

```
SELECT * FROM Customers
WHERE ContactTitle <> 'Owner'
```

```
SELECT * FROM Customers
WHERE ContactTitle NOT IN ('Owner', 'Sales Manager')
```

Most servers also allow wildcards in search conditions. One common convention is to use a percent sign to match zero or more characters:

```
SELECT * FROM Customers
WHERE CompanyName LIKE 'A%'
```

Or you can use an underscore to match a single character:

```
SELECT * FROM Customers
WHERE CustomerID LIKE 'A____'
```

To filter on dates, use the same syntax:

```
SELECT * FROM Orders
WHERE OrderDate = '7/12/1996'
```

And to filter on a numeric value, omit the quotes:

```
SELECT * FROM Orders
WHERE EmployeeID = 9
```

NOTE   If you're working with a Jet database, you use pound signs to quote dates in SQL statements.

The GROUP BY Clause

The GROUP BY clause also has a simple syntax:

```
GROUP BY {column_name}
[,...]
```

The purpose of the GROUP BY clause to is to create a resultset that somehow summarizes data in a table or set of tables. For example, here's a stripped-down version of the query that opened this appendix:

```
SELECT Customers.CustomerID,
  COUNT(Orders.OrderID)
FROM Customers INNER JOIN Orders
  ON Customers.CustomerID = Orders.CustomerID
GROUP BY Customers.CustomerID
```

This query joins the two tables, and then sorts them by CustomerID. For each CustomerID, it creates a single row in the resultset (that's the effect of the GROUP BY on the Customers.CustomerID field). Then it counts the number of OrderIDs that match that CustomerID, and fills that count in as the second field in the resultset. The net result is to show all the customers in the database together with the number of orders that they've placed.

If you include a GROUP BY clause, every column in the SELECT clause must either appear in the GROUP BY or have an aggregate function in the SELECT clause (COUNT is the aggregate function in this example). Table A.1 lists common aggregate functions.

TABLE A.1: SQL Aggregate Functions

Function	Returns
AVG	Average value
COUNT	Number of values
MAX	Largest value
MIN	Smallest value
SUM	Sum of all values
STDEV	Standard deviation of all values
STDEVP	Population standard deviation of all values
VAR	Variance of all values
VARP	Population variance of all values

The HAVING Clause

The HAVING clause works just like the WHERE clause, except that it's applied after aggregates have been computed (and can thus be included only in queries that contain a GROUP BY clause). For example, you could modify the query from the previous section:

```
SELECT Customers.CustomerID,
  COUNT(Orders.OrderID) AS OrderCount
FROM Customers INNER JOIN Orders
  ON Customers.CustomerID = Orders.CustomerID
GROUP BY Customers.CustomerID
HAVING COUNT(Orders.OrderID)= 17
```

This query still summarizes the number of orders per customer, but it includes only those whose total number of orders is 17 in the resultset.

Some SQL products would allow you to simplify this query by using the column alias in the HAVING clause:

```
SELECT Customers.CustomerID,
  COUNT(Orders.OrderID) AS OrderCount
FROM Customers INNER JOIN Orders
```

```
ON Customers.CustomerID = Orders.CustomerID
GROUP BY Customers.CustomerID
HAVING OrderCount = 17
```

The ORDER BY Clause

Finally, you can control the order that columns appear in the resultset with an ORDER BY clause:

```
ORDER BY column_name [ASC | DESC]
[,...n]
```

For example, to show data from the Customers table sorted in ascending order by CustomerID:

```
SELECT * FROM Customers
ORDER BY CustomerID
```

You can also specify a direction of sort by including ASC for ascending (the default) or DESC for descending:

```
SELECT * FROM Customers
ORDER BY CustomerID DESC
```

You can also sort on more than one column:

```
SELECT * FROM Orders
ORDER BY CustomerID DESC, OrderDate ASC
```

That statement sorts the results first in descending order by customer ID, then within each customer's orders by OrderDate in ascending order.

Data Modification Statements

Once you understand the syntax of the SELECT statement, you've got a large part of the syntax for the statements that modify data. These are:

- The DELETE statement to remove rows from a table

- The INSERT statement to add rows to a table

- The UPDATE statement to modify data already in a table

In this section, you'll learn the basic syntax for these three statements.

The DELETE Statement

The syntax of the DELETE statement is very similar to that of the SELECT statement:

```
DELETE
FROM table_name
WHERE <search_condition>
```

The FROM and WHERE clauses in a DELETE statement have the same syntax that they have in a SELECT statement. So, with just a few examples, you should be able to grasp the DELETE statement.

WARNING   If you're trying these examples, be sure you have a backup of your data before playing with the DELETE statement. There's no confirmation if you execute a DELETE statement directly from most query products.

To delete all the contents of a table, you use the simplest DELETE statement:

```
DELETE FROM Customers
```

Optionally, you can modify the DELETE statement to filter and only delete specific rows:

```
DELETE FROM Customers
WHERE ContactTitle IN ('Owner', 'Sales Manager')
```

This statement will delete all rows from the Customers table where the Contact-Title is either "Owner" or "Sales Manager."

The INSERT Statement

The INSERT statement is used to add new rows to a table. Here's the simplified syntax:

```
INSERT [INTO] table_name
{ [(column_list)]
{ VALUES ( { DEFAULT
| NULL
| expression
}[,...n]
)
```

In an INSERT statement, you supply a table, a list of columns, and a list of values for that column. If you want no data inserted in a particular column, you can use NULL in that position in the value list. If a column has a default value, you can use the special value DEFAULT to indicate that this default should be used. Otherwise, you must supply a literal value, or an expression that evaluates to the correct datatype for the column.

You don't have to list all the columns in a table in the INSERT statement. Any non-nullable column without a default value must be explicitly listed, and a value for it supplied.

For example, this statement will insert a new row in the Northwind Customers table:

```
INSERT INTO Customers
  (CustomerID, CompanyName)
VALUES
  ('ZOOFO', 'Zoo Foods')
```

This statement inserts a new row into the Customers table with a CustomerID of ZOOFO and a CompanyName of Zoo Foods. There are no defaults on any of the columns of this table, so all the other columns are set to NULL when the new row is inserted.

The UPDATE Statement

To modify an existing row in a table, you use the UPDATE statement:

```
UPDATE table_name
SET
{column_name = {expression | DEFAULT | NULL}
 } [,...n]
 [WHERE
<search_condition>]
```

Again, the WHERE clause has the same syntax that it does in a SELECT query.

You can use an UPDATE query to set any column to its default value, to NULL, or to a value you calculate within the UPDATE query. For example, to change the title of every customer to "Manager," you could use this query:

```
UPDATE Customers
SET ContactTitle = 'Manager'
```

Or, to make the same change only on rows where the current title is "Owner," you'd use this query:

```
UPDATE Customers
SET ContactTitle = 'Manager'
WHERE ContactTitle = 'Owner'
```

Other SQL Statements

It's not my purpose in this book to teach you SQL. This appendix is meant as only a quick introduction to enough SQL to help you make sense of the ADO examples in the rest of the book. For further details, you should refer to the documentation that came with your database server. But to give you some idea of the range of operations you can perform with SQL, I'll briefly list a few other important SQL statements here. Of course, not every database product supports every one of these statements.

- CREATE statements, such as CREATE TABLE, CREATE VIEW, CREATE DATABASE, and CREATE TRIGGER, can be used to create new database objects.

- ALTER statements, such as ALTER TABLE, ALTER VIEW, ALTER DATA-BASE, and ALTER TRIGGER, can be used to modify existing database objects.

- DROP statements, such as DROP TABLE, DROP VIEW, DROP DATABASE, and DROP TRIGGER, can be used to delete database objects.

- BACKUP and RESTORE can be used to make tape backups and to read backups into a server.

- BEGIN TRANSACTION, COMMIT TRANSACTION, and ROLLBACK TRANSACTION are used to group multiple statements into a single logical entity.

- IF, ELSE, and CASE can be used to do conditional processing within SQL statements.

- DECLARE CURSOR, OPEN, and FETCH can be used to work with cursors directly in SQL.

- GRANT and REVOKE can manage server-side security.

INDEX

Note to the Reader: Page numbers in **bold** indicate the principal discussion of a topic or the definition of a term. Page numbers in *italic* indicate illustrations.

M

P

W

X

GET MCSD CERTIFIED WITH SYBEX
THE CERTIFICATION EXPERTS

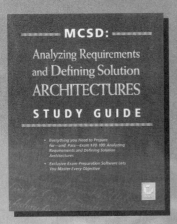

MCSD:
Analyzing Requirements
and Defining Solution
ARCHITECTURES
S T U D Y   G U I D E

*Everything you Need to Prepare
for—and Pass—Exam #70-100: Analyzing
Requirements and Defining Solution
Architectures*

*Exclusive Exam-Preparation Software Lets
You Master Every Objective*

Ben Ezzell
ISBN 0-7821-2431-3

- Complete coverage of every Microsoft objective

- Hundreds of challenging review questions, in the book and on the CD

- Hands-on exercises that let you apply the concepts you've learned

- Page count: 592-752; Hardcover; Trim: 7½" x 9"; Price: $44.99; CD included

Other MCSD Study Guides Available from Sybex:

*MCSD: Visual Basic® 6 Desktop Applications
Study Guide*
Michael McKelvy
ISBN 0-7821-2438-0

*MCSD: Visual Basic® 6 Distributed
Applications Study Guide*
Michael Lee with Clark Christensen
ISBN 0-7821-2433-X

MCSD: Access® 95 Study Guide
Peter Vogel & Helen Feddema
ISBN 0-7821-2282-5

MCSD: Windows® Architecture I Study Guide
Ben Ezzell
ISBN 0-7821-2271-X

MCSD: Windows® Architecture II Study Guide
Michael Lee & Kevin Wolford
ISBN 0-7821-2274-4
MCSD: SQL Server® 6.5 Database Design

Study Guide
Kevin Hough
ISBN 0-7821-2269-8

MCSD: Visual Basic® 5 Study Guide
Mike McKelvy
ISBN 0-7821-2228-0

*MCSE/MCSD: SQL Server® 7 Database
Design Study Guide*
Kevin Hough & Ed Larkin
ISBN 0-7821-2586-7

Available Summer '99:
*MCSD Visual Basic® 6
Core Requirements Box*
Michael McKelvy,
Michael Lee with
Clark Christensen &
Ben Ezzell
ISBN 0-7821-2582-4
$109.97
Contains:
*MCSD: Analyzing Requirements and
Defining Solution Architectures Study Guide*
*MCSD: Visual Basic® 6 Desktop
Applications Study Guide*
*MCSD: Visual Basic® 6 Distributed
Applications Study Guide*

A savings of $25!

Microsoft Certified
Professional
Approved Study Guide

SYB
www.sybex.

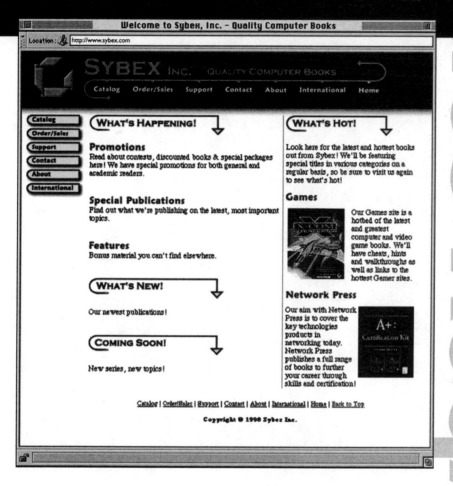